Alfred's

The Death
and Resurrection
of the Author?

The Death
and Resurrection
of the Author?

Edited by
William Irwin

GREENWOOD PRESS
Westport, Connecticut • London

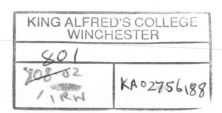
The Library of Congress has cataloged the hardcover edition as follows:

The death and resurrection of the author? / edited by William Irwin.
     p. cm.—(Contributions in philosophy, ISSN 0084–926X ; no. 83)
    Includes bibliographical references and index.
    ISBN 0–313–31870–0 (alk. paper)—ISBN 0–313–32275–9 (pbk. : alk. paper)
    1. Authorship—Philosophy. 2. Criticism. I. Irwin, William, 1970– II. Series.
PN175.D52   2002
  808'.02'01—dc21   2001058634

British Library Cataloguing in Publication Data is available.

Library of Congress Catalog Card Number: 2001058634
ISBN: 0–313–31870–0
    0–313–32275–9 (pbk.)

First published in 2002

Greenwood Press, 88 Post Road West, Westport, CT 06881
An imprint of Greenwood Publishing Group, Inc.
www.greenwood.com

Printed in the United States of America

The paper used in this book complies with the
Permanent Paper Standard issued by the National
Information Standards Organization (Z39.48–1984).

10 9 8 7 6 5 4 3 2 1

For Jack McSherry, S.J., who saved my life.

Contents

Preface

Like Friedrich Nietzsche's assertion of the "death of God," Roland Barthes's claim of the "death of the author" presents a challenge that cannot be ignored. Though Nietzsche was an atheist, "the death of God" was not a statement of God's nonexistence but rather a statement of God's unimportance in modern life. Similarly, Barthes's "death of the author" does not argue that men and women do not write plays, novels, and poems but that the "authors" of these texts are unimportant and even repressive in interpretation. Barthes's "La Mort de l'Auteur" ("The Death of the Author") appeared in 1968, followed by Michel Foucault's like-minded "Qu'est-ce Qu'un Auteur" ("What Is an Author?") in 1969. As Nietzsche's "death of God" has become both a rallying cry for atheists and a call for religious renewal by pastors and theologians, so too has Barthes's "death of the author" become both a springboard for poststructuralist and de-constructionist literary critics and a foil for intentionalists.

Jorge J.E. Gracia generously suggested the idea for this book when I was working on what was to become my first book, *Intentionalist Interpretation* (1999). My research had uncovered a wealth of provocative essays both supporting and criticizing the position of Foucault and Barthes. Although I devoted Chapter 2 of *Intentionalist Interpretation*, "A Critical Survey of Author Constructs: Does It Matter Who Is Speaking?" to the topic, this volume more fully addresses the author question, offering a representative sample of the best articles on the topic from both sides of the debate and from both Anglo-American and Continental philosophers.

Stephen Heath's English translation of the Barthes essay that started the debate begins the collection; Josué V. Harari's English translation of the equally important Foucault essay follows. Most of the subsequent essays have been previously published; three have been written specifically for this volume, and one, mine, is revised and compiled from previously published material. Page numbers in brackets in the endnotes for each essay direct the reader to pages in this volume. I have added these references to produce a free-standing and dialogical volume.

I am grateful to the "authors" of the previously published essays, many of whom provided valuable feedback on the project and assisted me in securing permission to reprint their material. I am also, of course, grateful to the editors and permissions directors at the journals and presses who granted permission to reprint the material in this volume. These generous and cooperative souls include: Philip A. Alperson (*Journal of Aesthetics and Art Criticism*), Nicola Boulton (Blackwell Publishers), Perry Cartwright (University of Chicago Press), Jennie Doling (SUNY Press), Victoria Fox (Farrar, Straus & Giroux), Heather Hart (Cornell University Press), Joseph Koterski, S.J. (*International Philosophical Quarterly*), Peter Lamarque (*British Journal of Aesthetics*), Heather L. Lengyel (Johns Hopkins University Press), and Fiona Willis (Oxford University Press).

I am indebted to Eric Bronson, Jason Holt, and David Weberman, who agreed to contribute essays to this volume when it was only a proposal without a publisher. I wish to thank the good folks at Greenwood Press for their patience with and faith in me as this volume took (and changed) shape. My editors Erin Carter, Rebecca A. Homiski, Elisabetta Linton, Margaret Maybury, and Gillian von Beebe provided crucial support, and Peter Kracht, like a cheerful though beleaguered father, continued to issue advance checks as my permission costs ran over budget. I am grateful to my colleagues at King's College for their insight and friendship and for tolerating my cigar smoke. Thanks also to my research assistants Trisha Allen and Jennifer O'Neill, who saved me from potentially embarrassing mistakes.

The love and encouragement of my parents and sister have carried me through more than they could know. Most of all I wish to thank my wonderful wife, Megan, who took on more than her fair share of everything as I completed work on this book. May we walk gently through each day together, always.

Introduction

The Death and Resurrection of the Author? The title of this volume is an intentionally ambiguous question. What does it mean to assert "the death of the author"? Is the assertion correct? Has there been a "resurrection of the author"? If so, what are its implications? This volume addresses all of these questions.

Since the translation of the Barthes and Foucault essays, which begin this collection, a stream of articles, influenced by and commenting upon them, have appeared in influential books and leading journals in the Anglophone world. A number of these articles (along with some new ones) are included in this collection. In a sense, Barthes's "The Death of the Author" and Foucault's "What Is an Author?" can be taken as primary texts for which the subsequent essays are secondary literature.

The aim of this volume is to examine the philosophical underpinnings and arguments of Barthes and Foucault and their supporters and critics. Although the essays that comprise the volume focus primarily on the implications of the death of the author for literature, they also bear significantly on the question of the place of the author and his or her intentions in the interpretation of literary, philosophical, and legal texts and the fine arts.

Most of the essays in this volume are written by philosophers rather than literary theorists, though the topic and the essays are sure to be of interest to both. The perspectives of both Anglo-American and Continental philosophy are represented—the tools, methods, styles, and approaches of each are employed. Peter Lamarque and Jason Holt, in particular, bring the tools of analytic philosophy to bear on the topic of the death of the author but with differing conclusions. I am unabashedly a critic of "the death of the author," and a defender of the importance of authorial intention in interpretation. Still, I hope I have given fair consideration to the death of the author, anti-intentionalist, and non-intentionalist interpretation, particularly with the inclusion of the essays by Barthes and Foucault, Westpahl's essay on Kierkegaard, Weberman's piece on Gadamer, and Nehamas's appropriation of Foucault. I hope and trust that the diversity of views in the present collection will encourage the reader to think open-mindedly and independently. No other collection, to my knowledge, in-cludes the full Foucault and Barthes essays on this topic. For this reason, along with the provocative contributions to the debate made by the other essays in-cluded, I hope this book will be a valuable resource to scholars and students alike.

Each essay stands independently; thus, one can read them in whatever order one chooses. Still, there is a definite logic to the sequence. The order of the essays brings a sense of dialogue to the book and encourages the reader to seek answers to the questions and engage in the issues raised. The two parts of the book are not sharply demarcated, though they tell different stories. Part One, "The Death of the Author?" presents the case for the elimination, or at least minimization, of the author in interpretation, concluding with some rather critical postmortem analyses. Part Two, "The Resurrection of the Author? A Look at Author Constructs," surveys the development of one of Foucault's legacies, the author construct. The term "author construct" refers to a theorist's answer to the question, "What is an author?" The author construct is just that, a construct (as opposed to the actual historical writer), a concept applied in interpretation. Part Two begins with Nehamas's sympathetic treatment of Foucault and moves through criticism of Nehamas and the value of author constructs to re-adoption of author constructs, ultimately in the service of intentionalism. Let us turn to a brief overview of the contents of each essay.

"What matter who's speaking, someone said, what matter who's speaking."[1] This often quoted line from Beckett suggests the positions of Roland Barthes and Michel Foucault on the author. Though there are subtle differences between Barthes and Foucault on this topic, by way of introduction let us focus on what they share. The idea that it is not the author but the text that matters in inter-pretation was to be found earlier, in the New Critics' intentional fallacy, among other places, but Foucault and Barthes push the issue further, asking what an author *is* and why we should put so much stock in him and in his intentions. They conclude that the author is a repressive figure, and it matters not at all who is speaking. Barthes and Foucault see the author as a product of the En-lightenment and the rise of individualism. According to Foucault, authors came to be seen as owners of their texts at the end of the eighteenth and beginning of the nineteenth centuries, when a system of ownership and copyright rules were established (p. 14).[2] For Barthes, "The author is a modern figure, a product of our society" (p. 4). To be clear, neither Foucault nor Barthes denies that men and women write texts; rather, they oppose a certain approach to the author-as-person. They oppose attempts at elaborate historical reconstruction of the author-as-person on the grounds that such a figure is repressive, limiting the freedom of the reader. Nietzsche's madman asks, "What festivals of atonement, what sacred games shall we have to invent?" in order to fill the void left by the death of God. Similarly, Barthes and Foucault ask what shall fill the empty space left by the death or disappearance of the author? Their answer, the reader. As Barthes says in concluding his essay, "the birth of the reader must be at the cost of the death of the Author" (p. 7).

In "Kierkegaard and the Anxiety of Authorship," Merold Westphal discusses Søren Kierkegaard as an important literary and philosophical precursor to Barthes and Foucault. Westphal points out, despite the common misinterpretations of the Kierkegaardian corpus, that *Either/Or*, for example, has five different authors, none of whom is Kierkegaard. Westphal explains Kierkegaard's pseudonymous literary practice by explicating it in terms of "the anxiety of authorship," making use of the critical theories of Gadamer, Barthes, Foucault, and Derrida. He carefully traces and discusses the theological imagery used by Foucault, Barthes, and Derrida to shed light on the very different theological imagery used by Kierkegaard. Westphal links the German to the French, saying, "We might consider Gadamer's *Truth and Method* (1960) to be the artillery barrage that softened up the stronghold for the author in preparation for the all out assault by the French" (p. 24). In "Gadamer's Hermeneutics and the Question of Authorial Intention," David Weberman lays out in considerable detail Gadamer's battery of reasons for rejecting the identification of a text's meaning with its author's intention. He shows that while not an intentionalist, Gadamer does concede that the original creation of the text has a heuristic and narrowly constraining role. He concludes that Gadamer is not as radically anti-intentionalist as Foucault and Barthes, but rather espouses what might be called a version of "non-intentionalism."

In "The Marginal Life of the Author," Jason Holt argues that the conclusions of Foucault and Barthes are largely justified but not for the reasons they suppose. The life of the author is a marginal one, consisting in the mere "presumption of intent" that the text is an artifact produced with intention but nonetheless an intention that we can, and indeed often should, ignore. In "The Death of the Author: An Analytical Autopsy," Peter Lamarque insightfully captures and critically examines the common themes of "The Death of the Author" and "What Is an Author?" in four theses: the Historicist Thesis, the Death Thesis, the Author Function Thesis, and the *Ecriture* Thesis. The Historicist Thesis claims that "the birth of the author" occurred in the modern period. Only at some point after the Middle Ages did texts come to be seen as authored in the way they are today. The Death Thesis, simply stated, is that the author is "dead" or has "disappeared," as Foucault is more apt to put it. Lamarque investigates what exactly this means and whether the claim is descriptive or prescriptive. The Author Function Thesis claims that the "author" of a text performs a classificatory and constraining function, rather than simply referring to the person who wrote the text. The *Ecriture* Thesis asserts that the nature of writing makes the author redundant; in writing, the text is freed from the author.

Beginning Part Two, in "Writer, Text, Work, Author," Alexander Nehamas understands and deciphers Foucault in an important and interesting way. In "What Is an Author?" Foucault had some difficulty in keeping the author function distinct from the author-as-person. For Nehamas the author is not necessarily an intruder but can be an aid. In forming his author construct he distinguishes between the "writer" and the "author" of a text. The writer is a historical person firmly situated within a specific context, the efficient cause of a text's production, whereas the author is whoever can be understood to have produced the text as the reader has construed it. The author, as Nehamas conceives this figure, allows for a great deal more freedom than Foucault realized was implicit in his own author function. Nehamas suggests that this essential confusion between the author function itself and the author function formed in strict accord with the historical producer is the weak point of Foucault's theory.

In "Authorship and Authority," Nickolas Pappas emphasizes resisting authority, a theme in Foucault to which, he believes, Nehamas does not pay adequate attention. He tells us that Nehamas "argues in ontological terms—concentrating on what the author is, instead of what our attachment to the author is like—and as a result fails to avoid Foucault's critique of authorship" (p. 119). Pappas wants to "shift attention from the author's intention to the reader's motivation for trying to know it" (p. 125). He discusses the escape from the author's authority in reading Proust, Nietzsche, and Plato, arguing that respect for authors such as these is not necessarily deference to their authority. In "Apparent, Implied, and Postulated Authors," Robert Stecker discusses Walton's "apparent artist," Nehamas's "postulated author," and Booth's "implied author." Stecker argues that the distinction between the author construct, in its various forms, and the actual historical author is generally unhelpful and even unnecessarily confusing. If one is concerned with authorial intention, there is no need to refer to an author construct.

In "Feminist Literary Criticism and the Author," Cheryl Walker notes the way in which the role of the author construct in interpretation poses an interesting dilemma for feminist critics. Should they take the side of Barthes and Foucault in fighting repression (as caused by author constructs, in this case), or should they preserve a place for the author-as-person and so further the cause of promoting lesser known women writers? Walker concludes, "Though I may not wish to treat texts as the private property of their authors, I am unwilling to lose the sense of vital links between women that only a practice which preserves authors in some form can provide" (p. 157).

In "A Theory of the Author," Jorge J.E. Gracia further clarifies the distinction between the historical agent who produces the text and the author construct, the figure we create of the historical agent in interpreting the text. He also has much of interest to say on the issue of authorial repression. Gracia rejects Nehamas's terminology of "author" and "writer" in favor of a more careful distinction between the "historical author" and the "pseudo-historical" author. The historical author is the actual agent who produced the text. The pseudo-historical author is a construct, not a real person; it is a composite of what we know or think we know about the historical author. Because our knowledge of the historical author is always limited and approximate, our pseudo-historical author will be an imperfect match for the historical author. Still, for Gracia, the author construct is no arbitrary figure but is based as far as possible on historical fact.

In "Intentionalism and Author Constructs," I argue that intentionalists such as Hirsch, Juhl, and Carroll have too readily dispensed with author constructs. Intentionalism can benefit from, and indeed needs, an author construct. I articulate such an intentionalist author construct, the "urauthor," and elaborate on the intentionalism such a construct makes possible. In the final essay of this volume, "The Death of Cervantes and the Life of *Don Quixote*," Eric Bronson critically discusses the life of this classic centuries after the demise of its author, in particular, musing on its use and interpretation by Borges and Unamuno. Bronson argues that the disparate interpretations of *Don Quixote* actually accord with the broad and open-ended intentions of Cervantes.

In closing, it is the intention of the editor (dead or alive) that this book begin rather than end the reader's pursuit of answers to the questions, What is an author? and Does it matter who is speaking? An ample bibliography brings an end to the volume though not to the quest.

NOTES

1. Samuel Beckett, *Texts for Nothing* (London: Carder and Boyars, 1974), p. 16.
2. Parenthetical numbers in the Introduction refer to page numbers in this volume.

PART ONE

THE DEATH OF THE AUTHOR?

CHAPTER 1

The Death of the Author

Roland Barthes

In his story *Sarrasine* Balzac, describing a castrato disguised as a woman, writes the following sentence: '*This was woman herself, with her sudden fears, her irrational whims, her instinctive worries, her impetuous boldness, her fussings, and her delicious sensibility.*' Who is speaking thus? Is it the hero of the story bent on remaining ignorant of the castrato hidden beneath the woman? Is it Balzac the individual, furnished by his personal experience with a philosophy of Woman? Is it Balzac the author professing 'literary' ideas on femininity? Is it universal wisdom? Romantic psychology? We shall never know, for the good reason that writing is the destruction of every voice, of every point of origin. Writing is that neutral, composite, oblique space where our subject slips away, the negative where all identity is lost, starting with the very identity of the body writing.

No doubt it has always been that way. As soon as a fact is *narrated* no longer with a view to acting directly on reality but intransitively, that is to say, finally outside of any function other than that of the very practice of the symbol itself, this disconnection occurs, the voice loses its origin, the author enters into his own death, writing begins. The sense of this phenomenon, however, has varied; in ethnographic societies the responsibility for a narrative is never assumed by a person but by a mediator, shaman or relator whose 'performance'—the mastery of the narrative code—may possibly be admired but never his 'genius'. The author is a modern figure, a product of our society insofar as, emerging from the Middle Ages with English empiricism, French rationalism and the personal faith of the Reformation, it discovered the prestige of the individual, of, as it is more nobly put, the 'human person'. It is thus logical that in literature it should be this positivism, the epitome and culmination of capitalist ideology, which has attached the greatest importance to the 'person' of the author. The *author* still reigns in histories of literature, biographies of writers, interviews, magazines, as in the very consciousness of men of letters anxious to unite their person and their work through diaries and memoirs. The image of literature to be found in ordinary culture is tyrannically centred on the author, his person, his life, his tastes, his passions, while criticism still consists for the most part in saying that Baudelaire's work is the failure of Baudelaire the man, Van Gogh's his madness, Tchaikovsky's his vice. The *explanation* of a work is always sought in the man or woman who produced it, as if it were always in the end, through the more or less transparent allegory of the fiction, the voice of a single person, the *author* 'confiding' in us.

   Though the sway of the Author remains powerful (the new criticism has often done no more than consolidate it), it goes without saying that certain writers have long since attempted to loosen it. In France, Mallarmé was doubtless the first to see and to foresee in its full extent the necessity to substitute language itself for the person who until then had been supposed to be its owner. For him, for us too, it is language which speaks, not the author; to write is, through a prerequisite impersonality (not at all to be confused with the castrating objectivity of the realist novelist), to reach that point where only language acts, 'performs', and not 'me'. Mallarmé's entire poetics consists in suppressing the author in the interests of writing (which is, as will be seen, to restore the place of the reader). Valéry, encumbered by a psychology of the Ego, considerably diluted Mallarmé's theory but, his taste for classicism leading him to turn to the lessons of rhetoric, he never stopped calling into question and deriding the Author; he stressed the linguistic and, as it were, 'hazardous' nature of his activity, and throughout his prose works he militated in favour of the essentially verbal condition of literature, in the face of which all recourse to the writer's interiority seemed to him pure superstition. Proust himself, despite the apparently psychological character of what are called his *analyses*, was visibly concerned with the task of inexorably blurring, by an extreme subtilization, the relation between the writer and his characters; by making of the narrator not he who has seen and felt nor even he who is writing, but he who *is going to write* (the young man in the novel—but, in fact, how old is he and who is he?—wants to write but cannot; the novel ends when writing at last becomes possible), Proust gave modern writing its epic. By a radical reversal, instead of putting his life into his novel, as is so often maintained, he made of his very life a work for which his own book was the model; so that it is clear to us that Charlus does not imitate

Montesquiou but that Montesquiou—in his anecdotal, historical reality—is no more than a secondary fragment, derived from Charlus. Lastly, to go no further than this prehistory of modernity, Surrealism, though unable to accord language a supreme place (language being system and the aim of the movement being, romantically, a direct subversion of codes—itself moreover illusory: a code cannot be destroyed, only 'played off'), contributed to the desacrilization of the image of the Author by ceaselessly recommending the abrupt disappointment of expectations of meaning (the famous surrealist 'jolt'), by entrusting the hand with the task of writing as quickly as possible what the head itself is unaware of (automatic writing), by accepting the principle and the experience of several people writing together. Leaving aside literature itself (such distinctions really becoming invalid), linguistics has recently provided the destruction of the Author with a valuable analytical tool by showing that the whole of the enunciation is an empty process, functioning perfectly without there being any need for it to be filled with the person of the interlocutors. Linguistically, the author is never more than the instance writing, just as *I* is nothing other than the instance saying *I*: language knows a 'subject', not a 'person', and this subject, empty outside of the very enunciation which defines it, suffices to make language 'hold together', suffices, that is to say, to exhaust it.

The removal of the Author (one could talk here with Brecht of a veritable 'distancing', the Author diminishing like a figurine at the far end of the literary stage) is not merely a historical fact or an act of writing; it utterly transforms the modern text (or—which is the same thing—the text is henceforth made and read in such a way that at all its levels the author is absent). The temporality is different. The Author, when believed in, is always conceived of as the past of his own book: book and author stand automatically on a single line divided into a *before* and an *after*. The Author is thought to *nourish* the book, which is to say that he exists before it, thinks, suffers, lives for it, is in the same relation of antecedence to his work as a father to his child. In complete contrast, the modern scriptor is born simultaneously with the text, is in no way equipped with a being preceding or exceeding the writing, is not the subject with the book as predicate; there is no other time than that of the enunciation and every text is eternally written *here and now*. The fact is (or, it follows) that *writing* can no longer designate an operation of recording, notation, representation, 'depiction' (as the Classics would say); rather, it designates exactly what linguists, referring to Oxford philosophy, call a performative, a rare verbal form (exclusively given in the first person and in the present tense) in which the enunciation has no other content (contains no other proposition) than the act by which it is uttered—something like the *I declare* of kings or the *I sing* of very ancient poets. Having buried the Author, the modern scriptor can thus no longer believe, as according to the pathetic view of his predecessors, that this hand is too slow for his thought or passion and that consequently, making a law of necessity, he must emphasize this delay and indefinitely 'polish' his form. For him, on the contrary, the hand, cut off from any voice, borne by a pure gesture of inscription (and not of expression), traces a field without origin—or which, at least, has no other origin than language itself, language which ceaselessly calls into question all origins.

We know now that a text is not a line of words releasing a single 'theological' meaning (the 'message' of the Author-God) but a multi-dimensional space in which a variety of writings, none of them original, blend and clash. The text is a tissue of quotations drawn from the innumerable centres of culture. Similar to Bouvard and Pécuchet, those eternal copyists, at once sublime and comic and whose profound ridiculousness indicates precisely the truth of writing, the writer can only imitate a gesture that is always anterior, never original. His only power is to mix writings, to counter the ones with the others, in such a way as never to rest on any one of them. Did he wish to *express himself*, he ought at least to know that the inner 'thing' he thinks to 'translate' is itself only a ready-formed dictionary, its words only explainable through other words, and so on indefinitely; something experienced in exemplary fashion by the young Thomas de Quincey, he who was so good at Greek that in order to translate absolutely modern ideas and images into that dead language, he had, so Baudelaire tells us (in *Paradis Artificiels*), 'created for himself an unfailing dictionary, vastly more extensive and complex than those resulting from the ordinary patience of purely literary themes'. Succeeding the Author, the scriptor no longer bears within him passions, humours, feelings, impressions, but rather this immense dictionary from which he draws a writing that can know no halt: life never does more than imitate the book, and the book itself is only a tissue of signs, an imitation that is lost, infinitely deferred.

Once the Author is removed, the claim to decipher a text becomes quite futile. To give a text an Author is to impose a limit on that text, to furnish it with a final signified, to close the writing. Such a conception suits criticism very well, the latter then allotting itself the important task of discovering the Author (or its hypostases: society, history, psyché, liberty) beneath the work: when the Author has been found, the text is 'explained'—victory to the critic. Hence there is no surprise in the fact that, historically, the reign of the Author has also been that of the Critic, nor again in the fact that criticism (be it new) is today undermined along with the Author. In the multiplicity of writing, everything is to be *disentangled*, nothing *deciphered*; the structure can be followed, 'run' (like the thread of a stocking) at every point and at every level, but there is nothing beneath: the space of writing is to be ranged over, not pierced; writing ceaselessly posits meaning ceaselessly to evaporate it, carrying out a systematic exemption of meaning. In precisely this way literature (it would be better from now on to say *writing*), by refusing to assign a 'secret', an ultimate meaning, to the text (and to the world as text), liberates what may be called an anti-theological activity, an activity that is truly revolutionary since to refuse to fix meaning is, in the end, to refuse God and his hypostases—reason, science, law.

Let us come back to the Balzac sentence. No one, no 'person', says it: its source, its voice, is not the true place of the writing, which is reading. Another— very precise—example will help to make this clear: recent research (J.-P. Vernant[1]) has demonstrated the constitutively ambiguous nature of Greek tragedy, its texts being woven from words with double meanings that each character understands unilaterally (this perpetual misunderstanding is exactly the 'tragic'); there is, however, someone who understands each word in its duplicity and who, in addition, hears the very deafness of the characters speaking in front of him— this someone being precisely the reader (or here, the listener). Thus is revealed the total existence of writing: a text is made of multiple writings, drawn from many cultures and entering into mutual relations of dialogue, parody, contestation, but there is one place where this multiplicity is focused and that place is the reader, not, as was hitherto said, the author. The reader is the space on which all the quotations that make up a writing are inscribed without any of them being lost; a text's unity lies not in its origin but in its destination. Yet this destination cannot any longer be personal: the reader is without history, biography, psychology; he is simply that *someone* who holds together in a single field all the traces by which the written text is constituted. Which is why it is derisory to condemn the new writing in the name of a humanism hypocritically turned champion of the reader's rights. Classic criticism has never paid any attention to the reader; for it, the writer is the only person in literature. We are now beginning to let ourselves be fooled no longer by the arrogant antiphrastical recriminations of good society in favour of the very thing it sets aside, ignores, smothers, or destroys; we know that to give writing its future, it is necessary to overthrow the myth: the birth of the reader must be at the cost of the death of the Author.

NOTE

1. [Cf. Jean-Pierre Vernant (with Pierre Vidal-Naquet), *Mythe et tragédie en Grèce ancienne*, Paris, 1972, esp. pp. 19–40, 99–131.]

CHAPTER 2

What Is an Author?

Michel Foucault

The coming into being of the notion of "author" constitutes the privileged moment of *individualization* in the history of ideas, knowledge, literature, philosophy, and the sciences. Even today, when we reconstruct the history of a concept, literary genre, or school of philosophy, such categories seem relatively weak, secondary, and superimposed scansions in comparison with the solid and fundamental unit of the author and the work.

I shall not offer here a sociohistorical analysis of the author's persona. Certainly it would be worth examining how the author became individualized in a culture like ours, what status he has been given, at what moment studies of authenticity and attribution began, in what kind of system of valorization the author was involved, at what point we began to recount the lives of authors rather than of heroes, and how this fundamental category of "the-man-and-his-work criticism" began. For the moment, however, I want to deal solely with the relationship between text and author and with the manner in which the text points to this "figure" that, at least in appearance, is outside it and antecedes it.

Beckett nicely formulates the theme with which I would like to begin: " 'What does it matter who is speaking,' someone said, 'what does it matter who is speaking.' " In this indifference appears one of the fundamental ethical principles of contemporary writing (*écriture*). I say "ethical" because this indifference is not really a trait characterizing the manner in which one speaks and writes, but rather a kind of immanent rule, taken up over and over again, never fully

Reprinted from Michel Foucault, "What Is an Author?" in *Textual Strategies: Perspectives in Post-Structuralist Criticism*, ed. Josué V. Harari. Copyright © 1979 by Cornell University. Used by permission of the publisher, Cornell University Press.

applied, not designating writing as something completed, but dominating it as a practice. Since it is too familiar to require a lengthy analysis, this immanent rule can be adequately illustrated here by tracing two of its major themes.

First of all, we can say that today's writing has freed itself from the dimension of expression. Referring only to itself, but without being restricted to the confines of its interiority, writing is identified with its own unfolded exteriority. This means that it is an interplay of signs arranged less according to its signified content than according to the very nature of the signifier. Writing unfolds like a game (*jeu*) that invariably goes beyond its own rules and transgresses its limits. In writing, the point is not to manifest or exalt the act of writing, nor is it to pin a subject within language; it is, rather, a question of creating a space into which the writing subject constantly disappears.

The second theme, writing's relationship with death, is even more familiar. This link subverts an old tradition exemplified by the Greek epic, which was intended to perpetuate the immortality of the hero: if he was willing to die young, it was so that his life, consecrated and magnified by death, might pass into immortality; the narrative then redeemed this accepted death. In another way, the motivation, as well as the theme and the pretext of Arabian narratives—such as *The Thousand and One Nights*—was also the eluding of death: one spoke, telling stories into the early morning, in order to forestall death, to postpone the day of reckoning that would silence the narrator. Scheherazade's narrative is an effort, renewed each night, to keep death outside the circle of life.

Our culture has metamorphosed this idea of narrative, or writing, as something designed to ward off death. Writing has become linked to sacrifice, even to the sacrifice of life: it is now a voluntary effacement which does not need to be represented in books, since it is brought about in the writer's very existence. The work, which once had the duty of providing immortality, now possesses the right to kill, to be its author's murderer, as in the cases of Flaubert, Proust, and Kafka. That is not all, however: this relationship between writing and death is also manifested in the effacement of the writing subject's individual characteristics. Using all the contrivances that he sets up between himself and what he writes, the writing subject cancels out the signs of his particular individuality. As a result, the mark of the writer is reduced to nothing more than the singularity of his absence; he must assume the role of the dead man in the game of writing.

None of this is recent; criticism and philosophy took note of the disappearance—or death—of the author some time ago. But the consequences of their discovery of it have not been sufficiently examined, nor has its import been accurately measured. A certain number of notions that are intended to replace the privileged position of the author actually seem to preserve that privilege and suppress the real meaning of his disappearance. I shall examine two of these notions, both of great importance today.

The first is the idea of the work. It is a very familiar thesis that the task of criticism is not to bring out the work's relationships with the author, nor to reconstruct through the text a thought or experience, but rather to analyze the work through its structure, its architecture, its intrinsic form, and the play of its internal relationships. At this point, however, a problem arises: What is a work? What is this curious unity which we designate as a work? Of what elements is it composed? Is it not what an author has written? Difficulties appear immediately. If an individual were not an author, could we say that what he wrote, said, left behind in his papers, or what has been collected of his remarks, could be called a "work"? When Sade was not considered an author, what was the status of his papers? Were they simply rolls of paper onto which he ceaselessly uncoiled his fantasies during his imprisonment?

Even when an individual has been accepted as an author, we must still ask whether everything that he wrote, said, or left behind is part of his work. The problem is both theoretical and technical. When undertaking the publication of Nietzsche's works, for example, where should one stop? Surely everything must be published, but what is "everything"? Everything that Nietzsche himself published, certainly. And what about the rough drafts for his works? Obviously. The plans for his aphorisms? Yes. The deleted passages and the notes at the bottom of the page? Yes. What if, within a workbook filled with aphorisms, one finds a reference, the notation of a meeting or of an address, or a laundry list: Is it a work, or not? Why not? And so on, ad infinitum. How can one define a work amid the millions of traces left by someone after his death? A theory of the work does not exist, and the empirical task of those who naively undertake the editing of works often suffers in the absence of such a theory.

We could go even further: Does *The Thousand and One Nights* constitute a work? What about Clement of Alexandria's *Miscellanies* or Diogenes Laertius's *Lives*? A multitude of questions arises with regard to this notion of the work. Consequently, it is not enough to declare that we should do without the writer (the author) and study the work itself. The word *work* and the unity that it designates are probably as problematic as the status of the author's individuality.

Another notion which has hindered us from taking full measure of the author's disappearance, blurring and concealing the moment of this effacement and subtly preserving the author's existence, is the notion of writing (*écriture*). When rigorously applied, this notion should allow us not only to circumvent references to the author, but also to situate his recent absence. The notion of writing, as currently employed, is concerned with neither the act of writing nor the indication—be it symptom or sign—of a meaning which someone might have wanted to express. We try, with great effort, to imagine the general condition of each text, the condition of both the space in which it is dispersed and the time in which it unfolds.

In current usage, however, the notion of writing seems to transpose the empirical characteristics of the author into a transcendental anonymity. We are content to efface the more visible marks of the author's empiricity by playing off, one against the other, two ways of characterizing writing, namely, the critical and the religious approaches. Giving writing a primal status seems to be a way of retranslating, in transcendental terms, both the theological affirmation of its sacred character and the critical affirmation of its creative character. To admit that writing is, because of the very history that it made possible, subject to the test of oblivion and repression, seems to represent, in transcendental terms, the religious principle of the hidden meaning (which requires interpretation) and the critical principle of implicit significations, silent determinations, and obscured contents (which gives rise to commentary). To imagine writing as absence seems to be a simple repetition, in transcendental terms, of both the religious principle of inalterable and yet never fulfilled tradition, and the aesthetic principle of the work's survival, its perpetuation beyond the author's death, and its enigmatic *excess* in relation to him.

This usage of the notion of writing runs the risk of maintaining the author's privileges under the protection of writing's *a priori* status: it keeps alive, in the gray light of neutralization, the interplay of those representations that formed a particular image of the author. The author's disappearance, which, since Mallarmé, has been a constantly recurring event, is subject to a series of transcendental barriers. There seems to be an important dividing line between those who believe that they can still locate today's discontinuities (*ruptures*) in the historico-transcendental tradition of the nineteenth century, and those who try to free themselves once and for all from that tradition.

It is not enough, however, to repeat the empty affirmation that the author has disappeared. For the same reason, it is not enough to keep repeating (after Nietzsche) that God and man have died a common death. Instead, we must locate the space left empty by the author's disappearance, follow the distribution of gaps and breaches, and watch for the openings that this disappearance uncovers.

First, we need to clarify briefly the problems arising from the use of the author's name. What is an author's name? How does it function? Far from offering a solution, I shall only indicate some of the difficulties that it presents.

The author's name is a proper name, and therefore it raises the problems common to all proper names. (Here I refer to Searle's analyses, among others.[1]) Obviously, one cannot turn a proper name into a pure and simple reference. It has other than indicative functions: more than an indication, a gesture, a finger pointed at someone, it is the equivalent of a description. When one says "Aristotle," one employs a word that is the equivalent of one, or a series, of definite descriptions, such as "the author of the *Analytics*," "the founder of ontology," and so forth. One cannot stop there, however, because a proper name does not have just one signification. When we discover that Rimbaud did not write *La Chasse spirituelle*, we cannot pretend that the meaning of this proper name, or that of the author, has been altered. The proper name and the author's name are situated between the two poles of description and designation: they must have a certain link with what they name, but one that is neither entirely in the mode of designation nor in that of description; it must be a *specific* link. However— and it is here that the particular difficulties of the author's name arise—the links between the proper name and the individual named and between the author's name and what it names are not isomorphic and do not function in the same way. There are several differences.

If, for example, Pierre Dupont does not have blue eyes, or was not born in Paris, or is not a doctor, the name Pierre Dupont will still always refer to the same person; such things do not modify the link of designation. The problems raised by the author's name are much more complex, however. If I discover that Shakespeare was not born in the house that we visit today, this is a modification which, obviously, will not alter the functioning of the author's name. But if we proved that Shakespeare did not write those sonnets which pass for his, that would constitute a significant change and affect the manner in which the author's name functions. If we proved that Shakespeare wrote Bacon's *Organon* by showing that the same author wrote both the works of Bacon and those of Shakespeare, that would be a third type of change which would entirely modify the functioning of the author's name. The author's name is not, therefore, just a proper name like the rest.

Many other facts point out the paradoxical singularity of the author's name. To say that Pierre Dupont does not exist is not at all the same as saying that Homer or Hermes Trismegistus did not exist. In the first case, it means that no one has the name Pierre Dupont; in the second, it means that several people were mixed together under one name, or that the true author had none of the traits traditionally ascribed to the personae of Homer or Hermes. To say that X's real name is actually Jacques Durand instead of Pierre Dupont is not the same as saying that Stendhal's name was Henri Beyle. One could also question the meaning and functioning of propositions like "Bourbaki is so-and-so, so-and-so, etc." and "Victor Eremita, Climacus, Anticlimacus, Frater Taciturnus, Constantine Constantius, all of these are Kierkegaard."

These differences may result from the fact that an author's name is not simply an element in a discourse (capable of being either subject or object, of being replaced by a pronoun, and the like); it performs a certain role with regard to narrative discourse, assuring a classificatory function. Such a name permits one to group together a certain number of texts, define them, differentiate them from and contrast them to others. In addition, it establishes a relationship among the texts. Hermes Trismegistus did not exist, nor did Hippocrates—in the sense that Balzac existed—but the fact that several texts have been placed under the same name indicates that there has been established among them a relationship of homogeneity, filiation, authentication of some texts by the use of others, reciprocal explication, or concomitant utilization. The author's name serves to characterize a certain mode of being of discourse: the fact that the discourse has an author's name, that one can say "this was written by so-and-so" or "so-and-so is its author," shows that this discourse is not ordinary everyday speech that merely comes and goes, not something that is immediately consumable. On the contrary, it is a speech that must be received in a certain mode and that, in a given culture, must receive a certain status.

It would seem that the author's name, unlike other proper names, does not pass from the interior of a discourse to the real and exterior individual who produced it; instead, the name seems always to be present, marking off the edges of the text, revealing, or at least characterizing, its mode of being. The author's name manifests the appearance of a certain discursive set and indicates the status of this discourse within a society and a culture. It has no legal status, nor is it located in the fiction of the work; rather, it is located in the break that founds a certain discursive construct and its very particular mode of being. As a result, we could say that in a civilization like our own there are a certain number of discourses that are endowed with the "author function," while others are deprived of it. A private letter may well have a signer—it does not have an author; a contract may well have a guarantor—it does not have an author. An anonymous text posted on a wall probably has a writer—but not an author. The author function is therefore characteristic of the mode of existence, circulation, and functioning of certain discourses within a society.

Let us analyze this "author function" as we have just described it. In our culture, how does one characterize a discourse containing the author function? In what way is this discourse different from other discourses? If we limit our remarks to the author of a book or a text, we can isolate four different characteristics.

First of all, discourses are objects of appropriation. The form of ownership from which they spring is of a rather particular type, one that has been codified for many years. We should note that, historically, this type of ownership has always been subsequent to what one might call penal appropriation. Texts, books, and discourses really began to have authors (other than mythical, "sacralized" and "sacralizing" figures) to the extent that authors became subject to punishment, that is, to the extent that discourses could be transgressive. In our culture (and doubtless in many others), discourse was not originally a product, a thing, a kind of goods; it was essentially an act—an act placed in the bipolar field of the sacred and the profane, the licit and the illicit, the religious and the blasphemous. Historically, it was a gesture fraught with risks before becoming goods caught up in a circuit of ownership.

Once a system of ownership for texts came into being, once strict rules concerning author's rights, author-publisher relations, rights of reproduction, and related matters were enacted—at the end of the eighteenth and the beginning of the nineteenth century—the possibility of transgression attached to the act of writing took on, more and more, the form of an imperative peculiar to literature. It is as if the author, beginning with the moment at which he was placed in the system of property that characterizes our society, compensated for the status that he thus acquired by rediscovering the old bipolar field of discourse, systematically practicing transgression and thereby restoring danger to a writing which was now guaranteed the benefits of ownership.

The author function does not affect all discourses in a universal and constant way, however. This is its second characteristic. In our civilization, it has not always been the same types of texts which have required attribution to an author. There was a time when the texts that we today call "literary" (narratives, stories, epics, tragedies, comedies) were accepted, put into circulation, and valorized without any question about the identity of their author; their anonymity caused no difficulties since their ancientness, whether real or imagined, was regarded as a sufficient guarantee of their status. On the other hand, those texts that we now would call scientific—those dealing with cosmology and the heavens, medicine and illnesses, natural sciences and geography—were accepted in the Middle Ages, and accepted as "true," only when marked with the name of their author. "Hippocrates said," "Pliny recounts," were not really formulas of an argument based on authority; they were the markers inserted in discourses that were supported to be received as statements of demonstrated truth.

A reversal occurred in the seventeenth or eighteenth century. Scientific discourses began to be received for themselves, in the anonymity of an established or always redemonstrable truth; their membership in a systematic ensemble, and not the reference to the individual who produced them, stood as their guarantee. The author function faded away, and the inventor's name served only to christen a theorem, proposition, particular effect, property, body, group of elements, or pathological syndrome. By the same token, literary discourses came to be accepted only when endowed with the author function. We now ask of each poetic or fictional text: From where does it come, who wrote it, when, under what circumstances, or beginning with what design? The meaning ascribed to it and the status or value accorded it depend on the manner in which we answer these questions. And if a text should be discovered in a state of anonymity—whether as a consequence of an accident or the author's explicit wish—the game becomes one of rediscovering the author. Since literary anonymity is not tolerable, we can accept it only in the guise of an enigma. As a result, the author function today plays an important role in our view of literary works. (These are obviously generalizations that would have to be refined insofar as recent critical practice is concerned.)

The third characteristic of this author function is that it does not develop spontaneously as the attribution of a discourse to an individual. It is, rather, the result of a complex operation which constructs a certain rational being that we call "author." Critics doubtless try to give this intelligible being a realistic status, by discerning, in the individual, a "deep" motive, a "creative" power, or a "design," the milieu in which writing originates. Nevertheless, these aspects of an individual which we designate as making him an author are only a projection, in more or less psychologizing terms, of the operations that we force texts to undergo, the connections that we make, the traits that we establish as pertinent, the continuities that we recognize, or the exclusions that we practice. All these operations vary according to periods and types of discourse. We do not construct a "philosophical author" as we do a "poet," just as, in the eighteenth century, one did not construct a novelist as we do today. Still, we can find through the ages certain constants in the rules of author construction.

It seems, for example, that the manner in which literary criticism once defined the author—or, rather, constructed the figure of the author beginning with existing texts and discourses—is directly derived from the manner in which Christian tradition authenticated (or rejected) the texts at its disposal. In order to "rediscover" an author in a work, modern criticism uses methods similar to those that Christian exegesis employed when trying to prove the value of a text by its author's saintliness. In *De viris illustribus*, Saint Jerome explains that homonymy is not sufficient to identify legitimately authors of more than one work: different individuals could have had the same name, or one man could have, illegitimately, borrowed another's patronymic. The name as an individual trademark is not enough when one works within a textual tradition.

How, then, can one attribute several discourses to one and the same author? How can one use the author function to determine if one is dealing with one or several individuals? Saint Jerome proposes four criteria: (1) if among several books attributed to an author one is inferior to the others, it must be withdrawn from the list of the author's works (the author is therefore defined as a constant level of value); (2) the same should be done if certain texts contradict the doctrine expounded in the author's other works (the author is thus defined as a field of conceptual or theoretical coherence); (3) one must also exclude works that are written in a different style, containing words and expressions not ordinarily found in the writer's production (the author is here conceived as a stylistic unity); (4) finally, passages quoting statements that were made or mentioning events that occurred after the author's death must be regarded as interpolated texts (the author is here seen as a historical figure at the crossroads of a certain number of events).

Modern literary criticism, even when—as is now customary—it is not concerned with questions of authentication, still defines the author the same way: the author provides the basis for explaining not only the presence of certain events in a work, but also their transformations, distortions, and diverse modifications (through his biography, the determination of his individual perspective, the analysis of his social position, and the revelation of his basic design). The author is also the principle of a certain unity of writing—all differences having to be resolved, at least in part, by the principles of evolution, maturation, or influence. The author also serves to neutralize the contradictions that may emerge in a series of texts: there must be—at a certain level of his thought or desire, of his consciousness or unconscious—a point where contradictions are resolved, where incompatible elements are at last tied together or organized around a fundamental or originating contradiction. Finally, the author is a particular source of expression that, in more or less completed forms, is manifested equally well, and with similar validity, in works, sketches, letters, fragments, and so on. Clearly, Saint Jerome's four criteria of authenticity (criteria which seem totally insufficient for today's exegetes) do define the four modalities according to which modern criticism brings the author function into play.

But the author function is not a pure and simple reconstruction made second-hand from a text given as passive material. The text always contains a certain number of signs referring to the author. These signs, well known to grammarians, are personal pronouns, adverbs of time and place, and verb conjugation. Such elements do not play the same role in discourses provided with the author function as in those lacking it. In the latter, such "shifters" refer to the real speaker and to the spatiotemporal coordinates of his discourse (although certain modifications can occur, as in the operation of relating discourses in the first person). In the former, however, their role is more complex and variable. Everyone knows that, in a novel narrated in the first person, neither the first-person pronoun nor the present indicative refers exactly either to the writer or to the moment in which he writes, but rather to an alter ego whose distance from the author varies, often changing in the course of the work. It would be just as wrong to equate the author with the real writer as to equate him with the fictitious speaker; the author function is carried out and operates in the scission itself, in this division and this distance.

One might object that this is a characteristic peculiar to novelistic or poetic discourse, a "game" in which only "quasi-discourses" participate. In fact, however, all discourses endowed with the author function do possess this plurality of self. The self that speaks in the preface to a treatise on mathematics—and that indicates the circumstances of the treatise's composition —is identical neither in its position nor in its functioning to the self that speaks in the course of a demonstration, and that appears in the form of "I conclude" or "I suppose." In the first case, the "I" refers to an individual without an equivalent who, in a determined place and time, completed a certain task; in the second, the "I" indicates an instance and a level of demonstration which any individual could perform provided that he accepted the same system of symbols, play of axioms, and set of previous demonstrations. We could also, in the same treatise, locate a third self, one that speaks to tell the work's meaning, the obstacles encountered, the results obtained, and the remaining problems; this self is situated in the field of already existing or yet-to-appear mathematical discourses. The author function is not assumed by the first of these selves at the expense of the other two, which would then be nothing more than a fictitious splitting in two of the first one. On the contrary, in these discourses the author function operates so as to effect the dispersion of these three simultaneous selves.

No doubt analysis could discover still more characteristic traits of the author function. I will limit myself to these four, however, because they seem both the most visible and the most important. They can be summarized as follows: (1) the author function is linked to the juridical and institutional system that encompasses, determines, and articulates the universe of discourses; (2) it does not affect all discourses in the same way at all times and in all types of civilization; (3) it is not defined by the spontaneous attribution of a discourse to its producer, but rather by a series of specific and complex operations; (4) it does not refer purely and simply to a real individual, since it can give rise simultaneously to several selves, to several subjects—positions that can be occupied by different classes of individuals.

Up to this point I have unjustifiably limited my subject. Certainly the author function in painting, music, and other arts should have been discussed, but even supposing that we remain within the world of discourse, as I want to do, I seem to have given the term "author" much too narrow a meaning. I have discussed the author only in the limited sense of a person to whom the production of a text, a book, or a work can be legitimately attributed. It is easy to see that in the sphere of discourse one can be the author of much more than a book—one can be the author of a theory, tradition, or discipline in which other books and authors will in their turn find a place. These authors are in a position which we shall call "transdiscursive." This is a recurring phenomenon—certainly as old as our civilization. Homer, Aristotle, and the Church Fathers, as well as the first mathematicians and the originators of the Hippocratic tradition, all played this role.

Furthermore, in the course of the nineteenth century, there appeared in Europe another, more uncommon, kind of author, whom one should confuse with neither the "great" literary authors, nor the authors of religious texts, nor the founders of science. In a somewhat arbitrary way we shall call those who belong in this last group "founders of discursivity." They are unique in that they are not just the authors of their own works. They have produced something else: the possibilities and the rules for the formation of other texts. In this sense, they are very different, for example, from a novelist, who is, in fact, nothing more than the author of his own text. Freud is not just the author of *The Interpretation of Dreams* or *Jokes and Their Relation to the Unconscious*; Marx is not just the author of the *Communist Manifesto* or *Das Kapital*: they both have established an endless possibility of discourse.

Obviously, it is easy to object. One might say that it is not true that the author of a novel is only the author of his own text; in a sense, he also, provided that he acquires some "importance," governs and commands more than that. To take a very simple example, one could say that Ann Radcliffe not only wrote *The Castles of Athlin and Dunbayne* and several other novels, but also made possible the appearance of the Gothic horror novel at the beginning of the nineteenth century; in that respect, her author function exceeds her own work. But I think there is an answer to this objection. These founders of discursivity (I use Marx and Freud as examples, because I believe them to be both the first and the most important cases) make possible something altogether different from what a novelist makes possible. Ann Radcliffe's texts opened the way for a certain number of resemblances and analogies which have their model or principle in her work. The latter contains characteristic signs, figures, relationships, and structures which could be reused by others. In other words, to say that Ann Radcliffe founded the Gothic horror novel means that in the nineteenth-century Gothic novel one will find, as in Ann Radcliffe's works, the theme of the heroine caught in the trap of her own innocence, the hidden castle, the character of the black, cursed hero devoted to making the world expiate the evil done to him, and all the rest of it.

On the other hand, when I speak of Marx or Freud as founders of discursivity, I mean that they made possible not only a certain number of analogies, but also (and equally important) a certain number of differences. They have created a possibility for something other than their discourse, yet something belonging to what they founded. To say that Freud founded psychoanalysis does not (simply) mean that we find the concept of the libido or the technique of dream analysis in the works of Karl Abraham or Melanie Klein; it means that Freud made possible a certain number of divergences—with respect to his own texts, concepts, and hypotheses—that all arise from the psychoanalytic discourse itself.

This would seem to present a new difficulty, however: is the above not true, after all, of any founder of a science, or of any author who has introduced some important transformation into a science? After all, Galileo made possible not only those discourses that repeated the laws that he had formulated, but also statements very different from what he himself had said. If Cuvier is the founder of biology or Saussure the founder of linguistics, it is not because they were imitated, nor because people have since taken up again the concept of organism or sign; it is because Cuvier made possible, to a certain extent, a theory of evolution diametrically opposed to his own fixism; it is because Saussure made possible a generative grammar radically different from his structural analyses. Superficially, then, the initiation of discursive practices appears similar to the founding of any scientific endeavor.

Still, there is a difference, and a notable one. In the case of a science, the act that founds it is on an equal footing with its future transformations; this act becomes in some respects part of the set of modifications that it makes possible. Of course, this belonging can take several forms. In the future development of a science, the founding act may appear as little more than a particular instance of a more general phenomenon which unveils itself in the process. It can also turn out to be marred by intuition and empirical bias; one must then reformulate it, making it the object of a certain number of supplementary theoretical operations which establish it more rigorously, etc. Finally, it can seem to be a hasty generalization which must be limited, and whose restricted domain of validity must be retraced. In other words, the founding act of a science can always be reintroduced within the machinery of those transformations that derive from it.

In contrast, the initiation of a discursive practice is heterogeneous to its subsequent transformations. To expand a type of discursivity, such as psychoanalysis as founded by Freud, is not to give it a formal generality that it would not have permitted at the outset, but rather to open it up to a certain number of possible applications. To limit psychoanalysis as a type of discursivity is, in reality, to try to isolate in the founding act an eventually restricted number of propositions or statements to which, alone, one grants a founding value, and in relation to which certain concepts or theories accepted by Freud might be considered as derived, secondary, and accessory. In addition, one does not declare certain propositions in the work of these founders to be false: instead, when trying to seize the act of founding, one sets aside those statements that are not pertinent, either because they are deemed inessential, or because they are considered "prehistoric" and derived from another type of discursivity. In other words, unlike the founding of a science, the initiation of a discursive practice does not participate in its later transformations.

As a result, one defines a proposition's theoretical validity in relation to the work of the founders—while, in the case of Galileo and Newton, it is in relation to what physics or cosmology *is* (in its intrinsic structure and "normativity") that one affirms the validity of any proposition that those men may have put forth. To phrase it very schematically: the work of initiators of discursivity is not situated in the space that science defines; rather, it is the science or the discursivity which refers back to their work as primary coordinates.

In this way we can understand the inevitable necessity, within these fields of discursivity, for a "return to the origin." This return, which is part of the discursive field itself, never stops modifying it. The return is not a historical supplement which would be added to the discursivity, or merely an ornament; on the contrary, it constitutes an effective and necessary task of transforming the discursive practice itself. Reexamination of Galileo's text may well change our knowledge of the history of mechanics, but it will never be able to change mechanics itself. On the other hand, reexamining Freud's texts modifies psychoanalysis itself, just as a reexamination of Marx's would modify Marxism.

What I have just outlined regarding the initiation of discursive practices is, of course, very schematic; this is true, in particular, of the opposition that I have tried to draw between discursive initiation and scientific founding. It is not always easy to distinguish between the two; moreover, nothing proves that they are two mutually exclusive procedures. I have attempted the distinction for only one reason: to show that the author function, which is complex enough when one tries to situate it at the level of a book or a series of texts that carry a given signature, involves still more determining factors when one tries to analyze it in larger units, such as groups of works or entire disciplines.

To conclude, I would like to review the reasons why I attach a certain importance to what I have said.

First, there are theoretical reasons. On the one hand, an analysis in the direction that I have outlined might provide for an approach to a typology of discourse. It seems to me, at least at first glance, that such a typology cannot be constructed solely from the grammatical features, formal structures, and objects of discourse: more likely there exist properties or relationships peculiar to discourse (not reducible to the rules of grammar and logic), and one must use these to distinguish the major categories of discourse. The relationship (or nonrelationship) with an author, and the different forms this relationship takes, constitute—in a quite visible manner—one of these discursive properties.

On the other hand, I believe that one could find here an introduction to the historical analysis of discourse. Perhaps it is time to study discourses not only in terms of their expressive value or formal transformations, but according to their modes of existence. The modes of circulation, valorization, attribution, and appropriation of discourses vary with each culture and are modified within each. The manner in which they are articulated according to social relationships can be more readily understood, I believe, in the activity of the author function and in its modifications than in the themes or concepts that discourses set in motion.

It would seem that one could also, beginning with analyses of this type, reexamine the privileges of the subject. I realize that in undertaking the internal and architectonic analysis of a work (be it a literary text, philosophical system, or scientific work), in setting aside biographical and psychological references, one has already called back into question the absolute character and founding role of the subject. Still, perhaps one must return to this question, not in order to reestablish the theme of an originating subject, but to grasp the subject's points of insertion, modes of functioning, and system of dependencies. Doing so means overturning the traditional problem, no longer raising the questions: How can a free subject penetrate the substance of things and give it meaning? How can it activate the rules of a language from within and thus give rise to the designs which are properly its own? Instead, these questions will be raised: How, under what conditions, and in what forms can something like a subject appear in the order of discourse? What place can it occupy in each type of discourse, what functions can it assume, and by obeying what rules? In short, it is a matter of depriving the subject (or its substitute) of its role as originator, and of analyzing the subject as a variable and complex function of discourse.

Second, there are reasons dealing with the "ideological" status of the author. The question then becomes: How can one reduce the great peril, the great danger with which fiction threatens our world? The answer is: one can reduce it with the author. The author allows a limitation of the cancerous and dangerous proliferation of significations within a world where one is thrifty not only with one's resources and riches, but also with one's discourses and their significations. The author is the principle of thrift in the proliferation of meaning. As a result, we must entirely reverse the traditional idea of the author. We are accustomed, as we have seen earlier, to saying that the author is the genial creator of a work in which he deposits, with infinite wealth and generosity, an inexhaustible world of significations. We are used to thinking that the author is so different from all other men, and so transcendent with regard to all languages that, as soon as he speaks, meaning begins to proliferate, to proliferate indefinitely.

The truth is quite the contrary: the author is not an indefinite source of significations which fill a work; the author does not precede the works; he is a certain functional principle by which, in our culture, one limits, excludes, and chooses; in short, by which one impedes the free circulation, the free manipulation, the free composition, decomposition, and recomposition of fiction. In fact, if we are accustomed to presenting the author as a genius, as a perpetual surging of invention, it is because, in reality, we make him function in exactly the opposite fashion. One can say that the author is an ideological product, since we represent him as the opposite of his historically real function. (When a historically given function is represented in a figure that inverts it, one has an ideological production.) The author is therefore the ideological figure by which one marks the manner in which we fear the proliferation of meaning.

In saying this, I seem to call for a form of culture in which fiction would not be limited by the figure of the author. It would be pure romanticism, however, to imagine a culture in which the fictive would operate in an absolutely free state, in which fiction would be put at the disposal of everyone and would develop without passing through something like a necessary or constraining figure. Although, since the eighteenth century, the author has played the role of the regulator of the fictive, a role quite characteristic of our era of industrial and bourgeois society, of individualism and private property, still, given the historical modifications that are taking place, it does not seem necessary that the author function remain constant in form, complexity, and even in existence. I think that, as our society changes, at the very moment when it is in the process of changing, the author function will disappear, and in such a manner that fiction and its polysemous texts will once again function according to another mode, but still with a system of constraint—one which will no longer be the author, but which will have to be determined or, perhaps, experienced.

All discourses, whatever their status, form, value, and whatever the treatment to which they will be subjected, would then develop in the anonymity of a murmur. We would no longer hear the questions that have been rehashed for so long: Who really spoke? Is it really he and not someone else? With what authenticity or originality? And what part of his deepest self did he express in his discourse? Instead, there would be other questions, like these: What are the modes of existence of this discourse? Where has it been used, how can it circulate, and who can appropriate it for himself? What are the places in it where there is room for possible subjects? Who can assume these various subject functions? And behind all these questions, we would hear hardly anything but the stirring of an indifference: What difference does it make who is speaking?

NOTE

1. *Ed.*: John Searle, *Speech Acts: An Essay in the Philosophy of Language* (Cambridge, Eng.: Cambridge University Press, 1969), pp. 162–74.

CHAPTER 3

Kierkegaard and the Anxiety of Authorship

Merold Westphal

The concept of author in our day has been distorted in an extremely immoral way. (S[ø]ren Kierkegaard)[1]

I

In his biography of Mozart, Wolfgang Hildesheimer tells us that Kierkegaard "wanted to start a sect to revere Mozart, not above others, but exclusively."[2] The footnote, as one might expect, is to *Either/Or*. The only problem is that *Either/Or* is written by five different authors, none of whom is Kierkegaard.[3]

The effusive encomium for Mozart is found in an ecstatic essay entitled "The Immediate Erotic Stages or the Musical Erotic," drawn from *The Marriage of Figaro, The Magic Flute*, and *Don Giovanni*. But the author of this piece is the young aesthete, identified only as A. This means that in the text in question it is not Kierkegaard who speaks. He is most emphatic about this. "Thus in the pseudonymous books there is not a single word by me . . . if it should occur to anyone to want to quote a particular passage from the books, it is my wish, my prayer, that he will do me the kindness of citing the respective pseudonymous author's name, not mine" (CUP 626–27; cf. JP VI, 6786, 6566).

Pseudonyms are sometimes a means whereby authors express their own views without getting into trouble with the censors or without embarrassing those

Merold Westphal, "Kierkegaard and the Anxiety of Authorship," *International Philosophical Quarterly* Vol. 34, No. 1, Issue No. 133 (March 1994), pp. 5–22. Used by permission of *International Philosophical Quarterly*, Fordham University.

whose names must be changed to protect the innocent. The point is to hide the true identity of the author. Because Kierkegaard denies that this is the point of pseudonymity (CUP 625), he can coherently insist, precisely while acknowledging publicly that he is the producer of these works, that they remain pseudonymous. He wrote them, but he is not their author. If we are to understand this, we must recognize that the authors and editors to whom the pseudonymous works are attributed are *personae* rather than disguises.[4]

Such *personae* are familiar to us in the characters produced by novelists and playwrights. Kierkegaard notes that "all poetic creativity would *eo ipso* be made impossible or meaningless and intolerable if the lines [spoken by such characters] were supposed to be the producer's own words" (CUP 627). What is different in Kierkegaard's case is that he creates fictitious authors, who in turn create their own characters, tell their own stories, present their own theories. His kind of poetic creativity would become "impossible or meaningless and intolerable" if the words of his authors were supposed to be his own.

This means that to attribute to Kierkegaard the enthusiasm for Mozart expressed by A is like attributing to Dostoyevsky the world view of Raskolnikov. Just think of the wonderful intellectual biographies of Dostoyevsky we could write, glorifying or demonizing him with reference to practically any ideology, if we could selectively attribute to him the beliefs, feelings, and actions of the characters in his novels. What is probably the most irresponsible book ever written on Kierkegaard is constructed on precisely this principle. Adorno's *Kierkegaard: Construction of the Aesthetic* ranges through the pseudonymous writings and assigns to Kierkegaard the views of first this and then that pseudonym, giving us a construction, to be sure, but not so much of the aesthetic as of a thoroughly fictitious Kierkegaard.

We can avoid Adorno's arbitrariness by simply following the injunction to attribute the pseudonymous texts to their respective authors. But if we would go beyond blind obedience we must try to understand the point of Kierkegaard's "polyonymity" (CUP 625). We might start from the theory of fiction in general, beginning with Aristotle's claim that poetry is more philosophical than history because [it is] more universal (*Poetics*, 1451b5 ff.), and then see what is involved in extending the fiction function from characters created by authors to the authors themselves. In this essay I shall adopt a different strategy. I shall seek to throw light on Kierkegaard's practice by relating it to a recurring theme in contemporary continental philosophy. We could with good reason call this motif either the assault on authorship or the death of the author, but I shall refer to it as the anxiety of authorship. In the midst of their often rancorous quarrels, structuralists like Barthes, poststructuralists like Foucault and Derrida, and hermeneuticists like Gadamer hold views of this topic that, if not identical, exhibit powerful family resemblances. We may be able to bring Kierkegaard's practice into sharper focus by relating it to the recurring foci of their discussions.[5]

We might consider Gadamer's *Truth and Method* (1960) to be the artillery barrage that softened up the stronghold of the author in preparation for the all out assault by the French. His target is the "romantic" hermeneutics of Schleiermacher, Dilthey, and, more recently, Betti, that makes the intent of the author (*mens auctoris*) the meaning of a text. A text is the *expression* of the life or experience or thought of the author, and interpretation is *divination* (the French will say deciphering), the re-creation or reproduction of the author's inner state on the basis of the text as clue (TM 196–97, 187). Betti, for example, makes this scheme "the first and basic canon" for all hermeneutics. "Since meaningfull [*sic*] forms, as the object of interpretation, are essentially objectivations of mind and, in particular, manifestations of some thought-content, it is clear that they have to be understood with reference to that other mind that has been objectivated in them, and not in relation to any meaning the form itself may acquire if abstracted from the representational function it had for that mind or thought. . . . May I suggest that we call this first canon the canon of the hermeneutical autonomy of the object" (HGM 58).

This canon has an important corollary and an absolutely fundamental presupposition. The corollary is that "an interpreter's task is to retrace the creative process, to reconstruct it within himself, to retranslate the extraneous thought of an Other, a part of the past, a remembered event, into the actuality of one's own life" (HGM 62). The presupposition is that interpretation is "the transposition of meaning from the original perspective of the author into the subjectivity of the interpreter" without any "transformation" by virtue of the mediation of past with present; for unless "the understanding arrived at corresponded fully to the *meaning underlying the text* as an objectivation of mind," the "objectivity of the result" would not "be *guaranteed* on the basis of a reliable process of interpretation" (HGM 81, 79, my emphasis).

Gadamer has a triple response to this view. First, in relation to the irony of a "romantic" hermeneutics so concerned with "guaranteed" objectivity, he suggests that it belongs to the Cartesian (Enlightenment) project of method in the service of the "control," "possession," and "domination" of its subject matter (TM 237–39, 378, 476). Its goal is not the professed autonomy of the text but that of the interpreter, who is enabled to claim "superiority over his object" (TM 195).

Second, he challenges the notion of an external relation between a text and a meaning "underlying" it. The works to be interpreted "become detached from their origins and, just because of this, begin to speak—surprising even their creators . . . neither the word nor the sentence nor, as one would say today, the discourse refers back to the intention of the author." This is because "the intention has, so to speak, 'gone into' the work, and can no longer be sought behind it or before it" (HL 123).

Finally, he challenges the notion of an external relation between a text and the event or process of its interpretation. "The mens auctoris is not admissible as a yardstick for the meaning of a work" because "the idea of a work-in-itself, divorced from its constantly renewed reality in being experienced, always has something abstract about it . . . in other words, *understanding belongs to the being of that which is understood*" (TM xxxi, my emphasis).

Gadamer develops this belonging with four analogies. The first is with music. He asks, "Does being understood belong to the meaning of a text just as being heard belongs to the meaning of music?" (TM 164). For him the question is rhetorical. If every performance of a work is a new "reading," so every reading of a text is a new "performance" of its meaning. The second analogy is with historical events. "The hermeneutical reduction to the author's meaning is just as inappropriate as the reduction of historical events to the intentions of their protagonists" (TM 373). The third analogy is with conversation. Reading a text is like conversing with another person. It is a subject-subject relation in which we are addressed and questioned. "A reconstructed question [one understood as addressed to the reader] can never stand within its original horizon." This is why "understanding is always more than merely re-creating someone else's meaning" (TM 374–75). Finally, there is the analogy of interpretation with translation. No matter how much the translator may have "empathized with his author," translation cannot be "simply a re-awakening of the original process in the writer's mind; rather it is necessarily a re-creation of the text *guided by the way the translator understands what it says*," which involves "a new light" or a "highlighting" of the text from the author's perspective (TM 385–87, my emphasis). Interpretation, like translation involves the fusion of horizons, not the immaculate conveyance of a determinate identity from one to another.

The conclusion these models are intended to support is simple. "Not occasionally but always, the meaning of a text goes beyond its author. That is why understanding is not merely a reproductive but always a productive activity as well" (TM 296). Does this support the notion that the interpreter understands the text better than its author does? No. "It is enough to say that we understand in a *different way, if we understand at all*" (TM 297; cf. 373).

II

Translated into French, this challenge to the author's control over the text does indeed come out differently, but nonetheless recognizably. We shall look first at two brief, but famous essays on the topic, "The Death of the Author" by Roland Barthes (1968) and "What Is an Author?" by Michel Foucault (1969). Barthes speaks of the "prestige" of the author (DA 143), and Foucault of the author's "privilege" (WA 103, 105, 117). (In doing so, both writers treat the author as a special case of the larger question of modernity's notions of the individual and the subject.) Since for Kierkegaard pseudonymity seems to be the voluntary renunciation of the perks of authorship, we will want to see as clearly as possible what this "prestige" and "privilege" amount to.

In the opening round Gadamer has challenged the claim that the author is the unilateral source of a text's meaning. Similarly, Barthes' target is the author as a special case of the prestige of the modern individual who "reigns," even "tyrannically" (DA 143, 147), in the realm of language. This sovereignty is as much economic as political. It is "the epitome and culmination of capitalist ideology."

This strange claim has nothing to do with royalties. Its meaning becomes clear with reference to Mallarmé, the first to see "the necessity to substitute language itself for the person, who until then had been supposed to be its owner. For him, for us too, it is language which speaks, not the author" (DA 143).[6] At issue is the prestige of presiding.

By asking whether language is not prior to its "user" Barthes and Mallarmé suggest that sovereignty of ownership is but the flip side of the sovereignty of origin. "Writing," Barthes tells us, "is the destruction . . . of every point of origin" (DA 142). According to the notion he is challenging, the author is before and the book is after. The two are related to each other as father and child or as subject and predicate because writing has the character of expression, giving outward and public form to what has already existed inwardly in the author's mind (DA 145–46).[7]

But structural linguistics, along with such writers as Mallarmé, Valery, Proust, the surrealists, and Brecht, have enabled us to see that the scriptor, Barthes' replacement for the author, "is born simultaneously with the text . . . in no way equipped with a being preceding or exceeding the writing." It follows that writing is not expression and inscription "traces a field without origin—or which, at least, has no other origin than language itself" (DA 144–46).

It is in terms of the author's alleged sovereignty of origin that Barthes makes it clear that the root metaphor he wishes to uproot is theological more than either political or economic. For he immediately continues, "We know that a text is not a line of words releasing a single 'theological' meaning (the 'message' of the Author-God) but a multi-dimensional space in which a variety of writings, none of them original, blend and clash . . . the writer can only imitate a gesture that is always anterior, never original" (DA 146). More fundamental than the relation of owner to property or of father to child is the relation of God to the world. What makes the meaning of a text "theological" here is not its content but its singleness, its unity. As created by God the world has a single, all-encompassing meaning. The author function is the attempt to give a similar unity to the text, derived from its pure origin. But if God is dead, as Nietzsche reminds us, there is only a plurality of interpretations. Correspondingly, Barthes insists that the writer is not godlike and that however creative he (and I use the masculine deliberately) may be, he is not a Creator.

But if there is no Alpha, there is no Omega either, and the same point can be made in terms of finality and completion. "To give a text an Author is to impose a limit on that text, to furnish it with a final signified, to close the writing." Previously the single meaning of the text was temporally *before* its inscription; now its "ultimate meaning" is to be found spatially *beneath* the work. The task of reading is thus "to decipher a text" by "discovering the Author . . . beneath the work." If writing is expression, reading is deciphering.

By contrast Barthes insists that "everything is to be *disentangled*, nothing *deciphered*" because "there is nothing beneath" the text. He is again explicit about the theological character of this denial. When we refuse "to assign a 'secret,' an ultimate meaning, to the text (and to the world as text)," we engage in "what may be called an anti-theological activity . . . since to refuse to fix meaning is, in the end, to refuse God and his hypostases—reason, science, law" (DA 147).

We must be wary of two confusions about the theological dimension of this discussion. First, there is a *non sequitur* to be avoided. The evidence to which Barthes appeals concerns the character of texts produced by human scriptors. If he is right (and I think he is) that they are never able to be Authors, the Alpha and Omega of their texts, nothing whatever follows about the possibility of God as the Alpha and Omega of the world. Of course, if, with Barthes, we deny that the "world as text" has an "ultimate meaning" we are denying God. But if Barthes wants to suggest that the case against treating human texts as having a single, fixed meaning is also a case against treating the world (as text) in that way, his argument is fallacious. Kevin Hart charitably attributes to his intention only what he is entitled to claim: "Perhaps Barthes's aim lies not so much in making out a case against theism but in developing another vocabulary for interpretation, one in which 'God' plays no important role."[8] The question whether the world has a single, ultimate meaning and the question whether human texts have this character are two different questions. It is wishful and confused thinking to infer the finitude of being as such from the finitude of human being.

But the main issue all along has been not God as Author of the world but the Author as God of the text. The Author whose death Barthes celebrates is the human writer to whom divine attributes are assigned. Thus the phrase "Author-God" (DA 146) expresses the theological character of a certain view of writing. The Author is the *archē* from whom the *telos* emerges in terms of which the text is at once a fixed identity and a totality.

It is here that a second confusion needs to be avoided. Is it "an anti-theological activity" to challenge this notion of the Author as God? Have not Jewish and Christian theologies in their doctrines of both creation and the fall insisted on the essential difference between the human and the divine? Have they not provided a conceptual framework conducive to seeing human writers as the Alpha and Omega of their texts in only a relative and highly qualified sense? Well, yes and no. When they have stayed close to their Hebrew roots they have done so. But when they have sold their soul to Plato or the Enlightenment it has been a different story.

Barthes insists that the Author is a modern figure (DA 142). To be more specific, the Author is a child of the Enlightenment insofar as that name signifies the attempt by an increasingly secular society to replace the divine with the human. Heidegger describes this context into which Barthes places the Author: "Into the position of the vanished authority of God and of the teaching office of the Church steps the authority of conscience, obtrudes the authority of reason. . . . Creativity, previously the unique property of the biblical god, becomes the distinctive mark of human activity. Human creativity [*Schaffen*] finally passes over into business enterprise [*Geschäft*]."[9] We might say there is a parallel between modern culture's Author as Creator and modern society's Entrepreneur as Providence. Romanticism's aesthetic "antidote" to the reign of capital and technique is but the flip side of the same project.

To challenge these ersatz gods, the Author and the Entrepreneur, is to challenge the humanistic theology of the Enlightenment. But it is not an anti-theological gesture as such, for any theology that stays close to its biblical roots will have theological motivations for precisely such a challenge. (Could this be what Kierkegaard is up to?) In talking about the theological character of the Author as Origin, it is important to distinguish the "enlightened" theologics that support such a notion of writing from the biblical theologies that undermine it. (Could the question of authorship be fundamental rather than peripheral to Kierkegaard's quarrel with Hegel?)

There is one final, crucial theme in Barthes' essay. He praises Mallarmé's poetics for "suppressing the author in the interests of writing (which is, as will be seen, to restore the place of the reader)" (DA 143). So he concludes his brief essay by saying, "We know that to give writing its future, it is necessary to overthrow the myth: the birth of the reader must be at the cost of the death of the Author" (DA 148).

How so? If a text does not have a fixed unity of meaning given to it from outside by its author, it is the reader who can provide the needed wholeness. So, "a text's unity lies not in its origin but in its destination," because "there is one place where this multiplicity is focused and that place is the reader, not as was hitherto said, the author," and "there is, however, someone who understands each word in its duplicity and who, in addition, hears the very deafness of the characters speaking in front of him—this someone being precisely the reader" (DA 148). Of course the unity given to a text by the reader is different from that given by an Author. For while there is but one Author, there are many readers (including the "same" reader at a different reading); hence a reader dependent unity in a text will not be a single, fixed unity outside the text but a plurality of unities that belong to the text's career.

Three themes from Barthes' essay reverberate through Foucault's. The first is the notion of writing as expression, which he limns in now familiar terms. The author is thought to "precede" the text and to occupy a position not only "outside" it, but "so transcendent with regard to all languages that, as soon as he speaks, meaning begins to proliferate" (WA 101, 118–19).

The second theme, already implicit in the first, is the theological role of the author. When writing is expression the author is the source of a text's unity, structure, and coherence (WA 103, 111). Writing is thought of as "sacred" and "creative" because of "the absolute character and founding role of the subject ... the originating subject ... the author [as] the genial creator of a work in which he deposits, with infinite wealth and generosity, an inexhaustible world of significations" (WA 104, 118). The Author is treated as an "intelligible being" from whom a text emerges as from "a 'deep' motive, a 'creative' power, or a 'design' " (WA 110). Correspondingly, reading or criticism is governed by "the religious principle of the hidden meaning (which requires interpretation) . . . [and] the religious principle of inalterable and yet never fulfilled tradition," along with their aesthetic correlates (WA 104–05).[10]

Needless to say, Foucault challenges this notion of the Author as Creator, a transcendent and absolute origin. In doing so he echoes a third theme from Barthes, the "creative" role of the reader. He suggests that such questions as "Who really spoke?" will be and should be replaced by such questions as "Who can appropriate the text for himself?" (WA 119–20).[11]

Finally, Foucault introduces a new theme not present in Barthes. He says that "today's writing has freed itself from the dimension of expression." We now know how heavily loaded a claim that is. But the fascinating commentary comes in the further claim: "Writing has become linked to sacrifice, even to the sacrifice of life: it is now a *voluntary effacement* . . . the effacement of the writing subject's individual characteristics . . . the writing subject cancels out the signs of his particular individuality" (WA 102, my emphasis). What is the meaning of this shift from viewing the death of the Author as a necessity that cannot be avoided to seeing it as a possibility that might be voluntarily chosen? Unfortunately, Foucault does not say. But he has raised a question we can address to Derrida as we turn to him.

Like Barthes and Foucault, Derrida attacks the metaphor of expression. This assault is the central theme of his early critique of Husserl, *Speech and Phenomena*.[12] It is not necessary, however, to follow the rather technical and very closely textual development of the argument there to get its general drift, which Derrida makes abundantly clear elsewhere. For example, in *Positions* he identifies Husserl's theory of communication, and thus of authorship, as an expression theory because of his commitment to meaning independent of language. Both as intentional act (*noēsis*) and intentional object (*noēma*), meaning is an intelligible something externally related to the sensible vehicles that become its bearers. "This layer of pure meaning, or a pure signified, refers, explicitly in Husserl . . . to a layer of prelinguistic or presemiotic (preexpressive, Husserl calls it) meaning whose presence would be conceivable *outside and before* the work of *différance, outside and before* the *process* or *system* of signification. The latter would only bring meaning to light, translate it, transport it, communicate it, incarnate it, express it, etc." (P 30–32; my emphasis).[13]

Here we encounter the postal metaphor that is the main target of *The Post Card*, the notion that communication "in effect implies a *transmission charged with making pass, from one subject to another, the identity of a signified* object, of a *meaning* or of a *concept* rightfully separable from the process of passage and from the signifying operation" (P 23). The commonsense idea here is that it does not matter whether I send this manuscript to the publisher by Federal Express or United Parcel or the U.S. Post Office, since its meaning is unconditioned by and indifferent to the system that conveys it from one place to another. The philosophically loaded move is to identify language with a series of such postal systems for conveying meanings from one mind to another, meanings which in their "pure" state exist "outside," "before," or "beneath" the texts of their linguistic incarnation (P 30–32, 63).

This notion of a meaning that "does not fall into the world" (of process and system) until it is already completed is the key to the history of metaphysics from Plato to Husserl (P 22).[14] Derrida calls it the idea of the transcendental signified, the notion of "a concept simply present for thought, independent of a relationship to language, that is of a relationship to a system of signifiers" (P 19–20).[15] Derrida's critique of pure meaning seeks to show, drawing on structural linguistics, "that the signified is inseparable from the signifier, that the signified and signifier are the two sides of one and the same production" (P 18). This means that the notion of a transcendental signified is a transcendental illusion, an impossibility for human knowledge toward which we are nevertheless ineluctably drawn (P 33).[16]

If the task of the Author were simply to encode or express a transcendental signified, a meaning already fixed and determinate prior to and outside of its linguistic embodiment, the Author would be the cause and master of the text (P 28–29). But if, as Derrida argues, following Saussure, "language . . . is not a function of the speaking subject" (P 29), how could an Author be the Alpha and Omega of a text? Dare one claim to be the author of books "whose *unfinished movement* assigns itself no *absolute beginning*" (P 3, my emphasis; cf. 45)?

It comes as no surprise that the concept of the Author is as much a theological idea for Derrida as for Barthes and Foucault.[17] The notion of "an Idea . . . as simply anterior to a work which would supposedly be the expression of it" is not merely the prejudice of idealism. "Divine creativity, in this case, would be reappropriated by a hypocritical humanism" (FS 11–12), since the Author's relation to the book would be like that of God to the world. The Author would be a "subject who supposedly would be the absolute origin of his own discourse and supposedly would construct it 'out of nothing,' 'out of whole cloth,' would be the creator of the verb, the verb itself" (SSP 285).

The "prestige" and "privilege" of the Author are those of a divine sovereignty. Derrida designates this godlike role of the Author with a series of interchangeable terms: (absolute) origin, *archai*, source, basis, end, beyond, presence, and center (P 14; SSP 278–87). Contrary to the myth of meaning before, beyond, or outside linguistic mediation, he argues that for the human author, "Being has always already begun." The temporality of writing means that the history of the work "is not only its *past*, the eve or the sleep in which it precedes itself in an author's intentions, but is also the impossibility of its ever being *present*, of its ever being summarized by some absolute simultaneity or instantaneousness [even in the author's intentions]" (FS 12–14). Archaeology cannot get us to an Alpha point, nor eschatology to an Omega point.[18] Writing is always *in medias res*.

It is one thing to claim that human authors are not prior to their texts and outside the linguistic systems that they merely use to express themselves, that they are, in Barthes' words, "born simultaneously" with their texts; it is quite another to say that there is no God prior to and thus transcendent to the world. It is the difference between saying that God the Creator is not an appropriate metaphor for the human author and saying that there is no Creator God. Derrida clearly wants to say both, and like Barthes he risks implying a *non sequitur* in discussing the theological aspect of a certain idea of the Author. He often sounds as if he thinks the linguistic case against the human author as an absolute origin is part of a theological case against God as Creator. So he runs together his denial that human books have a certain character with his quite different denial that there is or could be a divine book.

No doubt the most familiar version of the divine book is the book of nature underlying Renaissance science. But Derrida focuses our attention on another version, the one Leibniz presents in the *Theodicy*. It is the book that contains the "totality of the Universe," the "history of this world" as the record of the only choice the divine mind could make, namely, the best of all possible worlds. Thus one can say, "There is only one Book, and this same Book is distributed throughout all books," meaning "that there is only one book on earth, that is the law of the earth, the earth's true Bible. The difference between individual works is simply the difference between individual interpretations of one true and established text" (FS 9–10).

In opposition, Derrida says, "To write is not only to conceive the Leibnizian book as an impossible possibility. . . . To write is not only to know that the Book does not exist and that forever there are books. . . . To write is to know that what has not yet been produced within literality has no other dwelling place, does not await us in . . . some divine understanding" (FS 10–11).

This is, of course, a stipulative definition of writing, but Derrida does not think it merely arbitrary. It belongs, on his view, to our history. He claims that "this absence of divine writing . . . the absence of the Jewish God . . . the absence and haunting of the divine sign . . . regulates all modern criticism and aesthetics" (FS 10). It would be trivial to point to twentieth-century authors for whom this is not true, since they would be proven thereby only not to be "modern" in this sense. Like Nietzsche, whose "death of God" declaration is his model here, Derrida points to a historical phenomenon typical of modernity and professes it as his own credo.

In his essay on Jabès the contrast between Leibnizian and modern writing becomes the contrast between the rabbi and the poet. For the heteronomous Jew, as for the believer in Leibniz's book, writing can only be a matter of sacred text and commentary. For the autonomous poet, by contrast, writing grows as a "weed" between "the fragments of the broken Tables" (EJ 66–67). The poet's way is "preceded by no truth, and thus lacking the prescription of truth's rigor, is the way through the Desert . . . God no longer speaks to us; he has interrupted himself: we must take words upon ourselves . . . because we have ceased hearing the voice from within the immediate proximity of the garden" (EJ 68). Corresponding to this exile, this separation, this lost immediacy (EJ 67–68) is an active resistance to the Jewish God, for "the poetic revolution of our century" is the attempt "always in vain—to retake possession of [our] language (as if this were meaningful) by any means, through all routes, and to claim responsibility for it against a Father of Logos" (EJ 73). Indeed, the only sense in which either writing or reading is "originary" is that "they do not first have to transcribe or discover" the Logos, the truth as found in a divine understanding (OG 19; cf. OG 13–14, FS 11). What, he asks pointedly, if writing were preceded by an "original illegibility" (EJ 77)?

Derrida's is clearly an atheistic concept of authorship. He quotes Georges Canguilhem as saying, "The idea that man has of his poetic power corresponds to the idea he has about the creation of the world, and to the solution he gives to the problem of the radical origin of things" (FS 10). We can summarize his view in relation to the two ideas of the book with which he works:

Book = $_{df}$ writing with a fixed and finished meaning, a linguistic totality by virtue of its prelinguistic origin.

books = $_{df}$ writing with an inherently labile and unfinished meaning both in relation to their own lack of an absolute origin and in relation to other texts of the same sort.

Because there is neither a divine or a human author capable of producing a Book, there are only books. The "prestige" and "privilege" of the Author are transcendental illusions. Both the pre-Enlightenment piety of those who treat writing as commentary (on the Book of the divine Author) and the Enlightenment hubris of those who would replace the divine Author with the human Author are misguided. The end of the Book is the beginning of post-Enlightenment writing (see OG 6–26).[19]

The combination of the death of God and the death [of] Man as modernity's ersatz God, makes the replacement of Authorship and the Book with writing and texts a necessity that can be avoided only in the world of illusion. This necessity is experienced in anguish (FS 9) because "language itself is menaced in its very life, helpless, adrift in the threat of limitlessness," and has thereby ceased "to be self-assured, contained, and *guaranteed* by the infinite signified which *seemed* to exceed it" (OG 6, his emphasis, then mine). At first Derrida speaks of "an anxiety about language," only to correct himself and speak of "an anxiety of language," since the anxiety consists precisely in the awareness that we are not safely situated outside of language where we could be anxious *about* it but have an identity so inextricably linked to language that our anxiety cannot be distinguished from its (FS 3).

The autonomy of language vis-à-vis its users means that in fact we have no choice but "to emancipate [one's language] or lose one's hold on it, to let it make its way alone and unarmed," to say with Jabès, "*I am absent because I am the storyteller. Only the story is real*" (EJ 70). But just like parents in relation to children they once thought they owned, this release can be reluctant or willing.

Reluctant release takes the form of nostalgia, the sighing sadness for a past that never was. Derrida finds this nostalgia especially pronounced in Rousseau, Lévi-Strauss, and Heidegger (SSP 292, EM 123–34; cf. VM 88). But Nietzsche signals another possible response, an *amor fati*, a "joyous affirmation of the play of the world . . . the affirmation of a world of signs without fault, without truth, and without origin which is offered to an active interpretation. *This affirmation then determines the noncenter otherwise than as loss of the center.* And it plays without security" (SSP 292).[20]

Nostalgia, whether in the writer or in the parent, is a constant attempt to tempt oneself, a continuous invitation to lapse back, against one's own insight, into viewing the text or the child as a possession, to be controlled.[21] By contrast, to affirm with joy the text's majority is to set it free to make its way "alone and unarmed." This is the equivalent in Derrida to the "voluntary effacement" of the author's privilege that we found in Foucault. We can choose to live in nostalgia, constantly prey to the transcendental illusions of the Author's authority; but can also choose to face the reality of our situation and, instead of succumbing to anxiety, accept the risks of writing.

To do this, however, is not merely to liberate the text. It is also to liberate the reader. By abandoning the notion of writing as expression we abandon the notion of reading as deciphering and offer our texts "to an active interpretation" (SSP 292; cf. EJ 76). Then we acknowledge that "reading is transformational" (P 63; cf. 20), and, in so doing, we give to the reader an originality comparable to that of the author (OG 19; cf. FS 11).

III

For Kierkegaard as for Foucault and Derrida, the very limited ability of the author to control the process of communication is at once a structural necessity and a personal choice; it is a "voluntary effacement," a kind of self-denying ordinance in which the author, who in fact is not God, willingly agrees to play a role other than God vis-à-vis text and reader. For him as for the French the issue of authorship will be theologically loaded from start to finish.

Writing pseudonymously is one of the most dramatic ways in which Kierkegaard voluntarily forgoes the privileges of authorship. But the most inclusive expression of this posture is the constantly reiterated claim that he writes "without authority," for this claim applies in the first instance even to those writings published under his own name. During 1843–44, while producing the pseudonymous works, he published six small volumes of "upbuilding discourses," which in 1845 he published together as *Eighteen Upbuilding Discourses*. The six prefaces differ from one another, but each begins with these words, "Although this little book (which is called 'discourses,' not sermons, because its author does not have authority to *preach*, 'upbuilding discourses,' not discourses for upbuilding, because the speaker by no means claims to be a *teacher* . . . [)]" (EUD 5, 53, 107, 179, 231, 295; cf. POV 143n.).[22]

Sometimes authors derive their authority from being authorized by either the church or the university. Kierkegaard is here telling us that his writings are not authorized in either of these ways, that our respect for such teaching institutions of human society will not dispose us to take him seriously (cf. CUP 273; OAR 111). At the same time, he is disclaiming two other kinds of authorization, both of which occur outside the official institutions of society. While seeking to clarify the important difference between a genius and an apostle, he insists that he is neither (OAR 103–20). What distinguishes him from both the apostle, who is authorized directly by God, and the genius, who writes "without authority" from God or church or state and is authorized only by his unmistakable talent (POV 142n.), is the fact that he is not epistemologically above or ahead of his readers, but is, just like them, a learner (POV 75, 160; cf. 29, 73).

This motif of the writer as fellow learner with the reader occurs frequently in the journals (see JP I, 649 [p. 273], 1038; VI 6533, 6700, for example), and Kierkegaard puts the same idea in the mouth of Climacus (CUP 622–23). (N.B. In considering the view of authorship that Kierkegaard presents to us, we must be careful not to attribute to him what his pseudonyms say, even when, as in this case, it is obvious that they agree with him; but on the other hand we will not want to ignore their comments either, since we know that Kierkegaard presents them in the hopes that his reader will wrestle seriously with them.)

Kierkegaard's fourfold forfeiture of authorial authority, his voluntary refusal to claim the privileges of pastor, professor, genius, or apostle, has theological presuppositions. With regard to finite truth, hierarchical teaching relations based on human differences have their temporary place, though consensus is the ultimate criterion. Here a democratic theory of truth like that of Peirce or of Habermas holds. But with reference to ethical-religious matters, or what Kierkegaard calls eternal truth, "the crowd is untruth," that is, human consensus is not the final standard. Moreover, here a more radical democracy obtains, for here there are no experts and all are equally learners. This is why "it is only religion that can, with the help of eternity, carry human equality to the utmost limit . . . [and why] religion is the true humanity" (POV 107–18). The only teachers here are God and the apostle, who, by a miracle that can be believed but not guaranteed by either proof or social institution, speaks as the direct representative of God (OAR 109, 112, 117). In matters of the spirit, short of apostolic authority, the pastor, the professor, and yes, even the genius, are every bit as much learners as those they would instruct. Under the rubric "without authority" Kierkegaard voluntarily adopts this posture as an essentially religious act. There is a similar humility in our three French writers, but it is also very different. In both cases the author refuses to play God. But there is all the difference in the world between saying, "There is no God, so I am not God," and saying "There is a God, so I am not God."

We shall have to ask whether this theological difference plays a role when

Kierkegaard, as emphatically as either Gadamer or the French, denies that the intention of the author governs the meaning of the text. For him this is in the first instance an autobiographical discovery. In *The Point of View*, written after the *Postscript* between 1846 and 1849, but published only posthumously, Kierkegaard argues that his authorship as a whole, not just this book or that one, has the character of being written by an Author. In spite of its obvious diversity, it is a religious authorship from start to finish and it has a coherent, unified meaning. But he is not its origin. He insists repeatedly that he did not have the full meaning of his authorship in view at the outset, but only came to see it in retrospect, and he attributes the coherence of his writings to Governance or Providence (POV 13, 72–73, 150, 160; cf. JP V, 5991; VI, 6346, 6523, 6700).[23]

Out of this experience he anticipates twentieth-century critiques of making the *mens auctoris* the meaning of a text. He vigorously stresses the importance of keeping his own inner life separate from the reading of his texts (POV 9; TA 99), and he ridicules the idea that the religious character of his authorship could be established simply on his own say so (POV 15). Most importantly, he recognizes that "in spiritual things all receptivity is productivity" (JP I, 878).

Moreover, he has Climacus present us not only with this hypothesis that "all receiving is a producing" (CUP 78), but also with the thesis "that the reception intrinsic to inwardness is not a direct reproduction of what was communicated, since that is an echo" (CUP 260). To equate understanding with reproduction is to reduce it to "learning by rote" (CUP 263–64, 623). In keeping with this Climacus praises the pseudonyms for not misusing their prefaces "to take an official position on the production, as if in a purely legal sense an author were the best interpreter of his own words, as if it could help a reader that an author 'intended this and that' " (CUP 252).

Kierkegaard presents two corollaries to this refusal to let the writer's intention be equated with the meaning of the text. First, the writer is but a reader of his or her own texts. In "A First and Last Explanation," in which Kierkegaard publicly acknowledges that he is the author of the pseudonymous writings, that is, the creator of the pseudonyms, he says, "I have no opinion about them except as a third party, no knowledge of their meaning except as a reader" (CUP 625–26). In other words, for him pseudonymity is a device to distance the writer from his texts and to accentuate his role as *an* interpreter rather than *the* origin of their meaning. In *The Point of View*, when he repeats this claim to being only a reader of these texts, he explicitly links it not only with his rejection of the *mens auctoris* theory of hermeneutics, but also with two closely related themes presented above, his personal claim to write "without authority," and his understanding of his authorship as constituting "my own upbringing" (POV 15, 151). In linking the notion that he is just one of his own readers with the notion that he is a fellow learner with his readers, he introduces us to his understanding of the egalitarianism of the spirit.

To the corollary that he is but a (co)reader of his own writings Kierkegaard adds the corollary that the reader is a (co)writer of these texts. As with Gadamer and the French, the reader comes to share in producing their meaning. It turns out that distancing the author from the text is a means toward distancing the author from the reader and leaving the reader alone with the text. The Hongs have written that "no thinker and writer ever tried as Kierkegaard did to leave the reader alone with the work. The dialectic of thought and existence is properly that of the reader with the work, not of the reader's curious interest in the writer."[24]

Writing of *Either/Or*, Kierkegaard says he is happy for the readers not to know the author's identity, "for then they have only the book to deal with, without being bothered or distracted by his personality" (COR 16). He had already put this thought in the mind of his editor, Victor Emerita, who writes: "The point of view ought to speak for itself. . . . Thus, when the book is read, A and B are forgotten; only the points of view confront each other" (EO I, 14).

It is Johannes Climacus, however, who develops this theme most fully. He praises his own *Philosophical Fragments* for not solving the problem it poses; he praises *Either/Or* for not choosing between the aesthetic and the ethical; and he praises *Stages on Life's Way* for reaching no conclusion and leaving its question unanswered because, and this is the central point, instead of making the reader "safe and secure" vis-à-vis the dialectic of existence, "it is left to the reader to put it all together by himself, if he so pleases, but nothing is done for the reader's comfort" (CUP 15, 254, 289, 298).[25] So when Climacus constantly tells his readers that he has no opinion about the issues he raises (CUP 224, 226, 231, 271n., 273, 369, 379, 619), his purpose is clear even without the benefit of Kierkegaard's remark that Climacus "dialectically formulated the issue so sharply that no one could directly see whether it was an attack on Christianity or a defense, but it depended on the state of the reader and what he got out of the book" (JP VI, 6690).

Climacus takes it to be his task "first and last to watch himself lest he become important in relation to others" (CUP 278), and he spells out two dangers in this regard. A writer's "renown," "celebrity," or "fame" on the other hand (CUP 13, 14, 63, 65, 72) or the rhetorical skill which the writer employs on the other hand (CUP 12–14, 260, 278) can all too easily dispose the reader to accept what is written as true without examination or personal appropriation. To complete this thought by his pseudonym, Kierkegaard notes that the author's "personal actuality" might just as easily dispose the reader against the text, and he does not wish to be a "constraint" (or "embarrassment" as the older translation has it) to the ideas in his books (CUP 627). The distance he seeks from his readers is precisely to leave them alone with the text.

And yet this way of putting it is not quite right. Just as Kierkegaard is always trying to separate the individual from the "crowd," from the "public," from the "present age," so here he seeks to separate the reader from the writer. But in neither case is his purpose to leave the individual simply alone; and if we add "with the text" we have still left out the essential point. He wants to help the individual get *alone before God*, and to that end he both assaults the apotheosis of the age and deliberately forgoes the privileges of Authorship. His whole theory of indirect communication, in which pseudonymity plays such a prominent part, is necessary "because ethically the task is precisely this—that every man comes to stand alone in the God-relationship" (JP I, 649, p. 273). In this mode the author "shyly withdraws (for love is always shy), so as not to witness the admission which [the reader] makes to himself alone before God" (POV 25–26; cf. 111, 135, 150).

Strangely, Kierkegaard thinks that the author who in this way declines to play God in relation to the text and the reader, is nevertheless acting in a truly godlike manner. Our twentieth century writers can only wonder how this could be, since the Kierkegaardian writer, like their own, does not even try to be the Alpha and Omega of the text or the Teacher of the reader. The answer is that he has a different conception of God from theirs. Because he sees creation in the light of incarnation, he views it as *kenōsis* rather than as *imperium*. Climacus hints at this view when he writes that God "communicates creatively in such a way that in creating he *gives* independence vis-à-vis himself" (CUP 260). But it is Kierkegaard himself who spells this out more fully.

The greatest good, after all, which can be done for a being . . . is to make it free. In order to do just that, omnipotence is required. This seems strange, since it is precisely omnipotence that supposedly would make [a being] dependent. But if one will reflect on omnipotence, he will see that it also must contain the unique qualification of being able to withdraw itself again in a manifestation of omnipotence in such a way that precisely for this reason that which has been originated through omnipotence can be independent. That is why one human being cannot make another person wholly free. . . . Only omnipotence can withdraw itself at the same time it gives itself away, and this relationship is the very independence of the receiver. (JP II, 1251)

Human withdrawal does not have the same effect as divine withdrawal, but it has the same goal, and the author who withdraws to leave the reader alone with God is imitating, but not replacing, the Creator.

So, as promised, the understanding of authorship is as intensely theological an issue for Kierkegaard as for Barthes, Foucault, and Derrida, but in such a different direction that his important and impressive agreements with them take on a very different meaning. Authorship and anxiety are linked for him as for them, but as we might now expect, in a different way. They see a Cartesian anxiety about certainty and control as the underlying source of the idea of the Author as Alpha and Omega, and they seek to overcome this anxiety in the courage to be merely human, even when there is no other Origin or Center. They are Nietzscheans. For Kierkegaard the anxiety of authorship is the "fear and trembling lest one do anyone harm" (JP VI, 6230). This anxiety is not to be overcome but nourished as a constant warning against the danger of coming between the reader and the text, or, even worse, failing to withdraw so as to leave the reader alone before God.

NOTES

1. JP V, 5944. The sigla used for citing the works of S[ø]ren Kierkegaard in the text and notes, are as follows:

CA *The Concept of Anxiety*, trans. Reidar Thomte and Albert B. Anderson (Princeton: Princeton Univ. Press, 1980).

COR *The Corsair Affair and Articles Related to the Writings*, trans. Howard V. and Edna H. Hong (Princeton: Princeton Univ. Press, 1982).

CUP *Concluding Unscientific Postscript*, trans. Howard V. and Edna H. Hong (Princeton: Princeton Univ. Press, 1992). Citations are from Volume One unless otherwise indicated.

EO *Either/Or*, trans. Howard V. and Edna H. Hong (Princeton: Princeton Univ. Press, 1987).

EUD *Eighteen Upbuilding Discourses*, trans. Howard V. and Edna H. Hong (Princeton: Princeton Univ. Press, 1990).

JP *S[ø]ren Kierkegaard's Journals and Papers*, trans. Howard V. and Edna H. Hong (Bloomington: Indiana Univ. Press, 1967–78). Note that the number following the volume number will be the entry number, not the page number.

OAR *On Authority and Revelation*, trans. Walter Lowrie (New York: Harper & Row, 1966).

POV *The Point of View for My Work as An Author: A Report to History*, trans. Walter Lowrie (New York: Harper & Row, 1962).

SLW *Stages on Life's Way*, trans. Howard V. and Edna H. Hong (Princeton: Princeton Univ. Press, 1988).

TA *Two Ages: The Age of Revolution and the Present Age: A Literary Review*, trans. Howard V. and Edna H. Hong (Princeton: Princeton Univ. Press, 1978).

2. Wolfgang Hildesheimer, *Mozart*, trans. Marion Faber (London: J.M. Dent & Sons, 1983), p. 16.

3. There is Victor Eremita, the editor of the whole text but author only of the Preface. There is the aesthete, identified only as A, whose papers comprise most of Volume One. There is Johannes the Seducer, whose diary concludes Volume One and who [may] or may not be identical with A. Then there is Judge William, also referred to as B, author of the two long letters that make up all of Volume Two except for the concluding homily, which is by our final author, an unnamed pastor.

4. "A Kierkegaardian pseudonym is a *persona*, an imaginary person created by the author for artistic purposes, not a *nom de plume*, a fictitious name used to protect his personal identity from the threats and embarrassments of publicity . . . his purpose was not mystification but distance." Louis Mackey, *Kierkegaard: A Kind of Poet* (Philadelphia: Univ. of Pennsylvania Press, 1971), p. 247.

5. For the discussion of Gadamer, Barthes, Foucault, and Derrida, the following sigla will be used in the text and notes:

DA Barthes, Roland. "The Death of the Author," in *Image—Music—Text*, trans. Stephen Heath (New York: Noon Day Press, 1977).

HGM   Betti, Emilio. "Hermeneutics as the general methodology of the *Geisteswissen-schaften*," in *Contemporary Hermeneutics: Hermeneutics as Method, Philosophy, and Critique*, ed. Josef Bleicher (London: Routledge & Kegan Paul, 1980).

EM   Derrida, Jacques. "The Ends of Man," in *Margins of Philosophy*, trans. Alan Bass (Chicago: Univ. of Chicago Press, 1982).

OG   ————. *Of Grammatology*, trans. Gayatri Chakravorty Spivak (Baltimore: Johns Hopkins Univ. Press, 1976).

P   ————. *Positions*, trans. Alan Bass (Chicago: Univ. of Chicago Press, 1981).

PC   ————. *The Post Card: From Socrates to Freud and Beyond*, trans. Alan Bass (Chicago: Univ. of Chicago Press, 1987).

SP   ————. *Speech and Phenomena: And Other Essays on Husserl's Theory of Signs*, trans. David B. Allison (Evanston: Northwestern Univ. Press, 1973).
        ————. *Writing and Difference*, trans. Alan Bass (Chicago: Univ. of Chicago Press, 1978). Includes:

FS   "Force and Signification"

EJ   "Edmond Jabès and the Question of the Book"

VM   "Violence and Metaphysics"

SSP   "Structure, Sign, and Play in the Discourse of the Human Sciences."

        Foucault, Michel. *The Foucault Reader*, ed. Paul Rabinow (New York: Pantheon Books, 1984). Includes:

NGH   "Nietzsche, Genealogy, History"

WA   "What Is an Author?"

OT   ————. *The Order of Things: An Archaeology of the Human Sciences* (New York: Vintage Books, 1973).

HL   Gadamer, Hans[-]Georg. "Hermeneutics and Logocentrism," in *Dialogue and Deconstruction*, ed. Diane P. Michelfelder and Richard E. Palmer (Albany: SUNY Press, 1989).

TM   ————. *Truth and Method*, trans. revised by Joel Weinsheimer and Donald G. Marshall (New York: Crossroad, 1991).

        Kearney, Richard. *Dialogues with Contemporary Continental Thinkers: The Phenomenological Heritage* (Manchester: Manchester Univ. Press, 1984). The interview with Jacques Derrida is entitled:

DO   "Deconstruction and the Other."

    6. Cf. Heidegger's essay, "Language" and its recurring theme, "Language speaks," *Die Sprache spricht*. *Poetry, Language, Thought*, trans. Albert Hofstadter (New York: Harper & Row, 1971).
    7. In this passage Barthes suggests replacing the expression metaphor with that of the performative as described in speech act theory. Perhaps the notion of musical performance is closer to what he wants. Even a jazz performer, who has great "creative" liberty as an improvisor, is not the Creator of the work, but only one who passes on what precedes its performance without being already there. In this spirit Barthes tells us that "in ethnographic societies the responsibility for a narrative is never assumed by a

person but by a mediator, shaman or relator whose 'performance' . . . may possibly be admired but never his 'genius' " (DA 142). [3–4]

8. Kevin Hart, *The Trespass of the Sign* (Cambridge: Cambridge Univ. Press, 1989), p. 35. In other words, Barthes' analysis of human authorship provides no warrant for his own "refusal" of God.

9. Martin Heidegger, "The Word of Nietzsche: 'God is Dead,' " in *The Question Concerning Technology and Other Essays*, trans. William Lovitt (New York: Harper & Row, 1977), p. 64.

10. Foucault's rejection of hermeneutics as the search for deep meaning is a central theme of Dreyfus and Rabinow in *Michel Foucault: Beyond Structuralism and Hermeneutics* (Chicago: Univ. of Chicago Press, 1982, 1983). Foucault himself writes: "If interpretation were the slow exposure of the meaning hidden in an origin, then only metaphysics could interpret the development of humanity. But if interpretation is the violent or surreptitious appropriation of a system of rules, which in itself has no essential meaning, in order to impose a direction, to bend it to a new will, to force its participation in a different game, and to subject it to secondary rules, then the development of humanity is a series of interpretations" (NGH 86).

11. Foucault does not develop this suggestion, but the quotation in the previous note provides a scary commentary.

12. See especially SP 17–22, 32–37, 72–76, and 91–94.

13. This text illustrates the dual meaning of the term *différance* in Derrida, designating both temporal deferral and spatial distinction. As outside the "process" of signification, Husserlian meaning would be present all at once and would await no completion. As outside the "system" of signification Husserlian meaning would be, like Spinoza's substance, intelligible in itself without reference to any other. The term *différance* is designed to deny both forms of immediacy. Jack Caputo nicely summarizes the Husserlian theory that Derrida disputes as the claim that meaning "occurs essentially in transcendental solitude." *Radical Hermeneutics: Repetition, Deconstruction, and the Hermeneutic Project* (Bloomington: Indiana Univ. Press, 1987), p. 132.

14. We could say that the Husserlian *epoché* is the replacement for Plato's more literal asceticism as the means for separating the sensible from the intelligible world. Derrida's constant claim that the concept of the sign is a metaphysical concept refers to this notion of the external relation of signifier and signified. See, for example, P 17; OG 13–14.

15. Cf. P 22–23, 29, 44, 49, 65; OG 6, 13, 18–23, 49, 158; SSP 280.

16. "There is no conceptual realm beyond language which would allow the term to have a univocal semantic content over and above its inscription in language" (DO 111). Derrida's infamous claim, *"There is nothing outside of the text"* (OG 158), has two different, if closely related, meanings, depending on whether we take the signified to be, in Frege's sense, meaning (*Sinn*) or reference (*Bedeutung*). Most frequently in Derrida's usage, "signified" signifies Frege's *Sinn* or conceptual meaning. In that context, "There is nothing outside of the text" is equivalent to the sentence with which this note begins. But sometimes "signified" signifies Frege's *Bedeutung*, reference, and there is indeed a reference to "the absence of the referent or the transcendental signified" immediately preceding the infamous claim of OG 158. Here it is not just that "we have access to their [in this case Jean-Jacques, Mamma, and Thérèse] 'real' existence only in the text . . . [but also] that in what one calls the real life of these existences 'of flesh and bones,' beyond and behind what one believes can be circumscribed as Rousseau's text, there has never been anything but writing . . . substitutive significations which could only come

forth in a chain of differential references" (OG 158–59). Derrida is emphatic about what this does *not* mean: "It is totally false to suggest that deconstruction is a suspension of reference. Deconstruction is always deeply concerned with the "other" of language. I never cease to be surprised by critics who see my work as a declaration that there is nothing beyond language, that we are imprisoned in language; it is, in fact, saying the exact opposite. . . . Certainly, deconstruction tries to show that the question of reference is much more complex and problematic than traditional theories supposed" (DO 123). Hart makes a helpful suggestion about what Derrida's hard saying *does* mean: "Derrida's point is merely that any knowledge one can glean of the writer's life and intentions will not provide one with a privileged point of access to the text; it will involve one in yet another network, such as the writer's various relations with other writers. . . . The doctrine that there is nothing outside the text is neither esoteric nor difficult: it is merely that there is no knowledge, of which we can speak, which is unmediated. What Derrida adds to this familiar epistemological thesis is that the contention that this knowledge is always in a state of being constituted and never arrives at a state of final constitution: there is no immediacy, even in mediation; no self-identity, even in difference." *The Trespass of the Sign*, pp. 25–26. Like Peirce and the Renaissance *epistēmē* described by Foucault in *The Order of Things*, Derrida takes "things" to be signs and thus gives an expanded meaning to the concepts of text and writing. The one thing they exclude is the kind of immediacy presupposed by the theory of language as expression. Cf. P 34.

17. In speaking of the theological character of expression theory, Derrida sometimes uses the Heideggerian term, ontotheology, and makes it interchangeable with both metaphysics and logocentrism. See P 17, 34–35, 44.

18. The analogy between God and the Author can be put in these terms. At the divine level history is conceived "as a detour between two presences" (SSP 291), while at the human level knowledge is viewed as a similar detour "*for the purpose of* the reappropriation of presence" (OG 10).

19. Derrida often uses "text" as a technical term for this post-Enlightenment writing. Thus he contrasts text with both expression (P 33–34) and book, in the sense of Book (OG 18: "The idea of the book is the idea of a totality . . . this totality of the signifier cannot be a totality, unless a totality constituted by the signified preexists it, supervises its inscriptions and its signs, and is independent of it in its ideality. The idea of the book . . . is profoundly alien to the sense of writing").

20. On the risk involved in writing as Derrida conceives it, see EJ 74, P 14, and FS 11. Cf. his metaphor of the writer's home as the desert rather than the garden, EJ 68.

21. On the theme of control as central to the question of authorship, see Frank, "Limits of the Human Control of Language: Dialogue as the Place of Difference between Neo-structuralism and Hermeneutics," in *Dialogue and Deconstruction: The Gadamer-Derrida Encounter*, eds. Diane P. Michelfelder and Richard E. Palmer (Albany: SUNY Press, 1989), and Irene E. Harvey, *Derrida and the Economy of Difference* (Bloomington: Indiana Univ. Press, 1986), pp. 62–67.

22. Two of Kierkegaard's pseudonyms repeat the claim to write without authority, adding illuminating satirical comments in the process. Climacus asks that no one appeal to his book, since he is a humorist and not an authority, though he is comforted "that there are such great men who are able and willing to be the authority, from whom one has the benefit of accepting their opinion as a matter of course" (CUP 618–19); and Vigilius Haufniensis presents himself as "an author without any claims," though with regard to human authority "I am a fetish worshipper and will worship anyone with equal

piety, but with one proviso, that it be made sufficiently clear by a beating of drums that he is the one I must worship and that it is he who is the authority and *Imprimatur* for the current year" (CA 8).

23. On the translation of *Styrelse* as Governance rather than Providence, see POV 64n.

24. See the Preface to Malantchuk, *Kierkegaard's Thought*, trans. Howard V. and Edna H. Hong (Princeton: Princeton Univ. Press, 1971), p. viii. The Hongs add that the purpose of pseudonymity is "to make the author of the authors irrelevant and to leave the reader alone with the works and the various positions presented" (EUD xx). Climacus says, with reference to the pseudonymous authorship, "The absence of an author is a means of distancing" (CUP 252; cf. 263 on the "gap between reader and author"), and Mackey states that the purpose of pseudonymity "was not mystification but distance" (*A Kind of Poet*, p. 247).

25. In *The Point of View* he calls attention to the epigram of *Stages*, "Such works are mirrors: when an ape looks in, no apostle can look out" (POV 95n; cf. SLW 8).

CHAPTER 4

Gadamer's Hermeneutics and the Question of Authorial Intention

David Weberman

While Hans-Georg Gadamer has written on a wide array of philosophical topics and figures, it is his development of philosophical hermeneutics that lies at the heart of his thought and for which he is best known. The central issue in hermeneutics concerns the human activity of understanding or interpreting oneself, others, and the surrounding world—an activity that Gadamer, following Dilthey and Heidegger, views as fundamental and ever-present, not at all limited to theoretical inquiry. In his most important work, *Truth and Method* (1961), Gadamer focuses on the problem of understanding *human* products and phenomena, such as historical events, artworks, speeches, and especially written texts.[1] Of course, all human products and phenomena (that is, all intentional ones) have their designers, agents, or, in the case of texts, authors. As a result, the precise role of the agent or author becomes a question of great philosophical importance for Gadamer and for any hermeneutic theory.[2] The aim of this essay is to reconstruct Gadamer's unique and instructive answer to the question of the relation between authors' intentions and the meaning of their texts.

The fundamental thesis of Gadamer's hermeneutics is that our understanding or interpretation of objects and events is always conditioned or shaped by *our* historical situation in a way not fully transparent to us and that this circumstance does not so much impede as enable knowledge and experience. So when we understand something (a text, for instance), we always understand it differently from the way it is understood by others, without this difference necessarily amounting to an error in judgment. Gadamer's recognition of diverse, nonerroneous understandings makes him an advocate of pluralism. A text's meaning is always conditioned and constituted, in part, by its readers. Since readers bring different assumptions and interests to a text, textual meaning is not fixed. And if textual meaning is not fixed, then, of course, the intention of the author of the text does not and cannot uniquely determine its meaning. So Gadamer's theory is certainly a non-intentionalist one. Whether it is anti-intentionalist altogether—that is, whether Gadamer holds that the author's intention is absolutely irrelevant to textual meaning—is another matter. As we will see, Gadamer is not an absolute anti-intentionalist. Rather he holds a nuanced, middle position that many, even those unfamiliar with the German tradition, will likely find interesting and even persuasive.

Gadamer's discussion of the role of author is not direct or systematically sustained. For this reason, my presentation of his ideas involves a certain degree of reconstruction and, at times, an effort to fill in the gaps. I begin by explaining Gadamer's reasons for rejecting intentionalism (i.e., the view that authorial intention determines textual meaning). In the following section, I give Gadamer's reasons for not finding authorial intention altogether irrelevant and provide a way of making sense of Gadamer's position that allows for the ideas in the first two sections to sit comfortably with one another. What emerges, I hope, is a theory that is both loyal to Gadamer's work and attractive in its own right. The next section complicates matters by addressing the issue of the heterogeneity of types of texts. In the "Final Note" I deal with the possible objection to my presentation—that it engages in a performative contradiction by appealing to Gadamer's very intentions in order to reconstruct and defend a non-intentionalist position. I explain why the method of my analysis is nonetheless fully congruent with the argument it develops.

REJECTING INTENTIONALISM

If we begin by consulting common sense, then we might be inclined to believe that a text means what it says and it says what the author intended it to mean. Of course, many texts are complex, symbolic, vague, or ambiguous, which causes uncertainties to arise in the reader as to what the text is actually saying. In such cases, so the thinking goes, we should consult, whenever possible, the author's intention. All in all, then, common sense seems to tell us that a text means what its author intends. This is not only a commonsense view; it has also been carefully considered, adopted, and defended by philosophers and other theorists, perhaps most convincingly by the philosophically schooled literary critic E.D. Hirsch.[3] Along comes Gadamer, a meticulous reader of philosophical and literary texts and an exegete himself, who tells us that this intentionalist view is wrong about both textual meaning and the entire enterprise of reading and understanding texts. The question is why.

The first step in the argument comes with Gadamer's assertion that all understanding is historically situated and thus historically shaped. In *Being and Time*, Heidegger famously argues that understanding always involves a three-tiered forestructure of expectations that come out of a way of life, a conceptual/

linguistic scheme, and specific hypotheses about whatever object or event is being understood.[4] Gadamer adopts this idea and makes it the focal point of his hermeneutics when he insists on "the essential prejudgment-ladenness (*Vorurteilshaftigkeit*) of all understanding" (WM 254; TM 270). What Gadamer means by prejudgments or prejudices are not so much explicitly held theoretical positions, but a much more opaque and unreflected set of interests, assumptions, and attitudes shaped in large part by our cultural surroundings. As Gadamer puts it, "[H]istory does not belong to us; we belong to it. . . . The individual's self-reflection is only a flickering in the closed circuits of historical life" (WM 260f.: TM 276). So our understanding of texts (or anything else for that matter) is always inescapably embedded in particular historical circumstances in a way that cannot be made fully transparent to ourselves.

Now I think most of us would agree on the truth and tremendous importance of this point. It is, or should be, uncontroversial that our understanding and knowledge of everything is and will always be shaped, to some extent, by our reflected as well as unreflected, theoretical, and practical precommitments. But what follows from this fact? According to Gadamer, it follows that human understanding of texts, events, and so forth cannot be properly modeled along the lines of somehow restoring those things in our minds to what they really were, independent of us. Rather they can only be modeled along the lines of a "fusion of horizons" (WM 289; TM 306), that is, as a mediation of past and present or self and other. When it comes to texts and authors, the idea is that we should not hope to restore textual meaning by recreating the author's intentions since the intervention of our own precommitments into our understanding of the text does not allow this. So understanding the text is a matter of interacting with it in the light of our own situation.

However, this first step itself is sufficient neither for rejecting restoration as a model of understanding nor for displacing the authority of the author in reference to textual meaning. This is so for a very simple reason. Even if it is true that our own historical situatedness (both cultural and temporal) can never be left behind altogether, it can still be kept in check, at least to some extent, by careful study of the text, the author's situation, and the surrounding world from which it came. In other words, even if we cannot reconstruct the author's intention perfectly and with any real certainty that we have it right, we can and should try our best to do so because *that* is what it is to understand a text. So goes the initial objection to Gadamer's hermeneutics. It seems to be a perfectly reasonable response. Were one to try to defend Gadamer by saying that it makes no sense to try to accomplish what is impossible, the objection would still not be met. It may well make sense to strive for the impossible if it serves as a useful regulative ideal that enhances interpretive practices. So Gadamer must point to more than ineluctable historical embeddedness. And he does.

Gadamer rejects the identification of textual meaning with authorial intention on a number of grounds—by my count, six. Let me list these reasons before explaining them: (1) There is less in the text than the author had in mind. (2)

There is more in the text than the author had in mind. (3) The text, like all language, has the character of what Gadamer calls "ideality." (4) The text is relationally constituted. (5) The text is not about the author's mind, but about the truth of the subject matter. Each of these five reasons purports to show that textual meaning is different from authorial intention. The last reason is of another type. It assumes that difference and supports the claim that (6) *our interest* typically is and typically should be directed not at the author's intention, but at the text itself.[5]

Less in the Text than the Author Intended

Gadamer discusses the fact that in many cases "an author meant more than one was able to understand." He agrees with Chladenius that the task of interpretation lies in seeking "not to understand this 'more,' but to understand the true meaning of the books themselves" (WM 172; TM 184). The idea here is that the author's state of mind and intention may contain all sorts of personal or idiosyncratic associations that cannot really be said to belong to the meaning of the text. Thus, in writing "sky," the author may have in mind and intend the particular look of the sky out the window at the time of writing, but this cannot be properly said to be what the word "sky" in the text actually means. For one thing, that particular sky is irretrievable; for another, it seems extraneous to the text. This point is also noticed by some proponents of intentionalism. E.D. Hirsch writes:

Verbal meaning is, by definition, *that aspect of a speaker's "intention" which, under linguistic conventions, may be shared by others. Anything not sharable in this sense does not belong to the verbal intention or verbal meaning.* Thus, when I say, "The air is crisp," I may be thinking, among other things, "I should have eaten less at supper," and "Crisp air reminds me of my childhood in Vermont," and so on. In certain types of utterance such unspoken accompaniments to meaning may be sharable, but in general they are not, and therefore do not belong to verbal meaning.[6]

Hirsch's solution is to say that idiosyncratic associations, while they belong to the author's mental state accompanying the intention, are not part of his or her *intention* and thus are not part of the meaning of the text. We can see from the last quoted Gadamer passage that he would agree with this move to exclude the idiosyncratic from textual meaning. However, the point reveals a deep problem in the intentionalist position. Intentions are clearly mental states or at least start out as such. Yet how is one to decide what in the mental state of the author is a mere association and what truly belongs to the intention and thus to the textual or verbal meaning? Hirsch suggests that "sharability" is the key.[7] But most idiosyncratic associations are sharable, including, for example, memories of the crisp air of one's Vermont childhood. Perhaps the idea is that the criterion is not so much "sharability" but "what is shared in and by the text itself or can be shared through it *alone*" (without further testimony from the author). But once this becomes the touchstone, we have left the mental intention as such behind. That is, once we take seriously that there is less in the text than in the author's mental state, the author's mental state, or that part of it thought to be the intention, cedes to the words on the page. More precisely, the difference between the author's mental state and the intention as conceived by Hirsch is arrived at by consulting the words on the page. And if the words on the page do not succeed in *sharing* what was intended, it is the words that win out in the matter of deciding textual meaning.

More in the Text than the Author Intended

According to Gadamer, the reverse also holds. What is in the text is always more than was intended by the author. Gadamer writes:

What expression expresses is not merely what is supposed to be expressed in it—what is meant by it—but primarily what is also expressed by the words without its being intended—i.e., what the expression, as it were, "betrays." (WM 318; TM 335f.)

By "what is supposed to be expressed," Gadamer means something like the author's express intent. By what might be "betrayed," he means all sorts of things: things that the author may wish to conceal, things that he or she unconsciously represses, things that he or she is simply unaware of, or things about which the author is cognizant but which he or she is not explicitly intending at that moment (e.g., background beliefs). On one level, what is "betrayed" are psychological and social circumstances that escape the author. Any of this may be relevant, and often quite crucial, to what the text means. Yet, on another level, it is language itself that allows for more than was intended because language opens onto so much more. In fact, there is a long tradition in the history of hermeneutics from Chladenius through Schleiermacher and Droysen of seeing more in human actions and utterances than what is intended, where the unintended "extra" may be psychological/social or linguistic (or both).[8] Thus, Gadamer quotes and concurs with the eighteenth-century hermeneuticist Chladenius, who wrote that "men cannot be aware of everything, their words, speech and writing can mean . . . that they themselves did not intend to say or write" (WM 172; TM 183). In order to explain how a text's *language* can contain more than the author intended, let me depart for a moment from Gadamer to say something about what I will call the porous nature of language.

Language—that is "natural" as opposed to "artificial" language—is famously inexact, both in its connotative associations and its denotative scope. If I tell a person at a party to fetch from the other room all the ashtrays he or she can find, it may not be clear whether I mean to include under "ashtray" a plastic cup with a couple of cigarette butts in the remains of a drink. Not only is the word "ashtray" imprecise, but my intended use of the word is probably not fully determinate. I haven't already canvassed in my mind all possible "ashtray candidates" and come to a decision about whether the abandoned cup should count as an ashtray. In other words, mental intentions underdetermine linguistic meaning. This is no less true for texts, though for some texts more than others. Some of the best examples of textual porosity are the broadly phrased clauses in the U.S. Constitution, particularly the Bill of Rights (including the Fourteenth Amendment) with its famous limitations on the powers of government and its protection of individual rights. There one finds references to "freedom of speech," the prohibition of "cruel and unusual punishment," "due process," and "equal protection of the laws." Jurists have struggled to give determinate content to these phrases for two centuries now. The language itself is too porous (and too terse) to answer many of the questions put to it. This is what H.L.A. Hart calls the "open-textured" character of (legal) language. He writes:

[U]ncertainty at the borderline is the price to be paid for the use of general classifying terms in any form of communication concerning matters of fact. Natural languages like English are when so used irreducibly open-textured. . . . [W]e should not cherish, even as an ideal, the conception of a rule so detailed that the question whether it applied or not to a particular case was always settled in advance.[9]

Even an appeal to the intentions of the authors of the language—in this case, the Framers of the Constitution—fails to eliminate this open-textured character, and not just because the Framers are dead and gone. If they were here with us, we would certainly discover in many cases that their intentions simply did not anticipate a whole range of applications. Hart makes the same point when he underscores the "relative indeterminacy of aim" of legislators.[10] So language is porous and intentions are imprecise and incomplete. Partly for just this reason, Gadamer recognizes the importance of legal interpretation as a paradigm for interpretation in general and the central place of something like Aristotelian *phronesis* in understanding human language—that is, a kind of judgment that is irreducible to a mechanical subsumption of the particular to the universal (WM 310; TM 326f.). The underdetermined character of the text, owing to linguistic porosity as well as the incompleteness of intention, gives us another reason for thinking that textual meaning can encompass more than was originally intended by the author. So we see that intentionalism runs into trouble from both ends, texts can mean both less than and more than what their authors had in mind.

The Text Has the Character of Ideality

If a text's meaning is always possibly more or less than its author intends, then meaning must be detachable from the author and the circumstances of utterance.[11] This is where the notion of ideality comes in—a term and idea Gadamer borrows from Husserl.[12] Husserl explains the concept by distinguishing the "material," psychological content of an expression (e.g., your thought of a dog, my thought of a dog), which varies from act to act, from its "ideal," logical sense (the thought or idea of a dog), which remains identical in the manifold of expressive acts. As Husserl says, to call expressions ideal in this sense should not be thought to suggest that they "exclude reality"; rather, they underlie real acts and enable them to have meaning. Thus, the meaning of a linguistic item is separable from the utterer's intention as well as its meaning in a particular context of utterance. Its ideal aspect or sense is that which transcends, unites, and makes possible all specific instances in which a linguistic item occurs. The words "sky," "horse," "dignity," and "imagine" mean something distinct from and greater than any particular intended use of those words. Let me forestall two possible misunderstandings here. First, this notion of ideality has nothing to do with idealism in Plato's sense or in Berkeley's sense. Second, neither should it be associated with a deconstructionist commitment to the idea that linguistic meaning is constituted solely by the interrelatedness of signifiers without any appeal to the signified, that is, the world outside of language. As the assertion that the text concerns the truth about some subject matter (see below) indicates, Gadamer, unlike Derrida, makes the extra-linguistic and extra-textual an integral part of his theory of meaning and understanding. The important point is that Husserl's and Gadamer's notions of ideality say that meaning is not reducible to any or all actual psychological acts. As Gadamer writes: "It is the ideality (*Idealität*) of the word that raises everything linguistic above the finitude and transience that characterize the rest of past human existence" (WM 368; TM 390). In other words, once conceived as ideal in this way, language becomes autonomous and open-ended, suggesting not that a word can mean anything, but that it always means or refers to much more than was intended in a particular instance.

On Gadamer's view, this is especially evident in the case of written language (though it is also true of spoken language), since written language more often outlasts its moment of creation.

In writing, language gains its true ideality (*Geistigkeit*). . . . [W]riting is central to the hermeneutical phenomenon insofar as its detachment both from the writer or author and from a specifically addressed recipient or reader give [it] a life of its own. What is fixed in writing has raised itself into a public sphere of meaning in which everyone who can read has an equal share. . . . What is fixed in writing has detached itself from the contingency of its origin and its author and made itself free for new relationships. (WM 368, 369f., 373; TM 390, 392, 395)

When we read a text, its words have a meaning distinct from its specific instantiation in the author's mind. This quality of the ideality, abstractability, and, finally, autonomy of linguistic meaning is what underlies the preceding two arguments that textuality is less than and more than the original intention.

The Text Is Relationally Constituted

Gadamer argues, as we have just seen, that verbal meaning has "detached itself from the contingency of its origin and its author and made itself *free for new relationships*" (WM 373; TM 395, my emphasis). The point is not just that a text can and always will develop new relationships to other texts, historical events, differently situated readers, and so forth, but that textual meaning, as grasped, is always thoroughly relational. What is a text after all? It is more than marks on a page. Granted, the text springs from the mind of an author. But it employs language whose meaning and usage comes from outside itself, from the public. And it refers to a world beyond the text. We already have three relationships—to the author, to the public language, to the world about which it speaks. Should or can we stop there at the point of its creation? According to Gadamer, try as we might, we cannot. And why should we? Gadamer devotes a key section of *Truth and Method* to a novel treatment of temporal distance (*Zeitenabstand*):

The tacit presupposition of historical method, then, is that the permanent significance of something is only objectively knowable when it belongs to a closed context—in other words, when it is dead enough to have mere historical interest. Only then does it seem possible to exclude the subjective involvement of the observer.... [But] temporal distance obviously means something other than the extinction of our interest in the object. It lets the true meaning of the object emerge fully.... [T]he discovery of the true meaning of a text or a work of art is never finished; it is in fact an infinite process. (WM 282; TM 298)

Actually, the last line of this passage purporting that discovery of the text is never finished, emphasizes the point less strongly than Gadamer puts it elsewhere in arguing that it is not just the discovery of the text that is unfinished, but, in a sense, the text itself. For elsewhere Gadamer speaks of the text, and the object of research more generally, as a "phantom" and as something that in itself "clearly does not exist at all" (WM 283, 269; TM 299, 285). Texts do not exist in themselves; they are what they are partly as a result of their relation to other things, whether contemporaneous texts and events or later ones.[13] This is part of a broader metaphysical point. Objects and events, generally, are what they are not merely in virtue of their intrinsic properties, but also in virtue of their extrinsic or relational properties. Thus, a shooting at 9:00 A.M. is, or becomes, a killing if the victim dies at 11:00 A.M.[14] It is what it is in virtue of its relationships to earlier, later, and contemporaneous events of various kinds. The same goes for texts. In this sense, there is no text in itself. And for this same reason, the author's intention does not lock the text into a particular meaning once and for all.

The Text Concerns the Truth about Some Subject Matter

This claim would strike most intentionalists as bewildering—bewildering because it seems obviously true but just as obviously irrelevant since it does not seem to impugn intentionalism as such. After all, intentionalists will say: "Of course, the text is about something or other and the meaning of the text is simply what the author intended to say about that something." For Gadamer, however, that the text aims at the truth about some subject matter (*die Sache*) is a crucial point and one that deflects from the focus on intention. In reading a text, Gadamer says, what one understands is not just "an unfamiliar opinion; it is always possible truth" (WM 372; TM 394). Consider, for the sake of contrast, the idea of trying to get into an interlocutor's state of mind without any regard whatsoever for the truth set forth by that person. The example that comes to mind is that of a psychiatrist seeking to understand a delusional patient whose claims about the world cannot be taken at all seriously. Here utterances are symptoms, not candidates for truth. But a text's meaning is not a mere symptom or sign of the mental life of its author; it is a discourse, in some sense, about the world. The act of understanding texts actually has a triadic structure, a structure with three poles: the reader; the text created by an author; and the subject matter addressed by the text. This subject matter (Gadamer's *Sache*) is extra-mental and extra-linguistic and, in some sense, prior to and causative of both our mental states and our linguistic utterances. When we grasp the text, we do so not so much by speculation about the author's psychology, but by a tacit appeal to what it would make sense to say, given our logic and our prior understanding of the world. If the world were altogether different, a text would have to mean something else as well or perhaps lose its meaning together. Thus textual meaning is *weltbezogen* (i.e., not so much about expressing mental life, but making claims about the world).[15]

Our Deeper Interest Typically Is Directed at the Text, Not the Author's Psychology

So far we have encountered reasons for thinking that the meaning of a text is different from the mental intention of the text's author. Gadamer has not shown (nor has he tried to show) that there is no such thing as the author's intention, that it is an incoherent notion or that we cannot, to some extent, come to know it. This means that, to the extent that the preceding arguments have been successful, there are two different objects of research: (1) the meaning of the text as portrayed above (or "meanings," given the porosity of the text and its different relations to different times, cultures, and readers) and (2) the author's intended communication, which despite its possible vagueness still has some degree of determinacy. Now, what is to stop a person from devoting himself or herself to discovering the author's intention rather than the textual meaning(s)? Put differently, what is to stop a person from regarding the author's intended meaning as the real textual meaning and according the meaning as portrayed here to some place on the back burner (or ignoring it altogether)? This is something like the view of Hirsch, for whom the author's intention constitutes the text's meaning, while the text's relations to events and points of view outside it make up its so-called significance.[16] So, which of the two possible objects of attention deserve our study? Intentionalists such as Hirsch argue that the author's intention gives us a single, stable standard for correctness in interpretation and that without it we are at sea in a multitude of meanings.[17] Yet intentionalists often fail to recognize two assumptions built into this argument. First, they assume that it is always preferable to have a single standard and that this preference trumps all others. Second, they often take for granted (e.g., Hirsch in the pages just referred to) that where a single meaning is not available no criteria exist at all for distinguishing right from wrong interpretations. They fail to consider that porosity and relationality do not entail the total absence of guidelines since the text itself and its certifiable relations can still serve as touchstones.

Still, why not devote oneself chiefly to reconstructing the author's intention? It is not sufficient to say that the author's psychology is, in the end, unknowable because it can sometimes be fairly well pieced together on the basis of the text, diaries and letters, interviews, a study of the author's milieu, and so forth. It is possible to achieve (fallible) knowledge of the author's intention. So why not pursue that knowledge? Gadamer's point is that to study the psychology and intention behind the text is either separate from or only subordinate to the deeper motivation we have in reading texts, namely, to discover truths about the world and ourselves. As Gadamer puts it, "The task of hermeneutics is to clarify this miracle of understanding, which is not a mysterious communion of souls, but sharing in a common meaning" (WM 276; TM 292). This is what reading and grasping texts is finally about (besides the intrinsic pleasure that we derive from the activity). Biographically oriented scholars are concerned largely with reconstructing authorial intentions. Readers, by and large, are not. We misrepresent the act of reading and the nature of textual meaning if we take as our model the scholar's or biographer's efforts at getting into the state of mind of his or her creative subject. This process is sometimes worthwhile, but it is a rarified exercise that does not capture the more typical experience of reading a text. Scholarship serves reading; it is done at its behest. We should not think that it is the other way around.

So what is textual meaning, according to Gadamer, if it is not identifiable with what the author intended to say? The text is a verbal construct, created by an author, but a construct whose meaning transcends the author's particularity in that it employs publicly shared meanings (i.e., a language that is in a constant state of flux as is the world to which it refers).[18] Consequently, the reader of a text is always a different reader, and the meaning of the text, since it is constituted in part by its relations, is always, in a sense, a different one.

THE LIMITED RELEVANCE OF THE AUTHOR

Given Gadamer's adamant separation of textual meaning from authorial intention and his idea that understanding is typically and fundamentally directed at the former, one might conclude that Gadamer finds the author's intentions altogether irrelevant, that is, one might assume that he holds an extreme anti-intentionalist position in which the text begins, so to speak, with the death of the author.[19] In fact, Gadamer does not hold this view.[20] In his discussion of Schleiermacher's hermeneutics, there arises the issue whether it makes sense to try "to re-establish the 'world' to which [a work] belongs, to re-establish the original situation which the creative artist 'intended,' . . . [or] to reproduce the writer's original process of production" (WM 159; TM 166). As elsewhere, Gadamer doubts that one is really able to reconstruct the original process and questions whether doing so would give us the meaning of the work. However, he does admit:

Reconstructing the conditions in which a work passed down to us from the past was originally made to serve its purpose is undoubtedly a significant aid (*eine wesentliche Hilfsoperation*) to understanding it. But we may ask whether what we obtain in that case is really the *meaning* of the work of art. (WM 159; TM 167)[21]

This passage is important. Unfortunately, Gadamer does not explain it. And the rest of *Truth and Method* does not provide specific clues as to how exactly it should be understood. If the author's intention does not give us the meaning of the work, in what sense is reconstructing the intention a significant aid to understanding it? Gadamer says that Schleiermacher's reasons probably have to do with "guard[ing] against misunderstanding and anachronistic misinterpretation (*falsche Aktualisierung*)" (WM 159; TM 166). Yet since Gadamer holds, as a matter of fundamental principle, that understanding is always a fusion of the horizons (WM 289; TM 306) of past and present or of text and reader, he himself does not disapprove of anachronistic readings. On his theory, understanding always has an element of "anachronism" in a sense purged of anything pejorative.

In Gadamer's other works, there is occasional acknowledgment of the intentional dimension of meaning. For example, in an essay on poetry from 1961, he writes:

The ambiguous meaning of poetry is inseparably bound up with the unambiguous meaning of the intentional word. . . . [Its] elements . . . possess their appropriate mode of being as intentional language. . . . Language as the medium and material of expression can never fully emancipate itself from [such intentional] meaning.[22]

And in his 1981 debate with Derrida, Gadamer goes even further:

[L]ike one who is in a conversation, the writer tries to impart what he or she means. . . . *The other takes what is said as it is intended*, that is, he or she understands because he or she fills out and concretizes what is said and because he or she does not take what is said in its abstract, literal meaning. (my emphasis)[23]

These passages come close enough to intentionalism that one is tempted to scratch one's head and wonder if Gadamer has not recanted or changed his mind. Yet, he has not. There are several passages from his later works that unequivocally reassert the view that meaning is different from intention. For example, in a 1973 essay, Gadamer writes: "But is it necessary to have knowledge of what the poet himself thought about a poem? All that matters is what the poem actually says, not what its author intended."[24] So how can we give sense to his claim that authors' intentions are not definitive but are nonetheless relevant as an aid to understanding?

I want now to suggest that Gadamer finds authorial intent relevant in two senses: as a heuristic device and as a (narrowly applied) regulative constraint.[25] Heuristically, it is often useful for a reader to imagine an author with a single purpose so that the reader can aim at reestablishing a certain impulse and cohesiveness in the text. This is especially true when a textual unclarity is encountered, at which point one's discovery of meaning is aided by asking the question: What is the author trying to say here? Appeal to an intention encourages the reader to make sense of the work as a coherent whole.[26] It may even lead us to discover meaning by seeing it is as part of a more or less consistent *oeuvre* of the author's total production. In other words, reflection on the intent behind the text is a fruitful starting point and tool for the discovery of possible meanings and their coherence.

No less important, consideration of authorial intent can serve as a *regulative constraint* (my word choice, not Gadamer's) on interpretation. By this I mean that the author's intention can show certain interpretations of the text to be misinterpretations or misunderstandings. It is, however, a *narrowly applied* constraint. To see what this means, let us return to Gadamer's writings.

Gadamer's commentaries and essays on the poetry of Paul Celan are especially revealing. Early on in one of the essays he says (part of the first sentence of this passage was quoted above):

All that matters is what the poem actually says, not what its author intended and perhaps did not know how to say. Of course, a hint from the author regarding the raw material of his subject "matter" can be useful even for a perfectly self-contained poem, and can guard against misunderstanding. But such hints remain a dangerous crutch. When a poet shares his private and occasional motives, he basically displaces what has been balanced out as a poetic configuration toward the side of the private and contingent—which, in any case, is not even there.[27]

Notice that information about intention "guards against misunderstanding" but does not add anything to the words on the page. Its function seems to be wholly negative; it rules out but does not provide any positive content of its own. Later in the essay, we find an illustration of this idea. Gadamer notes that we now know that Celan's poem, "Flower," a poem about growth, was inspired by his son, though the poem makes no mention of a child. Gadamer goes on to say that this information is not relevant to the meaning of the poem:

Growing toward one another can occur in a wide range of different constellations. . . . Does "knowing" what the poet had in mind therefore mean one knows what the poem says? . . . [Celan himself] insisted that a poem must be left to its own existence and detached from its creator. Whoever does not understand more than what the poet could have said without his poetry understands far too little. Of course, outside information can often be valuable. It protects against blatant error in the attempt to interpret. It makes it easier to understand everything correctly, that is, with uniform coherence, at least on a preliminary level. But . . . [28]

The last sentence of this passage confirms the earlier point about heuristics. The sentence before tells us what kind of error or misunderstanding can be avoided: "blatant error." This is the point of what I have called the narrowly applied regulative constraint: to avoid blatant error.[29]

Consider three examples of blatant error. First, according to the Gospels (Matthew 19:24; Mark 10:25; Luke 18:25), Jesus says, "It is easier for a camel to pass through the eye of a needle than for a rich person to enter the kingdom of God." This line seems to imply that it is quite impossible for the wealthy to find salvation since a camel cannot pass through the eye of a needle. Some scholars have suggested, however, that "the eye of the needle" was the name of a gate in Jerusalem that was so low and narrow that camels had to unload their cargo and crouch down before passing through.[30] This claim is controversial but let us assume that we have solid evidence for its truth. Jesus, then, perhaps meant to say that the heavenly chances for the rich were not impossible, but quite difficult. Here, to disregard the original intent would result in a misunderstanding of the meaning of the maxim. Second, the First Amendment of the U.S. Constitution prohibits Congress from passing laws that would abridge "the freedom of speech, or of the press." Handwritten letters, however, are instances neither of speech nor of press, yet are reasonably taken to deserve equal protection.[31] We have every reason to believe that the authors of the amendment meant to imply all forms of communication and did not mean to leave letters vulnerable to state censorship. Say we had proof of that fact. In that case, we would misunderstand the provision if we did not take the intention into account. Third, we know that Jonathan Swift's "A Modest Proposal" was written with ironic intent. Once again, to treat it with indignation as an abominable political tract would amount to an act of simple misunderstanding. Instead, we take that ironic intent into account in our present reading and, if Gadamer is right, inevitably "fuse" the ironically intended work with our present historical horizon.

But this does not mean that whenever an interpretation diverges from the author's intention it is a misinterpretation. A writer may intend his stories to have a comforting effect on the reader; yet it could be that most readers find them unsettling in important ways and interpret them accordingly.[32] This would not be a misinterpretation, since it is not a blatant error of the sort mentioned above. The author may, in fact, misunderstand his own work in such cases or have only a diminished sense of it. Is there a sharp line dividing cases of blatant mistakes from intention-divergent interpretations that are not mistakes? Probably not. Perhaps, what is a mistake and what is not must be decided on a case-by-case basis, and, even then, consensus may be elusive. But this need not undermine the basic distinction.

I quoted a passage above in which Gadamer says that the reader "takes what is said [by the writer] as it is intended" but we should not forget that he goes on to say that the reader "fills out and concretizes what is said. . . . To be sure, everything that is fixed in writing refers back to what was originally said, but it must equally as much look forward" (TI, pp. 34, 36). For Gadamer, looking back to what was intended plays an ancillary role of facilitating discovery and averting simple error. Even then, Gadamer holds that we never really resurrect the original intention itself but always construe it through the prism of our own "relatedness" to it. Most of the work of interpretation concretizes, fills out, and looks forward, that is, beyond the intention, even allowing for circumstances where the intention is violated. So, intention may serve as a starting point, but not a stopping point.

We see, then, that Gadamer is neither an intentionalist nor an absolute anti-intentionalist. The author's intention has a heuristic and narrowly regulative role to play, but it is not determinative of the text's meaning. This is the core of Gadamer's non-intentionalism. It is a position I myself find very appealing, perhaps because I have been guided, in interpreting it, by my own ideas of what a textual theory should be—employing a principle of charity or, better yet, carrying out a fusion of horizons.

THE HETEROGENEITY OF TEXTS

Such is Gadamer's theory of the role of the author with regard to the meaning of texts. What kinds of texts? All kinds of texts. One might well ask at this point: Doesn't a good deal of the question of the relation between authorial intent and textual meaning depend on what kind of text we are talking about? Consider the variety of types: there are literary, legal, and philosophical texts, personal letters, diaries, and even instruction handbooks and interoffice memos. Consider also the variety of interpretive interests we bring to them. One might suspect that differences among these types require divergent theories about what it is for them to mean and to be understood. Does Gadamer address this issue?

The theory of textual meaning that we have examined is part of Gadamer's overall hermeneutic theory. Gadamer presents his theory as a *universal* one, that is, as one applicable to all understanding, whether the understanding of art, social and natural phenomena, or even extra-scientific, everyday experience.[33] As for texts, though *Truth and Method* discusses different types of texts, saying different things about them, it does not develop different theories for these different types or assign a different role to the author according to the type of text. In particular, it does not distinguish between meaning in literary texts and meaning in non-literary texts. On the contrary, *Truth and Method* takes the understanding of literature and art to be paradigmatic for understanding in general.[34] In later essays, especially his "Text and Interpretation" (1981), Gadamer proceeds differently. He accords literary texts a special status and a greater independence from the author than other texts. This may be because Gadamer changed his mind. Or it may be that his earlier theory of hermeneutics is universal as far as it goes, but that within it art and literature manifest a certain distinctiveness that was not specifically explored in Gadamer's earlier works. In any case, let us now turn to his later work to see how the special status of the literary text bears on the question of the author.

Gadamer's "Text and Interpretation," an essay prompted by an encounter with Derrida, deals in particular with different types or genres of texts, their different message-sending functions, and their different recipients or readers. He begins with scientific texts, pointing out that they are directed toward the specialist with whom the author shares knowledge and assumptions (TI 33). He then turns to personal letters and conversational utterances, observing that the former unlike the latter require particular care, given the absence of tone of voice and of the chance for response (TI 34). He considers speech in the form of military orders and, finally, legal texts (TI 35–36). Gadamer repeats the point made in *Truth and Method* that laws are not self-interpreting but always leave "an interpretive free space." Court stenographers have the task, he says, of doing justice to "the intended meaning of the speaker." In all of this, there is frequent talk of the purposes, wishes, and intentions of the speaker or writer. Intentions seem, at the very least, central to the communication's sender and recipient; whether or not they determine the meaning of the message itself is not stated here.

After explaining problems with texts that resist straightforward interpretation (e.g., jokes, rhetorical bridges, ideologically or psychologically distorted content), Gadamer takes up the literary text, where his treatment becomes passionate and unequivocal. He writes:

The point I have been trying to make, or prepare for, in everything I have said so far is that the connection between text and interpretation is fundamentally changed when one deals with what is called the "literary text." . . . In all the cases we have discussed . . . the so-called text itself was subordinated and ordered to the process of reaching agreement in understanding. . . . The interpreter steps in and speaks only when the text (the discourse) cannot do what it is supposed to do. . . . The interpreter has no other function than to disappear completely into the achievement of full harmony in reaching agreement in understanding. . . . But then there is literature! . . . A literary text does not refer back to an original expression of something. Rather, the literary text is text in the most special sense, text in the highest degree, precisely because it . . . exercises a normative function that does not refer back either to an original utterance or to the intention of the speaker but is something that seems to originate in itself, so that in the fortune and felicity of its success, a poem surprises and overwhelms even the poet. (TI 40–42)[35]

He goes on to say that literature, unlike ordinary discourse, "suspends a text's referential and message-conveying function" (TI 44).[36]

These remarks are noteworthy. First, in cases of nonliterary genres, Gadamer gives the interpreter a much smaller, more subservient role than in *Truth and Method*. This is probably because he has just been examining less historical and more pedestrian types of communication such as scientific reports, stenographers' transcripts, legal contracts, and so forth, not the works of cultural heritage that usually draw Gadamer's attention. Second, literary or artistic texts are given an absolutely unique status; they are autonomous (i.e., absolutely independent of the author's intentions). What is surprising is that if this is what makes literary texts unique, then, by implication, nonliterary texts are, in some sense and to some degree, dependent on author's intentions. So we see that on a rather important issue—the role of the author's intentions in textual meaning—Gadamer may have modified his position.

Perhaps we can make the view most coherent by summing it up as follows: First, Gadamer's theory of understanding, in general, does not take the meaning of human behavior, speech, and writing to be determined by the agent or author for all the reasons laid out in the first part of the chapter. Second, straightforward message-conveying texts such as military orders, scientific reports, or stenographers' transcripts are best understood with some kind of reference to their writers' supposed intentions. Third, literary texts, and artworks more generally, are best understood without appeal to their creator's intentions or with appeal only for the heuristic and narrowly regulative reasons discussed in the middle section of this chapter. This is because literature and art have an irreducible life of their own.[37] But what about the many other types of texts that are neither straightforward nor literary—texts such as philosophical treatises, political speeches, the Bill of Rights, even diary entries? It appears that Gadamer would assign them a place somewhere in between because they are less autonomous than literature. On the one hand, these texts surely cannot lay claim to whatever it is that makes aesthetic works and our experience of them so special. On the other hand, if the arguments in the beginning of the chapter successfully refute intentionalism concerning literary texts, they would seem no less successful with regard to these other types of texts. Gadamer's work does not provide a definite answer to this last question. Still, his work gives us a deep, detailed, and, I believe, quite persuasive account of the relation between textual meaning and authorial intent. It is an account of textual interpretation that articulates and defends a moderately non-intentionalist pluralism.

FINAL NOTE

I want to conclude on a self-referential note, by addressing a possible objection to my reconstruction of Gadamer's non-intentionalist position on textual interpretation. The reader of this chapter may have noticed that I appealed to, and could not easily avoid appealing to, locutions such as "Gadamer means to say this" or "his theory is put forth so as to show that." If intentionalism is wrong, why bother spending so much time and effort tracking down what Gadamer was trying to do and say? Perhaps, if I were writing about a literary text or artwork, I would not be so interested in the author's or artist's intended message. In the case of philosophical texts, though, I find that trying to get at what the author had in mind has tremendous heuristic value. Without it, it is harder to find a philosophical alter ego or a worthy opponent. With the idea of the author, things fall more neatly into place. Yet whether they fall into place just as the author intended them to is a further question. What if they do not? If the pursuit of truth has been furthered, does it matter? In any case, misconstruing intentions leaves something for a later commentator to work with. But it may be that the differences between readings of the written text, rather than a correct reconstruction of the intention behind it, is what makes the whole enterprise worthwhile. The important point, however, is that the text will mean more, less, and something other than what the author intended, even if tracking down that scent of intention is a fruitful way in which to advance understanding.[38]

NOTES

1. Hans-Georg Gadamer, *Wahrheit und Methode*, 4. Auflage (Tübingen: J.C.B. Mohr, 1975) *Truth and Method*, trans. Joel Weinsheimer and Donald G. Marshall (New York: Crossroad, 1990). Further references to this text will be indicated in parentheses, first to the German original (WM), then the English translation (TM). I have occasionally emended the translation for clarity.

2. In an essay from 1987, Gadamer writes: "[T]he issue of 'intentio auctoris' or the intention of the author . . . has for a long time especially occupied my attention." See "Hermeneutics and Logocentrism," in Diane P. Michelfelder and Richard E. Palmer, eds. *Dialogue and Deconstruction: The Gadamer-Derrida Encounter* (Albany: SUNY Press, 1989), p. 123.

3. See E.D. Hirsch, Jr., *Validity in Interpretation* (New Haven: Yale University Press, 1967); and, more recently, William Irwin, *Intentionalist Interpretation: A Philosophical Explanation and Defense* (Westport, CT: Greenwood Press, 1999).

4. See the passage on fore-having, fore-sight, and fore-conception (*Vorhabe, Vorsicht,* and *Vorgriff*) in *Sein und Zeit*, 15th ed. (Tübingen: Max Niemeyer Verlag, 1979), p. 150.

5. Some of Gadamer's reasons may not be altogether new, although their specific formulation and the overall picture that emerges is undoubtedly original.

6. Hirsch, *Validity in Interpretation*, pp. 218–19. Hirsch finds support for this point in Husserl's *Logical Investigations*.

7. Hirsch, *Validity in Interpretation*, pp. 218, 31, 50ff.

8. See both the "psychological" and "grammatical" sections of Friedrich Schleiermacher's *Hermeneutik und Kritik*, ed. Manfred Frank (Frankfurt am Main: Suhrkamp, 1977), as well as the reference to J.G. Droysen's *Historik* in Gadamer's *Truth and Method* (WM 200; TM 213).

9. H.L.A. Hart, *The Concept of Law*, 2nd ed. (Oxford: Oxford University Press, 1997), pp. 123, 127–28.

10. Hart, *Concept of Law*, p. 128. In *Intentionalist Interpretation*, p. 119, William Irwin argues that intentionalism can respond to this problem by appealing to counterfactual means: "Although the author of a text did not address a given issue we must sometimes counterfactually imagine what he would have said had he addressed it." While this may work some of the time, in very many cases it will not. This is so for two reasons: (1) there is often too little information about the original intention to guide the interpreter's imagination, and (2) the author's initial state of mind may simply underdetermine the counterfactual question that we might put to it.

11. I borrow here from my paper, David Weberman, "Reconciling Gadamer's Non-Intentionalism with Standard Conversational Goals," *The Philosophical Forum* 30 (1999): 317–28, specifically pp. 324–25.

12. See Edmund Husserl, *Logische Untersuchungen*, vol. 2, part 1, 6th ed. (Tübingen: Max Niemeyer Verlag, 1980), especially sections 31–32 entitled "Der Aktcharakter des Bedeutens und die ideal-eine Bedeutung" and "Die Idealität der Bedeutungen [ist] keine Idealität im normativen Sinne," pp. 99–102.

13. For a more detailed argument, see David Weberman, "A New Defense of Gadamer's Hermeneutics," *Philosophy and Phenomenological Research* 60 (2000): 45–65.

14. For a more complete defense of this idea, see David Weberman, "The Nonfixity of the Historical Past," *Review of Metaphysics* 50 (1997): 749–68; and idem, "Cambridge Changes Revisited: Why Certain Relational Changes Are Indispensable," *Dialectica* 53 (1999): 139–49.

15. These arguments for the ideality and subject matter relatedness of meaning and against a psychological and intentionalist position run parallel to Putnam's contention that "meaning just ain't in the head." See Hilary Putnam, "The Meaning of Meaning," in *Mind, Language and Reality: Philosophical Papers*, vol. 2 (Cambridge: Cambridge University Press, 1975).

16. Hirsch, *Validity in Interpretation*, pp. 8, 140ff.; and my criticism of the position in Weberman, "A New Defense of Gadamer's Hermeneutics," pp. 57ff.

17. Hirsch, *Validity in Interpretation*, p. 46.

18. The idea of flux is expressed by Gadamer in several passages, but perhaps most memorably by his claim that our relatedness to the object of understanding is "in beständiger Bildung begriffen" ("in a permanent process of formation") (WM 277; TM 293).

19. Perhaps the best known, though not best explained, statement of this position is in Roland Barthes, "The Death of the Author," in *Image, Music, Text*, trans. Stephen Heath (New York: Hill and Wang, 1977), pp. 142–48 [pp. 3–7].

20. Certainly not in *Truth and Method*. See, however, his comments on the literary text in his later essay, "Text and Interpretation" (1984), examined in the third section of this chapter.

21. These conditions include other facts surrounding the creation of the work besides the author's intention, but I focus only on the latter.

22. Hans-Georg Gadamer, "Composition and Interpretation," in *The Relevance of the Beautiful and Other Essays* (Cambridge: Cambridge University Press, 1986), p. 69.

23. Hans-Georg Gadamer, "Text and Interpretation," in Diane P. Michelfelder and Richard E. Palmer, eds. *Dialogue and Deconstruction: The Gadamer-Derrida Encounter* (Albany: SUNY, 1989), p. 34. Further references to this essay will be given as TI and page number in the body of the text.

24. "Who Am I and Who Are You" (1973), in Hans-Georg Gadamer, *Gadamer on Celan* (Albany: SUNY Press, 1987), p. 68. Further evidence follows: (1) "The unity of form so characteristic of the poetic work of art . . . cannot be reduced to the mere intention of meaning," from Gadamer, "Composition and Interpretation," p. 70; (2) "Certainly I share with Derrida the conviction that a text is no longer dependent on an author and his intention," from "Letter to Dallmayr"(1985), in *Dialogue and Deconstruction*, p. 96; and (3) "[R]eading is not a process of reproduction that permits a comparison with the original intention" from "Reflection on My Philosophical Journey," in Lewis Edwin Hahn, ed., *The Philosophy of Hans-Georg Gadamer* (Chicago: Open Court, 1997), p. 53.

25. I am compelled here to fill in a gap in Gadamer's argument.

26. See in this regard Gadamer's notion of the "Vorgriff der Vollkommenheit" ("anticipation of completeness") (WM 277; TM 293f.).

27. Gadamer, "Who Am I and Who Are You?" p. 68.

28. Gadamer, "Who Am I and Who Are You?" p. 133.

29. Some deconstructionists, unfettered by worries about blatant errors, sometimes disregard or deliberately subvert author's intentions. Gadamer does not go this far.

30. This information comes from Daniel Helminiak, *What the Bible Really Says about Homosexuality* (San Francisco: Alamo Press, 1994), p. 31.

31. I borrow the example from Antonin Scalia, *A Matter of Interpretation* (Princeton: Princeton University Press, 1997), pp. 37–38.

32. Thanks to Diane Michelfelder for this point.

33. See "Foreword to the Second Edition" (WM xvif.; TM xxviiif.) as well as "The Universality of the Hermeneutical Problem" (1966) and "On the Scope and Function of Hermeneutical Reflection" (1967), in David E. Linge, ed., *Philosophical Hermeneutics* (Berkeley: University of California Press, 1976), p. 38: "Hermeneutical reflection fulfills the function that is accomplished in all bringing of something to a conscious awareness."

34. See WM xxix; TM xxiii: "[The book] tries to develop from this starting point [aesthetic consciousness] a conception of knowledge and of truth that corresponds to the whole of our hermeneutic experience."

35. For a somewhat different conception of the special status of literature or poetry, see Gadamer's much earlier essay "Composition and Interpretation," p. 70.

36. What is important for the question of intention is the suspension of message conveying. However, the suspension of a referential function would seem to conflict with Gadamer's earlier commitment to texts being about the truth concerning some subject matter (*die Sache*). Furthermore, in his "Hermeneutics and Logocentrism," in *Dialogue and Deconstruction: The Gadamer-Derrida Encounter*, ed. Diane P. Michelfelder and Richard E. Palmer (Albany: SUNY Press, 1989), p. 123, Gadamer notes that he is very close to Schlegel's theory of the work as "detached from the producer and process of production." This seems closer to a formalist or textualist position than to the more dialogical conception in *Truth and Method*.

37. Regarding art and literature as uniquely independent of the creator or author is not at all uncommon, least of all, I think, among artists and writers. Here are two examples:

Hermann Hesse in his author's note to *Steppenwolf* (New York: Henry Holt, 1963), p. i, writes: "Poetic writing can be understood and misunderstood in many ways. In most cases, the author is not the right authority to decide on where the reader ceases to understand and the misunderstanding begins. Many an author has found readers to whom his work seemed more lucid than it was to himself." Thanks to Bill Irwin for this reference.

The poet Charles Simic writes (in *The New York Review of Books*, August 10, 2000, p. 52): "The true poet, one might say, gropes in the dark. Far from being omniscient on the subject of his work, he is merely a faithful servant of his hunches. The poem, with all its false starts and endless revisions, still mostly writes itself."

38. Part of an earlier version of this chapter was presented as a symposium paper at the APA Pacific meeting in San Francisco in March 2001. I would like to thank Christel Fricke, Bill Irwin, Ted Kinnaman, Diane Michelfelder, Beth Preston, Jason Prine, James Rosen, David Vessey, Brice Wachterhauser, and James Crosswhite for valuable comments and criticisms on earlier drafts. I am particularly grateful to Irwin for encouraging the project and defending intentionalism, Vessey for bringing my attention to the Celan essays, and Michelfelder for reminding me not to concede too much to intentionalist intuitions.

CHAPTER 5

The Marginal Life of the Author

Jason Holt

Though somewhat difficult to untangle, the death of the author thesis (DOA) is both provocative and important. Apart from certain critical analyses, however, it has not been given due attention from analytic philosophers. In this chapter I will defend DOA from an analytic perspective. I will argue that Barthes and Foucault are more or less right, though not for the reasons they think they are.

The ironies surrounding DOA may tempt one to ignore it as simply another postmodern indulgence. For one, the champions of DOA themselves avoidably fail to marginalize authors in the manner they prescribe. In "The Death of the Author," Barthes dubs his central example, an excerpt from Balzac's "Sarrasine," the *Balzac* sentence.[1] In "What Is an Author?" Foucault makes sure to cite Beckett's "What does it matter who's speaking?" as *Beckett's*.[2] Similarly, both credit Mallarmé with serving a pivotal role in the emergence, or reemergence, of authorial self-suppression.[3] If authors are so unimportant as to deserve metaphorical death, why bother mentioning them? Why credit the poet himself rather than the poetry? As authors, Barthes and Foucault have enlarged their own importance by denying that of authors generally. They eschew reason, yet offer arguments for the eschewal. By assailing authorial privilege, they have further cemented, in certain quarters at least, their own practically unassailable intellectual authority. The received view, by and large, has fostered not an explosion of creative interpretation but a sort of meaning nihilism, where delegitimation goes proxy for imaginative inquiry.[4] Telling as these ironies are, however, they do not bear on the defensibility of DOA, and this is the issue I will explore here.

I will begin by sorting out what DOA means and to what range of texts it applies. Following this, I will show how the arguments adduced for DOA by Barthes and Foucault are largely unsuccessful. Then I will develop a thought-experiment to the effect that while the content of authorial intentions is interpretively dispensable, the presumption of some intent or other is not. I will next offer an account of aesthetic meaning that allows for DOA as well as the disciplinary practice apparently threatened by it. My defense of DOA, then, will be somewhat limited, relegating the author not to the grave but to the margins. As it happens, more extreme measures in defense of DOA are neither necessary nor available.

WHAT IS DOA?

Although DOA is never stated clearly and constitutes a nexus of many descriptive, normative, and epistemological questions, there are clues as to what the thesis amounts to. One such clue is the work the thesis is meant to do. It is supposed to liberate us from interpretively restrictive views of literature, views "tyrannically centred on the author,"[5] where the author is that "functional principle" that "impedes the free circulation, the free manipulation, the free composition, decomposition, and recomposition of fiction."[6] Both advocate freedom from the author, Barthes more narrowly in interpreting texts, Foucault more generally in what one *does* with texts, which a fortiori includes interpreting them. Notwithstanding legitimate moral qualms with Foucault's overarching vision, in which anonymous texts are written irresponsibly, appropriated indiscriminately, and distorted unconscionably, the central purpose of DOA, shared by its progenitors, is reader liberation in interpreting texts. Concerns about authorial rights and responsibilities, while important, are independent of this central purpose and its subserving thesis.

If the purpose of DOA is reader liberation, then the thesis should be designed to lift such constraints as untowardly limit that freedom, specifically, constraints on textual meaning. Such constraints allegedly inhere in conceiving of texts as authored, which artificially "closes" the writing, fixing the meaning of a text so that successively improved interpretations of it will univocally converge. It is to this idea of textual closure that the advocates of DOA stand fundamentally opposed. Barthes denies that a text is "a line of words releasing a single 'theological' meaning (the 'message' of the Author-god)."[7] Foucault makes the same point indirectly. "The author," he says, "is the principle of thrift in the proliferation of meaning," and once the author is removed, "fiction and its polysemous texts will once again function according to another mode,"[8] one presumably in which they are recognized *as* polysemous. Seán Burke writes: "[N]o longer reduced to a 'single message,' the text is opened to an unlimited variety of interpretations. . . . This is the message—indeed the 'single message'—of 'The Death of the Author.' "[9] None of the interpretations to which a text is open is de facto privileged, much less canonical, and so there is no such thing as *the* meaning of a text. As a result, textual meaning can, and furthermore should, proliferate. While one may reasonably doubt that the author's fatal wound is either a necessary or sufficient opening of the text, the thesis itself is, as I hope to show, defensible.

On a superficial level, DOA may seem mere approbation for the "new writing," from which the author self-consciously withdraws in a refusal to fix meaning and in defiance of literary conventions, a trend beginning at least with Mallarmé and arguably culminating in the *nouveau roman* of Robbe-Grillet. His novel *Djinn* is a striking illustration—one might say vindication—of DOA. In the fictional prologue, *Djinn* is presented as a text of which, despite the most thorough investigative efforts, nothing is known of the author. The purpose of the text is also unknown. Is it fiction? A dream journal? The diary of someone not quite sane? A manual for learning grammatical structure? The point is, it doesn't really matter. Our ignorance of such things does not preclude interpretation but rather promotes it. The implication, it seems, is that where we have such information, we should not allow it to inhibit the proliferation of meaning in interpreting texts. It is not that authors of the *vieux roman* succeed in fixing meaning where they ought not to. Rather, they are mistaken to think they can, and disingenuous to pretend as much. DOA is meant to apply to literature broadly, and the new writing is to be lauded as a more honest and sanguine illustration of a thesis applying only inclusively to it.

Even so, it is not clear to what range of texts DOA applies. On the one hand, Barthes and Foucault draw examples almost exclusively from fiction, poetry, and plays, which suggests that DOA is meant to apply only to literary texts, that is, written art. Indeed, both often write as if this is precisely the range of texts they have in mind. On the other hand, Barthes claims that DOA collapses the distinction between literary and nonliterary texts,[10] and Foucault holds that DOA covers all authored texts, including scientific and philosophical works.[11] But extending the scope of DOA beyond literary texts is less pressing than the issue of whether it applies to literary texts in the first place. Art seems to lend itself, more readily than anything else, to interpretive variance, and aesthetics tolerates this without scandal. But if texts are open to a variety, indeed, an *unlimited* variety of interpretations, does this mean that, in interpretive matters, anything goes? If it does, then we cannot plausibly maintain that DOA applies to nonliterary texts, for these include "The Death of the Author" and "What Is an Author?" and we could then interpret these as affirming not DOA but precisely its negation. I take this to be a *reductio* of DOA as a statement that anything goes in interpreting any kind of text. In defending the thesis, I assume a narrow application to literary texts.

Another thing that is not so clear is the degree of textual openness mandated by DOA. Despite Foucault's spirit of unbridled textual freedom, he envisions some constraints in the wake of DOA, though he does not tell us what these might be.[12] For Barthes, textual meaning is a matter of reader response. Whatever serves the reader's pleasure in engaging the text is thereby justified, and here it seems anything goes, including not only multiple interpretation but avoidable contradiction and radical revision of textual data, that is, taking the words and sentences of a text, consistently or otherwise, to signify something else, a variety of things, or anything at all. In the unresigned spirit of Foucault, and quite in keeping with Barthes's view of reader response, DOA is the thesis that literary texts are interpretively open. To a certain extent, I will argue, this is not only defensible, it is perfectly compatible with disciplinary practice. It does not mean, however, that anything goes.

FIRST DEFENSE

Many of the arguments offered for DOA are far less persuasive than the thesis itself. In this section I criticize these arguments, most of them from ancillary theses usefully disambiguated by Peter Lamarque.[13] The first piece of support, which Lamarque calls the historicist thesis, is meant to establish that the concept AUTHOR is dispensable.[14] According to this thesis, AUTHOR is a concept that emerged only after a long history of textual production. As texts were once conceived without AUTHOR, it is not necessary to conceive of texts as authored, and so it is possible to dispense with AUTHOR.[15] Granted, a robust conception of authorial rights and responsibilities did emerge rather late in the game. Take, for example, early modern philosophers and scientists, many of whom appropriated their predecessors' ideas without what is now considered due acknowledgment or citation. In a more basic sense, however, an author is simply someone who produces a certain kind of text. Authorial rights and responsibilities are logically posterior to AUTHOR in this more basic sense, and it is far from obvious that *this* notion is a relatively new one. Even if it is, so is ELECTRON, and we can no longer dispense with ELECTRON if we are going to do physics. Perhaps, though, AUTHOR is rather more like PHLOGISTON than ELECTRON, but this suggestion, I take it, is not serious enough to merit rebuttal.

Foucault's author function thesis is meant to show not only that AUTHOR is dispensable, but that such dispensation is warranted. According to this thesis, the person designated "author" is inessential to AUTHOR, which is itself inessential to the discourses in which it functions to delimit textual meaning.[16] Anything, a computer say, could play the same role as the designated author, because although the designate is the proximal cause of the text, AUTHOR is really that function of discourse by which, among other things, various works are clustered in the same *oeuvre*.[17] To say that *x* is by Shakespeare is really to say no more than *x* is Shakespearean, a predicate that not only clusters texts and helps delimit meaning, but eliminates reference to Shakespeare himself. Without such reference to anchor it in discourse, the predicate becomes disposable, and because it stultifies meaning rather than proliferating it, the disposal is warranted. This is Foucault's "two step." Reduce the author to a function, then dispose of the function.

Such dispensation would naturally have undesirable consequences, including by hypothesis the loss of *oeuvres* and the classificatory, explanatory, and predictive work they do. The promissory note here, implausibly, is that the benefits would outweigh the necessary harms. But the harms are hardly necessary. AUTHOR would only inhibit interpretive practice if the meaning of "author" were radically different from what it is. We can and perhaps should abandon AUTHOR if, for instance, part of the meaning of "author" is that person whose intentions determine textual meaning. But this is not part of AUTHOR.[18] If it were, anti-intentionalist hypotheses would be incoherent, for they would assert that what determines textual meaning (i.e., authorial intention) does not bear on, and hence does not determine, textual meaning. But it is not incoherent to say that the author's intentions do not determine, or are not essentially relevant to, textual meaning. By this observation alone it is not clear that we can, much less that we should, dispense with the concept AUTHOR.

Another unsuccessful attempt to undermine the author is the claim that texts do not, and cannot, express the author's creative intentions, beliefs, desires, or other mental states. The text comes into being by an act that is not expressive per se but performative, preceded by, if anything, an elliptical *I write*, the "I" being something of a formal indicator. This is the *écriture* thesis, according to which the act of writing does not amplify but rather silences the author's "voice" or personality.[19] This is, to say the least, a tendentious claim. Authors are not misguided in seeing the publication of their writing as ampliative in this sense, nor are critics who speak of the author's voice, or infer psychological traits of the author from the text. Although the performative view of writing is provocative, and deserves further exploration,[20] the notion that texts are not psychologically expressive is clearly untenable. Autobiographical and confessional writings are not pure fictions, after all, and even the most impersonal text provides some evidence of its progenitor's mental state. Otherwise it would be pointless to subject a patient's diary or artwork to psychological analysis. The question is not whether texts are expressive, but rather whether the psychological states expressed in and evinced by a text have any bearing on the meaning we may ascribe to it. Similar considerations apply to the notion that textual signs purporting to have real-world reference merely establish reference, if any, to other signs. If the world itself really is a text, this is exactly what we should expect reference to amount to.

One piece of support Lamarque does not discuss is the attempt to undermine authors' originality. Barthes claims that a text is "a multi-dimensional space in which a variety of writings, none of them original, blend and clash," and goes on to say that "the writer can only imitate a gesture that is always anterior, never original. His only power is to mix writings" as, as it were, a mosaicist, a syntactician, one who merely arranges prefabricated semantic items according to established syntactic rules.[21] This means that the writer is not an originator but merely a proximal cause of the text. It also means that writers cannot be credited with writing original, that is, innovative texts. Without such originary powers, authors seem uninteresting, and the privileged status afforded them by author-based criticism erodes. But this view is implausible. There are innovative texts, and it is simply irresponsible not to credit their producers accordingly. Neologism, syntactic variation, thematic novelty, and procedural departures aside, originality is possible even relative to fixed vocabularies and syntax. A useful analogy here is the idea that a sufficiently long chain of deductions, each one trivial and uninformative in itself, can yield new, nontrivial knowledge, as with, for example, Gödel's proof.[22] In addition, allowing the author the sort of originality denied by Barthes in no way commits us to constraints, much less intentionalist constraints, on textual meaning. Either way, DOA is a non sequitur.

It is unfortunate that Barthes and Foucault focus so much of their attack on the author, for the author is not the only possible source of textual closure. Other candidates present themselves. In "The Intentional Fallacy," the *locus classicus* of anti-intentionalism, Wimsatt and Beardsley claim that author's meaning, a straightforward analog of speaker's meaning, is—literally "for all intents and purposes"—irrelevant to the meaning of a text.[23] Subject to the linguistic and literary conventions by which its meaning is publicly determinable, the text is not open but interpretively closed, and its meaning is that on which successively improved interpretations converge. It is odd for Barthes to claim, in this regard, that the reign of the author has coincided with the reign of the critic,[24] for if intentionalism is correct, the critic is beholden to the author, who has a significant if not indefeasible authority. But if anti-intentionalism is correct, and the text is interpretively closed, the critic stands unchallenged as *the* guru of literary significance. DOA is anathema to all such "tyrannies," authorial intention, the text itself, critical consensus, and—worst of all—readership majority. This accounts for Foucault's claim that certain notions intended to replace the author "actually seem to preserve that privilege and suppress the real meaning of his disappearance."[25]

THE PRESUMPTION OF INTENT

The concept AUTHOR is indispensable for conceiving of and indicating the subject who, with intent, even in automatic and afflatal writing, brings the text into being. The conditions of textual emergence cannot be denied or, per Barthes and Foucault, unduly diminished. While such intentions are causally relevant, what is not so clear is whether they are interpretively relevant. According to intentionalism, the meaning of a text is just what the author intended it to mean, and so interpretation ought to be accountable to what we can glean of the author's intent. Intentionalism is initially plausible, and as it implies textual closure, it is one of the views that must be undermined if DOA is to be successfully defended.

There are many reasons to reject intentionalism, not least Wimsatt's and Beardsley's classic distinction between author's meaning and textual meaning. The interpretations suggested by the author's avowed, secret, or subconscious intentions may preclude aesthetically preferable interpretations, even where these are relativized to writer-as-reader response.[26] As we know, we can interpret texts not only in ignorance but even in direct violation of the author's intentions. Dostoevsky wanted to transform Russia into a giant monastery, but his novels are better appreciated when his theological message—in Barthes' sense as well as the standard sense—is ignored. Alyosha is far less compelling than Ivan. Raskolnikov's redemption is a profound disappointment. Intentionalism is right to respect the author, but intentionalism is not the only means of doing so. We also respect authors by interpreting their work charitably, and the principle of charity requires that we not be limited to interpreting a text in accordance with the author's intentions. To be charitable to Dostoevsky, we must ignore him. One might claim that the most charitable interpretation of a text gives us access to the author's intentions, but this concedes the more important point that interpretation can proceed prior to an account of such intentions. Where a text is the only real evidence of the states of mind that produced it, as with certain anonymous texts, we can only access intentions, if we can at all, through a prior understanding of the text itself.

One might think intentionalism plausible if, for instance, one views communication as the proper function of texts. On this view, texts are designed to mediate the transmission of thoughts and feelings. Here one recalls from Prufrock, "That's not what I meant. That's not what I meant at all," and imagines Eliot himself replying, "So what?" No question, the proper function of most nonliterary texts is to communicate, but this is difficult to maintain for the literary text as a species of artwork. *The Trial* then becomes a terribly inefficient means of conveying the idea that life is bureaucratically oppressive, implacably irrational, and irremediably bleak. One might think that what Kafka wanted to communicate requires the perlocutionary effect of *The Trial*, but why then did Kafka want the manuscript destroyed? How do we square the novel's obvious literary success with the indeterminacy of the desired communiqué? Many artists explicitly disavow the intention to communicate, and many reveal in their work things they wish they had not revealed. Surely what an artist *betrays* in art is not a matter of communication. Obscurantism and the new writing are altogether pointless if the function of art is communicative. If literary writing has any single proper function, it is, quite trivially, to create a fictional, poetic, or dramatic world. Where the purpose is to communicate, success depends on the writer's competence in the use of, or, in the case of innovation, departure from linguistic and literary conventions. But here again, reader competence in engaging the text itself is sufficient for understanding the text. A good mystery is a good mystery even if the author, on our best hypothesis, intended to write a romance. If we know a romance was intended, we might well be disappointed in the author, and although this may detract from our appreciation of the text, it need not. Even if it does, and should, this does not by itself scotch our interpreting it as a mystery.

Another challenge faced by the intentionalist is what to say about accidentally produced original texts, or, if you prefer, quasi-texts. The monkey's *Hamlet* reproduces an already authored text where at least something of the author's intentions is already known. This scenario is far less interesting than that of a dramatically great, never before inscribed *Shamlet*, accidentally produced by a monkey or a computer programmed to generate random sentences. Naturally, *Shamlet* is not a work of art. Perhaps it is not even a text, although by hypothesis it is at least a quasi-text, interpretable *as if* it were a text.[27] As far as our aesthetic interest is concerned, it might as well have been written by a playwright. By hypothesis, we can interpret *Shamlet* in full view of the fact that there is no author whose intentions we can appeal to in determining the meaning of the quasi-text. Intentionalism requires us to ignore *Shamlet*, even though it is a literary interpretable. Yet it seems we have every reason not to ignore *Shamlet*. Had it been written by a playwright, it would count not only as literature, but as great literature, eminently worthy of dramatic performance and critical attention. It is not clear why the accidental emergence of *Shamlet* should delegitimate performances of it or critical commentary on it. There is nothing wrong with finding sunsets and other natural phenomena aesthetically piquant, and so there is no reason why the aesthetic rewards of *Shamlet* should be ignored, decried, or rejected out of hand. It might be more gratifying to interpret natural phenomena as artworks in the divine *oeuvre*, and one might even appeal to such beauty in an argument from aesthetic design. The point, however, is that the piquancy of sunsets and the like do not depend on their being intentionally produced.

It is for such reasons that a cluster of views loosely affiliated with intentionalism seems more plausible than the affiliate itself. These are varieties of constructivism, according to which interpretation of a literary text requires, not prior assessment of the author's intentions, which are often unknowable, or violable, but some kind of author construct. Examples include Booth's implied author, Walton's apparent artist, Nehamas's author figure, Gracia's pseudo-historical author, and Irwin's urauthor.[28] These constructs differ in explanatory purpose and power, constraints on historical plausibility, and degree of affiliation with intentionalism. What they share is the view that, without an author construct, interpretation is hamstrung. Ignorance or violation of the author's intentions is thus compatible, at least potentially, with textual closure via an author construct. Robert Stecker argues that such constructs are reducible to hypotheses about what the real author intended, in which case constructivism is on the same footing as intentionalism.[29] While Stecker's argument is persuasive, we might well construct a Dostoevsky whose message accords, not with the message of the man himself, but with our best, most charitable interpretation of his novels. Furthermore, it seems we can and perhaps should construct an author for *Shamlet*, in which case author constructs are not, generally speaking, reducible to hypotheses about what the real author intended. Constructivism thus has the relative advantage over intentionalism in allowing interpretation in ignorance or in violation of intended meaning, and of quasi-texts that merit literary attention.

What the *Shamlet* case shows, however, is that interpretation requires a *presumption of intent*, in that literary interpretables are taken to issue from, or as though from, intentions. Unlike interest in sunsets and other natural phenomena, our interest in *Shamlet* is asymmetrically dependent on our interest in written art, which, although produced under the auspices of bona fide intent, is interpretable irrespective of such intentional *content* as we may discover or ascribe. If we discovered that *Hamlet* really is a kind of *Shamlet*, this would undermine the belief that it is a work of art, not the belief that it is a literary interpretable. But the quasi-text is a literary interpretable in virtue of certain resemblances between it and genuine texts. Can we build an author construct for *Shamlet*? Of course. Must we? It seems not, given our knowledge of the accidental emergence of the quasi-text. If we must, our only means of doing so is by inference from what we can glean from *Shamlet*. But this means we derive the construct from the interpretation, not the other way around. What remains is a more or less empty constructivism. The one inescapable feature of the author construct, it seems, is that the text be treated as though it is an intentional artifact. This does not vindicate constructivism, however, for the requirement that a literary interpretable be taken as though intended does not mean that the content of such intent has any bearing on textual meaning. Without purchase on textual meaning, the presumption of intent yields an *abstractum* too minimal to count as a genuine author construct. Nonetheless, it is in this presumption that the marginal life of the author consists.

Intentionalism and constructivism are tempting because accessing the author's real or constructed intentions gives us an explanatory advantage vis-à-vis the text. Authorial vision, in other words, provides a top-down means to interpret textual data. But for reasons that should now be clear, this advantage may be illusory, unduly limiting, or superfluous. Robust author constructs are consequently dispensable. We do not need such a construct (i.e., God) to interpret the world, so why should we need one to interpret a literary world? Indeed, God-based worldviews, at least historically, have had the unduly limiting or superfluous role attributable to author-based and constructivist criticism. This is not to say that the DOA case has been won, or that traditional interpretive and critical practice is illegitimate *tout court*. It is rather to say that, at this point, DOA is defensible from two potential sources of textual closure.

AESTHETIC MEANING

According to Barthes, "a text's unity lies not in its origin but in its destination."[30] But as we have seen, we need not deny the author's antecedent creative vision to allow for liberation from authorial intention. Colin Lyas writes: "The alternative seems merely to replace authorial will with audience whim."[31] Short of reader response, however, we are now left with the text itself, subject to linguistic and literary conventions to which innovation is tractable as a departure. The text may provide its own interpretive closure, or rather convention might close it for us. The most difficult hurdle for advocates of DOA is not intentionalism and constructivism after all. It is rather the text itself, for textual data seem unrevisable, fixing meaning locally and determining the *gestalt*. Beyond mere underdetermination, indeterminacy in a literary world can be seen as an unimportant consequence of the fact that finite texts are incomplete. The meaning of a literary text might be said to consist in unrevisable textual data and such further determinable, though underdetermined, meaning as can be inferred from them.

The question now is how an advocate of DOA can dispose of the text itself as interpretively closed. One move is to grant that intentions do determine textual meaning while insisting that authorial intention is interpretively open. If the text is our best and sometimes only evidence of authorial intention, and evinces an indefinite disjunction of plausible intentions, then it is interpretively open. There are other kinds of evidence besides the text, however. These include biographical, historical, and psychological evidence, and in many cases these are usefully available for paring down the disjunction. Suppose that, from the initial conception of a text to its final execution, we know all there is to know about the author's brain. We might maintain that to build a profile of the author's intentions from this neurological knowledge is, at best, to engage in radical translation, where there is no canonical interpretation, no fact of the matter about the mental content we seek to discover. We might even say that all interpretation amounts to radical translation. Either way, the text will be interpretively open.

But suppose the advocate of DOA is quite rightly unpersuaded that radical translation is endemic either to a general theory of meaning or to the determination of an author's intentions. In other words, suppose the advocate rejects meaning holism in general and accepts psychological realism in particular. Certainly DOA would be far less interesting as a mere consequence of an otherwise unrelated theory of meaning. What is the DOA advocate to do? First, admit that the author's intentions and the text issuing from them are interpretively closed vis-à-vis the author's neuropsychology. Second, admit also that, relative to certain interpretive methods and purposes, literary conventions may tightly circumscribe textual meaning. Third, insist that none of this bears on textual meaning in the relevant sense, that of limiting how a reader may interpret a text. If nothing else, reader's meaning is, in principle at least, no less legitimate than writer's meaning, and it is after all in the *reading* of texts that multiple interpretability is fully appreciable. Various conventions may delimit acceptable interpretations, but readers concerned only with maximizing their own aesthetic experience have no other reason to bother with them, much less sacrifice their interpretations to those that are conventionally preferred. Relegating the sources of closure to other domains, the advocate has both the room, and the obligation, to formulate an account of such meaning as allows for the interpretive openness of literary texts.

As distinct from both intended and conventional meaning, the aesthetic meaning of a text can be understood in terms of those interpretations which variously and idiosyncratically facilitate the reader's appreciation, particularly what I elsewhere call *resolutive* experience—mutually coherent intellectual and emotional responses.[32] Piquant interpretations will vary from one person to another, and the more the individual reader allows meaning to proliferate, the more profound the resolutive experience. This latter claim is, within limits, psychologically plausible. The more meanings, or layers of meaning, are read into a text, the more one tends to appreciate it. In this way, aesthetic meaning is pluralistic, as DOA requires, both across individuals and, at least as a matter of psychological tendency, within individuals. I write "at least as a matter of tendency" because, in the name of reader liberation, it seems one cannot rule out either the possibility or the legitimacy of someone finding unisemous interpretation aesthetically optimal. Some have a need to simplify literary texts, finding them less pleasing otherwise. While this may betray a lack of refinement, neither Barthes nor Foucault can consistently rule it out of what the liberated reader may do.

DISCIPLINARY PRACTICE AND READER RESPONSE

The upshot of all this might seem to be that in interpreting literary texts, anything goes, and disciplinary practice is consequently groundless. If DOA implied this, it would not be defensible. But reader liberation does seem to imply that I may interpret a literary text any way I wish. I can stipulate, for instance, that *Ulysses* means "the cat is on the mat" or something equally absurd. In what ways might such a stipulation be defeasible? Stipulations are arbitrary assignments of meaning, and there is nothing wrong with them in principle. They have their uses, and that, indeed, is the point. Stipulation is purposive, and so is evaluable relative to the achievement and the value of such purposes. Stipulating that simulacra of the *Mona Lisa* will stand for some predicate in quantificational logic is pragmatically defeasible, as would be, in all likelihood, the *Ulysses* stipulation. The *Ulysses* stipulation might also be dismissed if it is put to an illicit purpose, to undermine the work by unfair means, to deceive a gullible audience, to interfere with fruitful discussion, and so on. In such cases, it is unclear that the stipulation would even count as an interpretation. So the *Ulysses* stipulation is potentially dismissible on a number of grounds. Although such grounds are extra-literary, they are sufficient to undermine idiosyncratic stipulations that are not in service of the stipulator's aesthetic appreciation.

In service of their own aesthetic experience, however, readers are free to interpret literary texts any way they want. Suppose, for instance, that someone finds the *Ulysses* stipulation piquant. We may dismiss the case as psychologically aberrant, and we may deny, for this reason, that the interpretation is likely to foster others' appreciation. At the same time, we have no legitimate grounds to deny readers what serves their legitimate aesthetic interest. In what sense then is there room for disciplinary practice? Plenty. Disciplinary practice needs criteria for better and worse interpretations, and nothing here prevents individuals from getting together and agreeing on the methods by which and the purposes for which they will proceed to interpret texts. Aesthetic interest may be provisionally sacrificed, by mutual agreement, for the investigation of the text-as-world, where such understanding is an end in itself or a means to augmenting deferred appreciation. Here, by default, the text loses some but not all of its plasticity as an erstwhile open interpretable, because the justification of interpretations will be constrained by intersubjective methods and purposes. With standards and purposes set, interpretations will be evaluable relative to those standards and purposes, and *gestalt* interpretations will ideally be successively improved in reflective equilibrium with low-level interpretations of textual data.

As different sets of readers can adopt different standards and purposes, there is plenty of room for disciplinary pluralism in an institutional context. This is a *desideratum* if one looks without a completely jaundiced eye at the present state of the art. However, just as in the case of the lone reader's stipulations, a subdiscipline can be evaluated relative to the achievement and the value of its purposes. On extra-literary grounds, some research programs simply will not cut it. But even within a legitimate subdiscipline, there is no reason to expect textual closure. From the perspective of Marxist criticism, is *Atlas Shrugged* a symptom of the medial stage of the dialectic, a *reductio* of nonmaterialist or nondeterminist views, propaganda, or dystopia? What various interpretations fit *Atlas Shrugged* from a feminist perspective? Is *Don Quixote* a satire or a celebration of self-ennoblement? Should textual ambiguities, like Othello's famous "Let it alone" be resolved as a matter of fact? Is there any textual datum so fixed that it is not in principle revisable? Procedures can always be developed to close a text, but the closure will be artificial, and may yield inferior interpretations when applied to other texts.

On a related track, there is nothing wrong with critics directing the reader's attention to good texts and to potentially piquant interpretations or interpretive procedures. Nor is there anything wrong with investigating the author in a psychology, history, or mechanics of the literary process, so long as what we discover of the author's vision, circumstances, or technique does not impede the pursuit of better textual interpretations. Assessing the extent to which a text realizes its author's vision requires this mutual independence. As meaning should proliferate within certain limits, so should disciplinary practice. To rule out disciplinary practice altogether, as Barthes and Foucault seem to imply, or to insist on one method or purpose as canonical, is not, after all, in the spirit or to the purpose of reader liberation. This is an important point to emphasize. DOA is in fact compatible with a virtuous mean between nihilism and dogmatism in disciplinary practice.

Although DOA is largely defensible, it is not so in virtue of the major arguments adduced by Barthes and Foucault. While literary texts are interpretively open, this does not mean that, in interpretive matters, anything goes. There are constraints on what counts as a viable interpretation, even for liberated readers in the privacy of their thoughts, for not just any interpretation will facilitate a reader's aesthetic appreciation, and those that do will, as a matter of human psychology, if not logical consistency, exclude many others. This is owing to the limits of attention and the relative implasticity of an individual's taste. But it is for a more important reason that the "D" in DOA turns out to be slightly inapt. What we cannot escape in interpreting a literary text or quasi-text is what I have called the presumption of intent, by which any literary interpretable is taken as, or as though, the product of intentions, the content of which, however, need not concern us. It is in this presumption, I have argued, that the marginal life of the author consists, leaving the author as good as dead, but not dead in fact, and leaving thanatophiles, aptly enough, with a polysemous challenge, to wit, and simply, *habeas corpus*.[33]

NOTES

1. Roland Barthes, "The Death of the Author," in *Image, Music, Text*, trans. Stephen Heath (New York: Hill and Wang, 1977), p. 147 (hereafter DA); Roland Barthes, "La Morte de l'Auteur," *Manteia* 5 (1968): 16 (hereafter MA) [p. 7].

2. Michel Foucault, "What Is an Author?" trans. Josué V. Harari, in Paul Rabinow, ed., *The Foucault Reader* (New York: Pantheon, 1984), p. 101 (hereafter WIA); Michel Foucault, "Qu'est-ce Qu'un Auteur?" *Bulletin de la Société Francaise de Philosophie* 63 (1969): 77 (hereafter QA) [p. 9].

3. DA, p. 143; MA, p. 13 [p. 4]; WIA, p. 105; QA, p. 79 [p. 12].

4. Donald Keefer, "Reports of the Death of the Author," *Philosophy and Literature* 19 (1995): 81–82.

5. DA, p. 143; MA, p. 13 [p. 4].

6. WIA, p. 119; QA, p. 95 [p. 21].

7. DA, p. 146; MA, p. 16 [p. 6].

8. WIA, p. 119; QA, p. 95 [p. 22].

9. Seán Burke, *The Death and Return of the Author: Criticism and Subjectivity in Barthes, Foucault and Derrida*, 2nd ed. (Edinburgh: Edinburgh University Press, 1998), p. 43.

10. DA, pp. 144–45; MA, p. 14 [p. 5].

11. WIA, p. 101; QA, p. 76 [p. 9].

12. WIA, p. 119; QA, p. 95 [p. 22].

13. Peter Lamarque, "The Death of the Author: An Analytical Autopsy," *British Journal of Aesthetics* 30 (1990): 319–31 [pp. 79–91].

14. I use capital letters to indicate the concept (e.g., "AUTHOR"), a convention used often in the philosophy of mind.

15. DA, p. 142; MA, p. 12 [pp. 3–4].

16. WIA, pp. 118–19; QA, pp. 94–95 [p. 21].

17. WIA, p. 107; QA, p. 82 [p. 13].

18. Knapp and Michaels agree that the text-as-authored implies intentionalism. See Steven Knapp and Walter Benn Michaels, "Against Theory," in W.T.J. Mitchell, ed., *Against Theory: Literary Studies and the New Pragmatism* (Chicago: University of Chicago Press, 1982), p. 12. Barthes and Foucault (implausibly) deny the author in favor of a (plausible) anti-intentionalism, while Knapp and Michaels claim (plausibly) that the author is indispensable, concluding (implausibly) that intentionalism is tautologous. In both cases the suspect premise is the conditional.

19. DA, p. 142; MA, p. 12 [p. 3].

20. I think there is something quite provocative in the *écriture* thesis, to wit, the idea that the very act of writing is sufficient to bring a literary world into existence. If, as I

hope to show, aesthetic meaning is both open and distinguishable from what it evinces of the author's psychology, then the literary text is at once expressive *and* performative, psychologically closed, aesthetically open.

21. DA, p. 146; MA, p. 16 [p. 6].

22. For an excellent introduction to Gödel's proof, see Ernest Nagel and James R. Newman, *Gödel's Proof* (New York: New York University Press, 1983).

23. W.K. Wimsatt and Monroe C. Beardsley, "The Intentional Fallacy," in *The Verbal Icon: Studies in the Meaning of Poetry* (Lexington: University of Kentucky Press, 1954), pp. 3–18.

24. DA, p. 147; MA, p. 17 [p. 6].

25. WIA, p. 103; QA, p. 78 [p. 10].

26. Stephen Davies, "The Aesthetic Relevance of Authors' and Painters' Intentions," *Journal of Aesthetics and Art Criticism* 41 (1982): 65.

27. I use "quasi-text" and "literary interpretable" to remain neutral on the question of whether texts must be intentionally produced. Many think not, but for an argument to the contrary see Jorge J.E. Gracia, *A Theory of Textuality: The Logic and Epistemology* (Albany: SUNY Press, 1995), pp. 59–70.

28. Wayne C. Booth, *The Rhetoric of Fiction* (Chicago: University of Chicago Press, 1961), p. 73; Kendall L. Walton, "Style and the Products and Processes of Art," in Berel Lang, ed., *The Concept of Style* (Philadelphia: University of Pennsylvania Press, 1979), p. 53; Alexander Nehamas, "Writer, Text, Work, Author," in Anthony J. Cascardi, ed., *Literature and the Question of Philosophy* (Baltimore: Johns Hopkins University Press, 1987), p. 285 [p. 110]; Gracia, *Theory of Textuality*, p. 4; William Irwin, *Intentionalist Interpretation: A Philosophical Explanation and Defense* (Westport, CT: Greenwood Press, 1999), p. 30.

29. Robert Stecker, "Apparent, Implied, and Postulated Authors," *Philosophy and Literature* 11 (1987): 258–71 [pp. 129–40].

30. DA, p. 148; MA, p. 17 [p. 7].

31. Colin Lyas, "Intention," in D.E. Cooper, ed., *A Companion to Aesthetics* (Oxford: Blackwell, 1996), p. 230.

32. Jason Holt, "A Comprehensivist Theory of Art," *British Journal of Aesthetics* 36 (1996): 427.

33. For helpful comments I thank William Irwin, Deborah Knight, and Rhonda Martens. For useful discussion I thank Elana Geller, Larry Holt, Carl Matheson, and Adam Muller.

CHAPTER 6

The Death of the Author: An Analytical Autopsy

Peter Lamarque

I

It is now over twenty years since Roland Barthes proclaimed the 'death of the author' and the phrase, if not the fact, is well established in the literary critical community. But what exactly does it mean? I suspect that many Anglo-American aestheticians have tended, consciously or otherwise, to shrug off Barthes's formulation as a mere Gallic hyperbole for their own more sober 'intentionalist fallacy' and thus have given the matter no further attention. In fact, as I will show, the significant doctrines underlying the 'death of the author' are far removed from the convivial debate about intentions and have their sights set not just on the humble author but on the concept of literature itself and even the concept of meaning.

My aim is to identify and analyse the main theses in two papers which are the seminal points of reference for the relevant doctrines: Roland Barthes's 'The Death of the Author' and Michel Foucault's 'What Is an Author?'.[1] I will be asking what the theses mean and whether they are true. I will not be discussing in any detail the broader context of the papers either in relation to general currents of thought or with regard to other work by the two theorists. My interest is with the arguments not the authors. I believe that the ideas as formulated in these articles—ideas about authorship, texts, writing, reading—are fundamental to the movement labelled post-structuralism yet are imprecisely expressed and

Peter Lamarque, "The Death of the Author: An Analytical Autopsy," *British Journal of Aesthetics* Vol. 30, No. 4 (October 1990), pp. 319–31. © Oxford University Press 1990. Reprinted by permission of Oxford University Press.

often misunderstood. Submitting them to an analytical study I hope will be instructive not only to those sceptical of [post-structuralism] but also for those supporters who might be unclear about the precise implications.

I will focus on four main theses which strike me as prominent in the papers. These I will dub The Historicist Thesis, The Death Thesis, The Author Function Thesis, and The *Ecriture* Thesis. All are closely interwoven and each has sub-components which will need to be spelt out. It is not my contention that Barthes and Foucault agree at every point—they clearly don't—but in combination they do present a case about authors and texts which has had a powerful influence on the development of a whole school of modern thought.

II

The Historicist Thesis

I will use Barthes's own words as a general characterization of the thesis:

The author is a modern figure, a product of our society. (p. 142)

Foucault speaks of the 'coming into being of the notion of "author" ' at a specific 'moment . . . in the history of ideas' (p. 101). Both locate the birth of the author in post-mediaeval times, a manifestation of the rise of the individual from the Reformation through to the philosophical Enlightenment. I am less concerned with the historical details than with the status (and meaning) of the Historicist Thesis. The idea that written works only acquired authors at a specific time in history clearly needs some explanation. I suggest there are at least three possible explanations, not mutually exclusive, and they will have a bearing on how to interpret the other theses in the overall argument. I should add that I am going to eliminate as uninteresting a merely lexicographical interpretation of the Historicist Thesis, i.e., an interpretation that sees the thesis as about the *word* 'author'. I take it that there could be authors prior to there being a word 'author' just as there can be writers before the word 'writer' and thoughts before the word 'thoughts'. No doubt for some even this is controversial but I do not believe that Barthes and Foucault had lexicography in mind in their defence of the Historicist Thesis.

The first (plausible) interpretation, then, is this:

A certain conception of a writer (writer-as-author) is modern.

For Foucault this conception is highly specific; in effect it is a legal and social conception of authorship. The author is seen as an owner of property, a producer of marketable goods, as having rights over those goods, and also responsibilities: 'Texts, books, and discourses really began to have authors . . . to the extent that authors became subject to punishment' (p. 108). In a similar vein Barthes identifies the author with 'capitalist ideology' (p. 143). I will call this interpretation of the Historicist Thesis the 'social conception', the point being that at a determinate stage in history, according to the thesis, writers (of certain kinds of texts) came to acquire a new social status, along with a corresponding legal and cultural recognition.

Again, I will not debate the truth of this historical claim—I suspect the actual details would not stand up to close scrutiny—but only comment on its theoretical implications. For example, it entails a distinction between an unrestricted notion of writer-*per-se* (any person who writes) and a more restricted notion of writer-as-author, the latter conceived in social or ideological terms. That distinction is useful in showing that the mere act of writing (writing on the sand, jottings on an envelope) does not make an author. An author so designated is a more weighty figure with legal rights and social standing, a producer of texts deemed to have value. Significantly, the thesis on this interpretation is about social conventions and a class of persons engaged in particular acts: it is not about a persona, a fictional character, or a construct of the text. Being about the personal status of authors it can offer no direct support, as we will see, for either the Author Function Thesis or the *Ecriture* Thesis, both of which conceive the author in impersonal terms.

The second interpretation of the Historicist Thesis I will call the 'criticism conception':

A certain conception of criticism (author-based criticism) is modern

Here the idea is that at a certain stage of history the focus of criticism turned to the personality of the author. Thus Barthes:

The image of literature to be found in ordinary culture is tyrannically centred on the author, his person, his life, his tastes, his passions, while criticism still consists for the most part in saying that Baudelaire's work is the failure of Baudelaire the man, Van Gogh's his madness, Tchaikovsky's his vice. (p. 143)

This state of affairs arose, according to Barthes, only after the bourgeois revolution which gave prominence to the individual. We can leave it to historians to debate the historical development of author-based criticism. No doubt it is a matter of degree how much critical significance is given at different periods of history to an author's biographical background or personality. Although the author as person (writer, cause, origin, etc.) is again evoked in this interpretation, it is nevertheless distinct from the 'social conception'. No direct implications about criticism follow from the fact that the author comes to be viewed as having rights over a text. Purely formalist criticism is compatible with a state of affairs where an author is accorded a secure legal and social identity.

The third interpretation is the most controversial but also the most interesting:

A certain conception of a text (the authored-text) is modern.

This I will call the 'text conception' of the Historicist Thesis. The idea is this, that at a certain point in history (written) texts acquire significance in virtue of being 'authored'. 'There was a time,' Foucault writes, 'when the texts which we today call "literary" (narratives, stories, epics, tragedies, comedies) were accepted, put into circulation, and valorized without any question about the identity of their author' (p. 109). He contrasts this with the case of scientific discourses which, in the Middle Ages, owed their authority to a named prove-nance (Hippocrates, Pliny, or whoever). A radical change occurred, so Foucault claims, in the seventeenth and eighteenth centuries when literary texts came to be viewed as essentially 'authored', while scientific writing could carry authority even in anonymity.

These are of course sweeping generalizations which again invite substantial qualification from the scrupulous historian of ideas. For our purposes further clarification is in order. The text conception is itself open to different interpre-tations. At its simplest it is just the claim that at a specific point in history (perhaps a different point for different discourses) it became important that texts be attributed. A stronger claim is that this attribution actually changed the way texts were understood. That is, they could not be properly understood except as by so-and-so. The author attribution carried the meaning, perhaps as personal revelation, expression of belief, seal of authority, or whatever. Foucault probably has in mind at least this latter claim. But from the evidence of his Author Function Thesis, which we will look at later, he seems to want something stronger still for the text conception. The suggestion is that the personal aspects of author attribution disappear altogether. It is not actual causal origins which mark the difference between an authored and an unauthored text but rather certain (emergent) properties of the text itself. The authored-text is viewed as the manifestation of a creative act but what is important is that this yields or makes accessible a distinctive kind of unity, integrity, meaning, interest, and value. And it is these qualities themselves, rather than their relation to some particular authorial performance, which are given prominence under this strengthened version of the Historicist Thesis.

There is a slide then in the text conception from the mere association of text and author to the much fuller conception of a text as a classifiable work of a certain kind fulfilling a purpose, expressing a meaning and yielding a value. I suggest that the plausibility of the Historicist Thesis weakens as it progresses along this scale. In other words the conception of certain pieces of writing as having meaning, unity and value seems much less datable historically (was there ever a time when there was no such conception?) than the mere inclination to highlight author attribution.

III

The Death Thesis

Against this background we can now turn to the second substantive thesis, which I have called the Death Thesis. At its simplest, this merely claims:

The author is dead

The meaning of the claim, and assessment of its truth, can only be determined relative to the Historicist Thesis, under its different interpretations. The underlying thought is this: that if a certain conception (of an author, a text, etc.) has a definite historical beginning, i.e., arises under determinate historical conditions, then it can in principle come to an end, when the historical conditions change.

One complication is that the Death Thesis can be read either as a statement of fact or as wishful thinking, i.e., either as a description of the current state of affairs (we simply no longer *have* authors conceived in a certain way) or as a prescription for the future (we no longer *need* authors so conceived, we can now get by without them).[2] Both Barthes and Foucault seem to waver on the question of description and prescription. Barthes, for example, admits that 'the sway of the Author remains powerful' (p. 143) yet in speaking of the 'modern scriptor', in contrast to the Author (pp. 145, 146), he suggests that (modern) writing is no longer conceived as the product of an author. Similarly, Foucault tells us 'we must locate the space left empty by the author's disappearance' (p. 105), the latter thus taken for granted, yet makes a prediction at the end of his paper that the author function, which is his own conception of the author, 'will disappear', i.e., sometime in the future, 'as our society changes' (p. 119).

To see what the Death Thesis amounts to, let us run briefly through the different permutations.

(A) [In relation to the social conception of the Historicist Thesis] the writer-as-author is dead, or should be

Does the conception of writer-as-author, with a certain social and legal status, still obtain? Surely it does. Authors are still, in Foucault's words, 'subject to punishment' (they can even be sentenced to death); there are copyright laws and blasphemy laws; authors can be sued for libel or plagiarism; they attract interest from biographers and gossips. Authors under this conception are certainly not dead. But should they be killed off? Should we try and rid ourselves of this conception? The question is political and moral, not philosophical. Should we promote a society where all writing is anonymous, where writers have no legal status and no obligations? Maybe. But the point is quite independent of any theoretical argument about *écriture* or the author function, for it is a point about the treatment of actual people in a political and legal system.

(B) [In relation to the criticism conception of the Historicist Thesis] author-based criticism is dead, or should be

Here we come closest to the Intentionalist Fallacy in that anti-intentionalists can be seen as advancing some such version of the Death Thesis. But note, first, that anti-intentionalists are not committed to a version based on the social conception of authorship, nor indeed to the text conception. Also, second, they are committed only to the normative element (author-based criticism should be dead) not to the descriptive element (it is in fact dead).

Although there is certainly an overlap here between the anti-intentionalists and Barthes and Foucault it seems to be the only point of contact. If the Death Thesis simply records and endorses the decline of crude author-based criticism then it is of only modest theoretical interest. Of course the debate continues about the proper role of authorial intention in literary criticism but there does seem to be a general consensus that concentration on purely biographical factors—or the so-called personality of an author—is not integral to a serious critical discipline. In fact, as we shall see, it is quite clear that Barthes and Foucault had something more substantial in their sights when they advanced the Death Thesis. Nevertheless, much of the credibility of the thesis undoubtedly trades off the more secure intuitions within the literary critical community that pure author-based criticism is a legitimate target. It is thus important to identify the real Death Thesis as intended by Barthes and Foucault so that we don't find ourselves forced to assent through a mistaken interpretation.

(C) [In relation to the text conception of the Historicist Thesis] the authored-text is dead, or should be

Does the conception of the authored-text still obtain, that is, the text conceived as having a determinate meaning, as the manifestation of a creative act? Certainly the qualities of unity, expressiveness and creative imagination are still sought and valued in literary works, indeed they are bound up with the very conception of literature. If possession of these is sufficient for something's being an authored-text, then authored-texts are not dead. Remember, though, that an authored-text, on the strong interpretation, is defined independently of its relation to an actual author (or author-as-person). The meaning and unity of an authored-text are explicable not in terms of some real act of creation, some determinate psychological origin, but only as a projection of these in the text itself. This is the import of the Author Function Thesis.

Foucault would accept that literary criticism still retains its conception of the authored-text: in fact he perceives this conception as the foundation of literary criticism. The Death Thesis, then, in this version, must be seen as a prescription not a description. Foucault's project is to get rid of the authored-text itself (along with its concomitant notions of meaning, interpretation, unity, expression, and value). The Author Function, which is the defining feature of an

authored-text, is, according to Foucault, 'an ideological product' (p. 119), a repressive and restricting 'principle of thrift in the proliferation of meaning'
(p. 118). In effect Foucault's death prescription is aimed at the very concept of
a literary work which sustains the practice of literary criticism (it is also aimed,
more broadly, at any class of work subject to similar interpretative and eval-
uative constraints). The prescription has little to do with the role or status of
authors as persons.

Seen in this light, it is no defence against Foucault's attack to point out that
the literary institution has long ceased to give prominence to an author's personality. That would be to give undue weight to the weaker versions of the
Death Thesis. There is no room for the complacent thought that Foucault is just
another anti-intentionalist. On the other hand, Foucault cannot find support for
his attack on the authored-text merely through an appeal to the inadequacy of
crude author-based criticism. He has in effect pushed the debate beyond the
author altogether.

IV

The Author Function Thesis

The Author Function Thesis is intended to provide further support for the
strong version (i.e., version (C)) of the Death Thesis. Although the notion is
never explicitly defined by Foucault, the central idea is that the author function
is a property of a discourse (or text) and amounts to something more than its
just being written or produced by a person (of whatever status): 'there are a
certain number of discourses that are endowed with the "author function", while
others are deprived of it' (p. 107).

We can identify a number of separate components of the thesis which help
to clarify the notion of 'author function'. First there is the distinctness claim:

(1) The author function is distinct from the author-as-person (or writer).

Foucault makes it clear that the author function 'does not refer purely and simply
to a real individual' (p. 113). He complicates the exposition by often using the
term interchangeably with 'the author'; however, the term 'author' itself is not
intended as a direct designation of an individual. He says that 'it would be . . .
wrong to equate the author with the real writer' (p. 112) and he speaks of the
author as 'a certain functional principle' (p. 119).

What are the grounds for postulating an impersonal conception of an author
as distinct from a personal conception? Foucault does not simply have in mind
the literary critical notion of an 'implied author', i.e., a set of attitudes informing
a work which might or might not be shared with the real author. For one thing
Foucault's author function is not a construct specific to individual works but
may bind together a whole *oeuvre*; and whereas an implied author is, as it were,

just one fictional character among others in a work, the author function is more broadly conceived as determining the very nature of the work itself.[3]

One of the arguments that Foucault offers for the distinctness claim (1), indeed it is also his justification for describing the author as an 'ideological product' (p. 119), rests on a supposed discrepancy between the way we normally conceive the author as a person (i.e., as a genius, a creator, one who proliferates meaning) and the way we conceive texts which have authors (i.e., as constrained in their meaning and confined in the uses to which they can be put). But this argument is unsatisfactory simply because there is no such discrepancy. To the extent that we conceive of an author as offering 'an inexhaustible world of significations' (p. 118), as a proliferator of meaning, then we expect precisely the same of the work he creates.

It is more promising to read Foucault as proposing a semi-technical sense of the term 'author', one which conforms to the following principle:

(2) 'Having an author' is not a relational predicate (characterizing a relation between a work and a person) but a monadic predicate (characterizing a certain kind of work).

This principle signals the move from 'X has an author' to 'X is authored' or more explicitly from 'X has Y as an author' (the relational predicate) to 'X is Y-authored' (the monadic predicate). The author function becomes a property of a text or discourse not a relation between a text and a person. We need to ask what the monadic predicate 'being authored' or being 'Y-authored' actually means in this special sense.

First, though, it might be helpful to offer a further elaboration of (2) in terms of paraphrase or reduction:

(3) All relevant claims about the relation between an author-as-person and a text are reducible to claims about an authored-text.

In this way the author disappears through a process comparable to ontological reduction by paraphrase. In place of, for example, 'the work is a product of the author's creative act' we can substitute 'the work is an authored-text' and still retain the significant cognitive content of the former. Such a semantic manoeuvre is not intended, of course, to show that authors (as persons) are redundant. At best its aim is to show that *relative to critical discourse* references to an author can be eliminated without loss of significant content. I take it that some such thesis underlies Foucault's statement that the

aspects of an individual which we designate as making him an author are only a projection, in more or less psychologizing terms, of the operations that we force texts to undergo, the connections that we make, the traits that we establish as pertinent, the continuities that we recognize, or the exclusions that we practice. (p. 110).

Foucault is thinking of such aspects as an author's 'design' and 'creative power', as well as the meaning, unity and expression with which the author informs the text. He believes, as we have seen, that these features can be attributed directly to an authored-text without reference back to the author-as-person. This is the heart of the Author Function Thesis.

What support can be offered for propositions (2) and (3)? After all, they are not obviously true and they depart from the more familiar meaning of 'author'. The main logical support that Foucault offers is an argument about authors' names. An author's name, he suggests, does not operate purely referentially; rather than picking out some individual person, it has, he says, a 'classificatory function', it 'serves to characterize a certain mode of being of discourse' (p. 107). I think he has something like the following in mind:

(4) (Some) author attributions (using an author's name) are non-extensional.

If we say that a play is by Shakespeare we mean, or connote, more than just that the play was written by a particular man (Shakespeare); for one thing we assign a certain honorific quality to it (it is likely to be a play worthy of our attention); also we relate the play to a wider body of work, to *Hamlet*, *King Lear*, *Twelfth Night*, and so on. Being 'by Shakespeare' signals not just an external relation but an internal characterization. We move from 'X is a play by Shakespeare' to 'X is a Shakespeare play' or even 'X is Shakespearean'. The latter formulations are non-extensional, or at least have non-extensional readings, in the sense that substitution of co-referential names is not always permissible (does not preserve truth); if Shakespeare turns out to be Bacon it doesn't follow that the plays become Baconian, where that has its own distinctive connotations.

Let us suppose that stated like this the argument has some merit. Does it in fact support the Author Function Thesis? Certainly it provides an illustration of the move from a relational predicate to a monadic predicate: in this case from 'by Shakespeare' to 'Shakespearean'. Is this an instance of the move from 'X has Y as an author' to 'X is Y-authored'? Maybe. But what it shows is that we are not obliged to make the move. 'X has Shakespeare as an author' has both a non-extensional, classificatory meaning *and* a fully extensional, relational meaning. In other words the reference to Shakespeare the person still stands. By pointing, quite rightly to the classificatory function of authors' names Foucault mistakenly supposes that this in itself eliminates the referential function.

What about the move, in (2), from 'X has an author' to 'X is authored'? This move is not directly supported by the argument from authors' names but hangs on a distinctive conception of an 'authored-text'. This takes us back to the Historicist Thesis. Foucault, as we saw, has in mind not just the attribution of an author to a text, nor in the more sophisticated version of (4) a text classified through a non-extensional attribution, but rather a notion of an authored-text conceived more broadly:

(5) An authored-text is one that is subject to interpretation, constrained in its meaning, exhibiting unity and coherence, and located in a system of values

It is precisely this notion he is attacking when he attacks the author function. But now we can begin to see how uncomfortably the pieces fit together for Foucault. For one thing the author as a person—with a personality, a biography, a legal status and social standing—has no role in (5). The reductive theses (2) and (3) see to that, as does the distinctness thesis (1). In effect, Foucault has recognized, in postulating the author function and the notion of an authored-text, that the qualities in (5) are *institutionally based* qualities, i.e., part of the conception of literature, and not *individualistically based*, i.e., formulated in terms of individual psychological attitudes.[4] There is no need to see the constraints on interpretation, nor the source of unity and coherence, nor the criteria of value, as directly attributable to an individual (the author-as-person).

   If that is the point of the Author Function Thesis then it has some force, albeit reiterating a position well-established in anti-intentionalist critical theory. But Foucault cannot have it both ways: he cannot distance the authored-text from the author-as-person and yet at the same time mount his attack on the authored-text on the grounds that it perpetuates the bourgeois ideology of the individual, that it elevates the author into a position of God-like power and authority, enshrined in law. It is as if Foucault has not fully assimilated the implications of his own Author Function Thesis; he speaks as if his main target is still the author-as-person behind and beyond the work informing it with a secret and inner meaning. Perhaps the source of the problem is the misleading invocation of the author in the terms 'author function' and 'authored-text'. Strictly speaking, authors have nothing to do with it; the authored-text, so-called, at least in its most obvious manifestation, is a literary work, defined institutionally. Literary works have authors, of course; they are the product of a creative act (a real act from a real agent) but the constraints on interpretation, and the determination of coherence and value, are independent of the individual author's will. That is the lesson of the Death Thesis in its more plausible versions and it should be the lesson too of the Author Function Thesis.

V

The *Ecriture* Thesis

   Barthes's version of the author function is what he calls the 'modern scriptor' who is 'born simultaneously with the text' (p. 145). But Barthes bases his move from the relational author to the non-relational scriptor—i.e., his version of the Author Function Thesis—on a thesis about writing (*écriture*). The basic claim of what I have called the *Ecriture* Thesis is this (in Barthes's words):

Writing is the destruction of every voice, of every point of origin. (p. 142)

The implication is that the very nature of writing makes the author—i.e., the author-as-person—redundant. What arguments does Barthes offer to support this thesis?

The first is an argument from narrative:

> As soon as a fact is *narrated* no longer with a view to acting directly on reality but intransitively, that is to say, finally outside of any function other than that of the very practice of the symbol itself . . . the voice loses its origin. (p. 142)

The trouble is, it is difficult to conceive of any act of narration which in fact satisfies the condition of having no other function than the 'practice of the symbol itself'. Nearly all narration has some further aim, indeed the aim in some form or other to 'act . . . directly on reality': be it to inform, entertain, persuade, instruct, or whatever. Narration is by definition an *act* and no acts are truly gratuitous. Strictly speaking the narrative argument collapses here.

Still, one might suppose, charitably, that certain kinds of *fictional* narrative come close to Barthes's specification: narratives where playfulness is paramount. It is a convention of some kinds of fiction that they draw attention to their own fictional status, that they point inward rather than outward, that they teasingly conceal their origin, and so forth. But even if we grant that in these special cases attention focuses only on the 'symbol itself', there is nothing here to support a general thesis about writing (or authors). For one thing, there are different kinds of conventions governing written (like spoken) narratives, often far removed from the tricks of fiction, and in many such cases narrative purpose (and thus the 'voice of origin') is manifest. Also of course not all writing is in narrative form.

A second argument for the *Ecriture* Thesis rests on the characterization of writing as performative:

> *writing* can no longer designate an operation of recording, notation, representation, 'depiction' . . . ; rather, it designates . . . a performative . . . in which the enunciation has no other content . . . than the act by which it is uttered. (pp. 145–6)

But the claim that writing has the status of a performative utterance, instead of supporting the *Ecriture* Thesis, in fact directly contradicts it. A performative utterance only counts as an act—a promise, a marriage, a declaration of war—under precisely specified contextual conditions; and one of those conditions, essential in each case, is the speaker's having appropriate intentions. Far from being the destruction of a 'voice of origin' the successful performative relies crucially on the disposition and authority of the speaker. The analogy, then, to say the least, is unfortunate.

Clearly what impressed Barthes about the performative utterance is another feature: that of self-validation. If I say 'I promise' I am not reporting some external fact but, under the right conditions, bringing a fact into existence. However, even if we set aside the requirement of the speaker's authority, and focus only on the feature of self-validation, the analogy with performatives is still inadequate. Once again Barthes is led to an unwarranted generalization about the nature of writing by taking as a paradigm a certain kind of fictive utterance, which creates its own facts or world, and ignoring more commonplace illocutionary purposes.

The third argument is about meaning. The thought is this, that writing *per se*, in contrast to the constrained authored-text, does not yield any determinate meaning:

a text is not a line of words releasing a single 'theological' meaning (the 'message' of the Author-God) but a multi-dimensional space in which a variety of writings, none of them original, blend and clash. (p. 146)

We find the same idea in Foucault, even though he voices some scepticism later on about *écriture*: 'today's writing has freed itself from the dimension of expression', 'it is an interplay of signs', it 'unfolds like a game' (p. 102). How does this support the thesis that writing has destroyed the voice of origin? The argument seems to go something like this: determinate meaning is always the product of authorial imposition, where there is no determinate meaning there is no author, writing *per se* (*écriture*) has no determinate meaning (it is a mere play of signs), so writing *per se* shows the author to be redundant. The reasoning is bizarre. Its formal validity is suspect and it also begs the question that there is such a thing as writing *per se*. *Ecriture* is in effect stipulated to be authorless, to be lacking in determinate meaning, to be free of interpretative constraints. But this very conception of *écriture* needs to be challenged.

The key is the idea of a 'text'. A 'text', as Barthes conceives it, is a specific manifestation of *écriture*. It is to be contrasted with a 'work'; a work belongs in a genre, its meaning is constrained, it has an author, it is subject to classification. A text, Barthes tells us, is 'always *paradoxical*'; it 'practises the infinite deferment of the signified';[5] 'it answers not to an interpretation, even a liberal one, but to an explosion, a dissemination' (p. 159); 'it cannot be contained in a hierarchy, even in a simple division of genres' (p. 157); and 'no vital "respect" is due to the Text: it can be *broken*' (p. 161). This idea of a text as an explosion of unconstrained meaning, without origin and without purpose, is a theoretician's fiction. Perhaps we could, by abstraction, come to look at writing in this way but it would be quite idle to do so. It would be like trying to hear a Mozart symphony as a mere string of unstructured sounds. More importantly, though, it is no part of the concept of writing (or language) that it should be so viewed. Writing, like speech, or any language 'performed', is inevitably, and properly, conceived as purposive. To use language as meaningful discourse is to perform speech acts; to understand discourse is, minimally, to grasp what speech acts are performed. Barthes's view of *écriture* and of texts tries to abstract language from the very function that gives it life.

An underlying assumption in both Barthes and Foucault is that there is intrinsic merit in what Foucault calls the 'proliferation of meaning'. Perhaps the fundamental objection to their combined programme is that this assumption is unsupported and untenable. By prescribing the death of the author and by promoting the text over the work, both writers see themselves as liberating meaning from unnatural and undesirable restrictions. They both assume that more is better. Part of the problem is that they are trapped by a gratuitous, and inappropriate, political vocabulary: 'repression', 'authority', 'control'. But deeper still they reveal a predilection for a peculiarly sterile form of literary criticism, exemplified perhaps by certain passages in Empson's *Seven Types of Ambiguity* and pressed almost *ad absurdum* in Barthes's own *S/Z*, where the literary work is seen as a limitless and unrestricted source of connotation and allusion. What is objectionable is that they have set up this conception as a paradigm not only of criticism but, worse, of reading itself.

The critical community at large soon tired of the simplistic proliferation of meaning and outside the literary institution it never even got a foothold. It is a non-starter—pointless if not impossible—to conceive of scientific or historical or philosophical discourse as *écriture*. It is always more interesting, more demanding, more rewarding for understanding, to consolidate meaning, to seek structure and coherence, to locate a work in a tradition or practice. This has nothing whatsoever to do with reinstating some bullying authoritarian author. But then that figure was always just a fiction anyway.[6]

REFERENCES

1. I will be using the following texts: Roland Barthes, 'The Death of the Author', in *Image—Music—Text*, Essays Selected and Translated by Stephen Heath (Fontana/Collins, 1977); Michel Foucault, 'What Is an Author?' in *The Foucault Reader*, edited by Paul Rabinow (Peregrine Books, 1986). All citations and page references are from these editions.

2. A similar ambiguity lies in the origin of the Death Thesis, namely Nietzsche's proclamation that 'God is dead'. Was Nietzsche describing a new human consciousness already in evidence or was he heralding a radical break with the past?

3. I am guided here, indeed throughout this essay, by the useful discussion in Alexander Nehamas, 'Writer, Text, Work, Author', in Anthony J. Cascardi, ed. *Literature and the Question of Philosophy* (Johns Hopkins U.P., 1987).

4. For a clear account of institutional qualities in the literary context, see Stein Haugom Olsen, 'Literary Aesthetics and Literary Practice', in *The End of Literary Theory* (Cambridge U.P., 1987).

5. Roland Barthes, 'From Work to Text', in *Image—Music—Text*, op. cit., p. 158.

6. An earlier version of this paper was presented at a conference of the Nordic Aesthetics Society in Helsinki in May 1989.

PART TWO

THE RESURRECTION OF THE AUTHOR? A LOOK AT AUTHOR CONSTRUCTS

CHAPTER 7

Writer, Text, Work, Author

Alexander Nehamas

> Of persons artificial, some have their words and actions *owned* by those whom they represent. And then the person is the *actor*: and he that owneth his words and actions, is the Author: in which case the actor acteth by authority. For that which in speaking of goods and possessions, is called an *owner*, and in Latin *dominus*, in Greek κυριος; speaking of actions, is called author. And as the right of possession, is called dominion; so the right of doing any action, is called AUTHORITY.

This passage from the *Leviathan* (bk. 1, chap. 16) concerns social roles, "persons artificial," in general. But though it does not specifically mention literature, it is easy to see that it can apply to the case of the literary author as well. It expresses, with the disarming straightforwardness so characteristic of Hobbes, his view of the relationship between all authors and what he takes to be their products. Authors, according to Hobbes, own their words and actions. The writings of literary authors, therefore, are also their own, their possession and property.[1]

This conception of the author as owner and of authority as possession constitutes the specific background against which we must read Roland Barthes's view that the author is "a modern figure, a product of our society insofar as, emerging from the Middle Ages with English Empiricism, French Rationalism and the personal faith of the Reformation, it discovered the prestige of the

Cascardi, Anthony J., ed. Literature and the Question of Philosophy, pp. 267–291. © 1989 The Johns Hopkins University Press. Reprinted by permission of The Johns Hopkins University Press.

individual, of, as it is more nobly put, the 'human person.' "[2] Hobbes's posses-
sive conception supplies at least part of the motivation for Barthes's negative
attitude toward the author.

Ownership involves the right to dispose of one's property as one wishes. In
addition to the institutions surrounding the ideas of intellectual property and
copyright, and from which we must try to keep it distinct, disposition in the
literary case emerges as interpretation, to which the author is often assumed to
bear a special relationship. But any such right or privilege can be exercised only
within the law, and it therefore entails responsibility for one's actions and for
what is subsequently made of them. Hobbes makes it clear that from his view
"it followeth that when an actor makes a covenant by authority, he bindeth the
author, no less than if he had made it himself; and no less subjecteth him to all
the consequences of the same" (*Leviathan*, bk. 1, chap. 16).

This connection between ownership and responsibility, in turn, constitutes the
background against which we must read another attack against the author closely
related to that of Barthes. This is the view of Michel Foucault, who begins from
the thesis that "this type of ownership has always been subsequent to what one
might call penal appropriation. Texts, books, and discourses really began to have
authors . . . to the extent that authors became subject to punishment."[3]

Such an approach seems almost calculated to shock and to startle. Since, as
we shall see, it faces some deep difficulties, it should be defended against some
obvious misunderstandings. First, we must notice that the conception of the
author as a historical phenomenon is not by itself intended to, and cannot, undermine the author's reality. To argue that this figure emerged at a particular
time for particular reasons is only to argue that our notion of the author is part
of our history. And being a part of history is not an alternative to reality: it is
one of its modes. Yet, though historicity does not undermine reality, it does
undermine necessity. If something has a history, if, that is, it has a beginning,
then it may also have an end. If the world did not contain authors at some time,
then perhaps someday it can be without them again.

Second, the historicist conception of the author is not the view that one day
we made the empirical discovery (as if we had not known this before) that
certain texts were composed by individuals. Rather, this conception asks why
these texts began to be treated in certain specific ways at some time, what
purposes such treatment served, what values such purposes promoted. In pro-
claiming the author "dead," writers like Barthes and Foucault do not claim, as
William Cain has correctly pointed out, "that authors don't exist at all or that
texts (as if by magic) write themselves."[4] Their argument, particularly Foucault's, which will mainly occupy me in what follows, is more subtle and more
complicated.

Schematically and in abstract terms, this argument consists of two stages.
Beginning with the idea that the notion of the author is a historical phenomenon
and that the way of reading texts associated with it has a definite temporal
beginning, the first stage concludes that this notion *can* come to an end. The

second stage then produces what it considers as good reasons for actually bringing this possible end about. The argument finally concludes that both the notion of the author and the treatment of texts it underwrites, that is to say, literary interpretation, *must* come to an end.

The second part of this argument, in my opinion, is more important than the first. Nevertheless, Foucault's historical claims raise some serious questions. He writes, for example, that the author emerged, that literature ceased being "authorless," only during the seventeenth and eighteenth centuries (149).[5] Yet, though perhaps Foucault is right in claiming that literature was accepted simply on the grounds of its "ancientness" during the Middle Ages, this clearly represented a radical departure from the practices of late antiquity. A complicated author figure, though of course one quite different from present-day notions, is implicit in Diogenes Laertius's *Lives of the Philosophers*, in the scholia to the tragic poets, or in the complex discussions of Homer's allegorical interpreters. Foucault also believes that the figure of the literary author that was established during the Enlightenment represents a direct transposition of the scientific author of earlier times. Now it may be true that scientific texts "were accepted in the Middle Ages, and accepted as 'true,' only when marked with the name of their author" (149). But this transportation, if such it was, was anything but direct. The role of the scientific author, who was supposed to guarantee the truth of a treatise, is very different from that of the literary author, the truth of whose texts has not been the central concern of modern criticism. In addition, the literary texts of antiquity did actually make claims to truth, though such claims were more often based on divine inspiration than on the author's identity. Plato's attacks on poetry in the *Republic* (bk. 10) and in the *Ion* show that the relationships between literature, science, and philosophy are immensely more complicated than Foucault's admittedly schematic discussion suggests. Finally, Foucault's view that in St. Jerome's *De viris illustribus* we can find, in naive and primitive form, all the criteria by means of which we attribute and evaluate texts today, is questionable (150–51). Jerome seems to me to rely exclusively on only two of Foucault's four criteria of authorship, that is, only on linguistic and stylistic features of texts.[6] In short, though the figure of the modern literary author may well be, not surprisingly, a modern phenomenon, the figure of the author in general has a much longer and more complex history than Foucault allows.[7]

Nevertheless, simply to dispute such historical claims and to rest content with pointing out that their truth is far from certain is to avoid facing the serious challenge Foucault's discussion presents to current literary practice. This challenge consists, first, in showing that whenever and however the author emerged in modern times, it is not so much a person as a figure or a function or a role—to use Hobbes's term again, though not only in its legal sense, a "person artificial."[8] This absolutely crucial distinction, which, I will argue below, Foucault himself sometimes overlooks, will occupy much of the discussion that follows. Though all texts have writers, not all texts have authors: "A private letter," Foucault writes in a passage to which we shall have to return, "may have a signer—it does not have an author; a contract may well have a guarantor—it does not have an author. An anonymous text posted on a wall probably has a writer—but not an author" (148). To consider that a text has an author, therefore, is not to make a discovery about its history. It is to take a particular attitude toward that text, to be willing to ask certain questions of it, and to expect certain types of answers from it. Texts that have authors are for Foucault texts that since the Enlightenment have been construed in a particular manner.

This particular manner of construing texts is reflected, according to Foucault, in the "aspects of an individual which we designate as making him an author" and which "are only a projection, in more or less psychological terms, of the operations that we force texts to undergo, the connections that we make, the traits that we establish as pertinent, the continuities that we recognize, or the exclusions that we practice" (150). And since the author, "at least in appearance, is outside . . . and precedes" the text (141), we come to think of literary texts as the products of an independent conscious agent, important for what they show us about that agent, and study them "only in terms of their expressive value or formal transformations"(158).

The second constituent of Foucault's challenge, and the real target of his attack, is just this particular manner in which, since the Enlightenment, authored (as opposed to merely written) texts have been construed: the expectations we have had and the questions we have asked of texts to which, as in the case of literature, we assign authors. The historical part of Foucault's argument aims to show that this manner of construing texts is not inevitable and that it can be abandoned. The second part argues that current critical practice must in fact be abandoned.

According to Foucault, our critical practice is centrally characterized by an effort to show that the texts of an author are continuous and not inconsistent, internally or with one another. This practice, he believes, is motivated by the hope that in this manner we may capture what the author really meant and that thus we may recapture the unique mental state, meaning, or message, which we assume all authored texts to express and communicate. But this vain hope directs us to the wrong enterprise. In thinking of the author as the preexisting seat of the single and coherent meaning which every text is assumed to possess, we tend to impose such a meaning on every text and we therefore actually use the author as a repressive "principle of thrift in the proliferation of meaning" (153).

According to this view, the figure of the author is the concrete expression of the idea that the purpose of criticism is to provide definitive interpretations of texts, revelations of their meaning. As such, the essential function of criticism is to exclude possible but "implausible" uses of literature, suggestive but "inaccurate" interpretations. The author is at the center of construing criticism as an activity that aims to describe literature and that is thus located on a different level from the object it describes, much as natural science is thought to be radically distinct from the reality it represents. The author, for Foucault, prevents us from thinking of criticism as an extension and elaboration of literature, as an activity essentially continuous with its object, aiming to produce new meanings and not to describe old ones. It prevents us from thinking of criticism as literature whose subject, unlike the case of other genres, is explicitly literature. Foucault's attack on the author is nothing less than an attack on this descriptive and interpretive conception of criticism as a whole.

This is the heart of Foucault's view. In order to come to terms with it, we must immediately press the distinction between writer and author. A writer is a historical person, firmly situated within a specific context, the efficient cause of a text's production. Writers often misunderstand their own texts, and they commonly utter little more than vague platitudes about them. They are no more knowledgeable about them than most of us are about the sense and significance, and sometimes the very nature, of our most complex and opaque actions. Writers (but not, as we shall see, authors) exist outside their texts and precede them in truth, not in appearance only. And precisely for this reason, writers are not in a position of interpretive authority over their writings, even if these are, by law, their property. We must keep the legal version of ownership, with which we began, clearly apart from what we might well call its "hermeneutical" aspect.

Writers are extrinsically related to their texts. This is reflected in the possibility that Henri Beyle, for example, never wrote the works that are commonly attributed to him. Perhaps throughout his life he was an ardent admirer of the *ancien régime* who, through some curious mixup, came to be thought of as Stendhal. It is, so to speak, not necessary for Henri Beyle to have written Stendhal's works, to have been Stendhal. But notice how we must construe the expression "to have been Stendhal" in this context: it simply specifies the feature of having been the author of Stendhal's works, and nothing more; it is not, despite appearances, a reference to an actual person. This, in turn, reflects the essential connection between Stendhal and the texts of which, necessarily, he is the author. Stendhal is whoever can be understood as the author of these texts; it is these texts that point us to him, and it is in this sense that he precedes them only in appearance. Stendhal, and every author so construed, is to a great extent the product and not the producer of the text, its property and not its owner.

This line of thought might seem to suggest that the author is completely constituted by properties of the text. As J. Hillis Miller has written, "There is not any 'Shakespeare himself.' 'Shakespeare' is an effect of the text . . . The same can be said of the texts published under the name of any author."[9] If this is so, it may now appear that the author cannot readily be distinguished from the very characters of fiction, since fictional characters, too, emerge out of texts in such a manner. Charlus does just what Proust's text says he does; he *is* just what the text says he does—there is no more to him than that. One of the purposes of literary interpretation is, precisely, to establish just what it is that Charlus is said to do in the text and so, in a literal sense, to determine who he is. And just as everything we understand Charlus to have done (itself, of course, a matter of continuing debate) is essential to his being the character he is, so, we might think, is the case with his author, Proust himself. Proust, and the author in general, seems to be whoever can be understood to have produced the text as we have construed it. According to this reasoning, the author is one more fictional character, totally immanent, like all fictional characters, in the text out of which he emerges.

This is a conclusion I would like to resist. Though we have generally identified the author of each text with its writer too quickly and too easily, it is no less quick and easy to infer from this that the author is therefore nothing over and above the text, a pure and total product of the peculiar language of fiction. The relation between authors and texts is much more complex than the relation between texts and fictional characters. The first cannot be reduced to the second; it is not, in particular, an immanent relation. Though an author, too, is a character, it is a character manifested or exemplified in a text and not depicted or described in it. The distinction is significant. "The author," John Sturrock has written, "can never finally appear in the text as subject. The representation of a subject is, inevitably, an object, requiring a further, invisible subject as its representer."[10] The relation between author and text can be called, not simply because a better word is lacking, "transcendental." Unlike fictional characters, authors are not simply parts of texts; unlike actual writers, they are not straightforwardly outside them.

In order to understand this equivocal relationship, we must distinguish the author figure from the notion that Wayne Booth has introduced by means of the term "implied author." The main differences are three. First, as Booth's very term suggests, the implied author is the product of the text and the creature of the writer. In this respect, at least, the implied author is very close to a fictional character. Second, the implied author is immanent in the text in the further sense that even if several texts have been composed by a single writer, their implied authors are held to be distinct. A writer's different works, Booth writes, "will imply different versions, different ideal combinations of norms . . . the writer sets himself out with a different air depending on the needs of particular works."[11] Third, though Booth emphasizes the distinction between implied and actual author, he sometimes suggests that the distinction is a practical matter. In discussing *Emma*, for example, he refers to the " 'author himself'—*not necessarily* the real Jane Austen but an implied author, represented in this book by a reliable narrator" (256, emphasis added). This statement leaves open the possibility that actual and implied author may coincide—if, for example, the views expressed by the narrator and Jane Austen's actual views turn out to be the same. "A great work," according to Booth, "establishes the 'sincerity' of its implied author regardless of how grossly the man who created that author may belie in his other forms of conduct the values embodied in his work. For all we know, the only sincere moments of his life may have been lived as he wrote his novel" (75). This shows that if a writer did actually accept whatever propositions are expressed in a text, then no logical reason compels us to distinguish a real from an implied author.

Booth originally introduced the implied author in order to account for the relationship between the general views, propositions, and norms expressed in a literary text and the views, propositions, and norms accepted by the writer of that text, since these need not be the same. The author figure, with which we are now concerned, is broader in two interconnected respects. First, in contrast to the implied author, this figure is not correlated only with individual works. On the contrary, the author is a figure that emerges from a whole *oeuvre*. It in fact constitutes the very principle that allows us to group certain individual works together and to consider them as parts of such an internally related collection. Since the author, as we have seen, is never depicted, but only exemplified, in a text, this figure is transcendental in relation to its whole *oeuvre* as well as to the individual texts of which that *oeuvre* consists. This, in turn, leads naturally to the second main difference between these notions. The author figure is relevant not only to the attribution of general views to particular texts but also, as we shall see, to every question of interpretation. Both the implied author and the author figure are interpretive constructs. But the latter plays a broader, more directive, and more regulative role in interpretation.

I now want to articulate and defend this transcendental conception of the author and to argue that it is very important for our understanding of literary interpretation. The distinction between writer and author, on which this conception depends, owes a great deal to Foucault's discussion, though, as I shall claim, Foucault, ironically, seems to collapse the two into each other after he has opened a gap between them. And it is, I shall also claim, just this collapse that prompts him to take so negative an attitude toward interpretation that he ends his essay with a call for its abolition. My own view is that just as the author must be consistently distinguished from the writer, so interpretation must be separated from the search for meanings concealed within the text and located in the writer's intention or experience.

We have already seen that to say that a text has an author is to say that it is subject to literary interpretation. If this is true, then it is plausible to claim that though all texts are written, since not all are given literary readings, not all texts are authored. Could we perhaps give a general account of the texts that belong to this class? Interestingly, this is just what is implied in Foucault's statement that private letters, contracts, and anonymously posted texts lack authors (148). This is not, of course, a general theory, but it suggests that some texts are essentially incapable of having authors, and therefore of being interpreted.

Yet private letters do sometimes offer themselves to interpretation. Often, of course, these are the letters of established authors. But the extraordinarily personal and private letters of Madame de Sévigné show that this is not necessarily the case, since it is just these letters that constitute her as an author: apart from them she makes no claim to our attention. And though it does seem unlikely that many anonymously posted texts will have authors, I still cannot think of any general argument that shows that none ever can.

Whether a particular text has an author depends, then, not only on its genre

but also on some additional factors, which seem extremely difficult to characterize both generally and informatively. Fictional texts are likely to generate
author figures, but not all of them need to. Broadly speaking, texts that, either
by imitating or by explicitly flouting literary convention, invite their readers to
consider them as literary works make such claims. But, again, the connection
does not appear necessary unless we trivialize it by simply defining literary
works as authored texts. Much of the literature sold under the heading of "Popular Fiction" in bookstores, for example, may well be authorless.

The reason for this is not that such writings are subliterary or of poor quality
but that there is a distinction to be made between understanding in general and
interpretation in particular. The view I am developing implies that we can read
texts, learn from them, disagree with them, perhaps even like or dislike them,
without necessarily interpreting them. The difference, actually, is one of degree.
Understanding does involve interpretation, but it appeals only to obvious, generally shared, and uncontroversial conventions or background assumptions. All
such conventions, of course, must be learned, and not all of them are shared by
everyone. Each person belongs to a number of different interpretive communities,[12] and each community accepts some of its own basic conventions. Such
conventions are always in the background, and they constitute the various contexts with which, necessarily, we engage in the effort to interpret and to understand. Since all understanding presupposes some such conventions, it is always
to that extent interpretive. But in many such cases only the most basic conventions of a particular context are involved, and interpretation can be so automatic
that it constitutes a limiting, null case. Depending on who one is, this can apply
to a sign warning hikers that a cliff is dangerous, to an article on genetic pro-
gramming, or even to a fictional account of an Elizabethan Englishman ship-
wrecked on the shores of Japan. Cases like these can often require no special
assumptions, no idiosyncratic hypotheses on our part; and this is why we speak
of understanding without interpretation. The difficulties begin when we try to
specify which cases require understanding that is genuinely interpretive.

It is often said (and more often believed) that interpretation is required when
a particular text conceals an implicit and, ideally, profound meaning differing
from the meaning that text appears to have. Literary texts in particular demand
to be interpreted because these surface meanings differ from their real significance, because, as Susan Horton has written, "a text means beyond itself . . . a
railroad is more than a railroad."[13] Such views hold that interpretation is needed
when the meaning of a text is somehow "beyond" or "behind" it. But this
distinction, which is subject to all the difficulties that face any distinction between what merely appears and what really is the case, has been the reason why
so much recent criticism has attacked the very notion of interpretation. If interpretation does in fact presuppose this distinction, of which there is good reason
to be suspicious, then perhaps there also is good reason to be suspicious of
interpretation itself.

I believe, however, that interpretation does not depend on such metaphors of depth and concealment and that it does not involve a radical distinction between the apparent and the real meaning of a text. I would like to articulate an alternative account of interpretation which is connected to the transcendental conception of the author I have been discussing. If such a view is acceptable, interpretation need not be seen as the revelation of a text's hidden meaning. And if this is so, perhaps we can see that much of the suspiciousness with which interpretation has recently been regarded is not really justified.

On the account I propose, interpretation is the activity by means of which we try to construe movements and objects in the world around us as actions and their products. The movement of an arm may, though it need not, be a greeting; the accidental forgetting of a name may, though it need not, be an unconscious aggressive gesture; a long written text may, though it need not, be a novel. But to construe something as an action is not to discover a meaning distinct from its apparent one, a meaning that underlies its seeming sense. Rather, it is to take that movement, or object, or text to be susceptible to a certain sort of question and to a certain sort of account and explanation. It is to want to ask "Why?" of it and to expect an answer that refers to an agent, to intention and to rationality. In most cases, this activity is automatic: we appeal only to general assumptions and classify our object as an action of an obvious, general, and not idiosyncratic sort. When my friend waves her arm at the station as my train is beginning to move, the waving is a farewell. My understanding is not interpretive in the strict sense. But in interpretation strictly conceived we account for the features of an object by appealing to the features of an unusual, original agent whose action we take it to be and who is manifested in it. We take the action, by means of an explicit and often complex process, as an unusual, original event—an event characteristic of its agent, to be sure, but not of many (or any) others. And even in those cases where we say that an action or a text means something other than what it appears to mean, we do not have two meanings, one real and one apparent. All we have, even in the case of psychoanalytic or Marxist interpretation, is a series of progressively more complicated, detailed, and sophisticated hypotheses aimed at construing a text as an action, at trying to find the meaning it does have in its relationship to its agent and to that agent's other actions, or texts. To identify the results of an automatic, early, rough, and general guess at the significance of something with its "surface," as opposed to its "real," meaning is like arguing that when we think that a square tower, seen at a distance, seems round, there is such a thing in the world as a round appearance in addition to the tower's square reality. Both reifications are equally unjustified.

Interpretation can and must be separated from the metaphors of depth and uncovering, which create this metaphysical difficulty. If we think of it instead in terms of breadth and expansion, we may be able to resist attacks that, like Foucault's, are motivated by the rejection of the distinction between appearance and reality. And by connecting this view of interpretation to the figure of the author, we may also be able to resist Foucault's attack against a naively psychological conception of this latter notion.

Of this proposal, to take a text or one of its parts as the product of an action is to undertake to relate it to other actions and their products, to account for its features by appealing to theirs and for their features by appealing to its own. We become interested in whoever it is who can be said to have produced that text and to be manifested in its characteristics. We assume that the text's characteristics, unusual as they may be, are as they are because the agent who emerges through them is as he is. Interpretation so construed is not an effort to take a stretch of language which means one thing and to show that it means something else instead. There are no surface meanings, just as there are no appearances—except in the trivial sense that we can be wrong about what texts mean, just as we can be wrong about what things are.

Interpretation, therefore, must be pictured not as an effort to place a text within a continually deepening context but as an attempt to place it within a perpetually broadening one. Nietzsche's comment is perfectly appropriate: "The most recent history of an action is related to this action; but further back lies a pre-history that covers a wider field: the individual action is at the same time a part of a much more extensive, later fact. The briefer and the more extensive processes are not separated."[14] The more extensive process of which an action can be seen as a part can in turn generate a different interpretation of at least part of the original action. This, again, can indicate that a new, more extensive process, perhaps containing at least part of the original one as its own part, must now be invoked. Such a process of continual adjustment has no end. Interpretation ends when interest wanes, not when certainty is reached. Nietzsche's comment, "one acquires degrees of Being, one loses that which *has* Being," is at least as apt when applied to meaning instead.[15]

One of the most striking examples of this understanding of interpretation is provided by the practice of the narrator of Proust's *Remembrance of Things Past*. As a child and later as an adolescent, the narrator is obsessed with the idea that not only books but all objects, natural as well as artificial, conceal messages of various sorts. He is convinced that happiness no less than literary success depends on the ability to decipher these messages. But the messages always remain elusively inaccessible. His fascination and frustration with the hawthorns along Swann's way is a famous case in point:

But it was in vain that I lingered beside the hawthorns—inhaling, trying to fix in my mind (which did not know what to do with it), losing and recapturing their invisible and unchanging colour, absorbing myself in the rhythm which disposed their flowers here and there with the lightheartedness of youth and at intervals as unexpected as certain intervals in music—they went on offering me the same charm in inexhaustible profusion, but without letting me delve any more deeply, like those melodies which one can play a hundred times in succession without coming any nearer to their secrets . . . in vain did I make a screen with my hands, the better to concentrate upon the flowers, the feeling they aroused in me remained obscure and vague, struggling and failing to free itself, to float across and become one with them. They themselves offered me no enlightenment.[16]

As long as the narrator searches for such hidden messages, he fails to find them and, of course, to write about them. Only when (much later in life) he succeeds in writing about the flowers' very silence and in seeing his experience of that silence as part of the process that finally enables him to become an author, that is, only when he takes this experience of "incomplete" understanding itself and gives it a place with the complete account of his life and his effort to become able to write, does his writing begin.

We should not, I suggest, accept the child narrator's point of view and try to decipher the underlying meaning of the perceptions of the young author-to-be. This is nowhere more obvious than in the well-known episode of the steeples of Martinville and Vieuxvicq.[17] Once again the narrator recalls the intimation of a message:

In noticing and registering the shape of their spires, their shifting lines, the sunny warmth of their surfaces, I felt that I was not penetrating to the core of my impression, that something more lay behind that mobility, that luminosity, something which they seemed at once to contain and to conceal. (196)

But all of a sudden the message seems to become clear; without warning,

their outlines and their sunlit surfaces, as though they had been a sort of rind, peeled away; something of what they had concealed from me became apparent; a thought came into my mind which had not existed for me a moment earlier, forming itself in words in my head . . . I could no longer think of anything else. (197)

Here, if anywhere in this book, we should expect to find at least an intimation of what such messages are like. This is especially true because the narrator tells us that he decided to write that thought down then and there and, once in this whole work, he reproduces his early prose for his readers to read. The passage that follows is therefore the earliest part of the book that he composed (198). But the fragment that is reproduced is stunning in that it nowhere contains the slightest mention of any such meaning. The narrator describes the three steeples as "three flowers painted upon the sky" and likens them to "three maidens in a legend, abandoned in a solitary place over which night has begun to fall" (ibid.). But these similes do not constitute the underlying secret, the covert meaning for which this text keeps urging us to search, always in vain.

What, then, is the thought that comes into the narrator's mind as he is looking at the three steeples? What is the thought that was not in his mind before but is there now? Proust's text dictates one answer to that question, and that answer does not in any way involve a message behind the steeples' changing appearance. The thought that the narrator now has is simply the thought contained in the passage that he goes on to compose and that he reproduces for us here. The thought is just the ability, and the exercise of the ability, to write about the steeples. It is the description of their surfaces and of their appearance, their incorporation, incomplete as they seem both to him and to us, into the narrative. The message hidden in the steeples, a message that is not obvious to the young narrator even as he writes his account but that becomes apparent once the account is embodied in the completed text, is that nothing really hides behind appearance. It is "appearance" *itself* that is difficult to understand: the very distinction between obvious appearance and obscure reality may therefore be untenable. The narrator's thought is simply the articulate account of the steeples which he is able to write down. The steeples are neither flowers nor maidens, nor is that what they have been trying to intimate. In calling such images to mind, they allow themselves to become part of the narrative in which we are engaged. Their significance, their meaning, docs not consist in the message, the search for which constantly leaves Proust's narrator not only frustrated and unhappy but also literally unable to write. Their significance is their very ability to become part of this text, their susceptibility to description, even if this description is exhausted by their surface. For the text is nothing over and above the juxtaposition of many such surfaces, the meaning of which is to be found in their interrelations. The steeples' meaning for the narrator is their ultimate contribution to his completed text, their inclusion in it. The meaning of the episode within the narrative itself is that the meaning of such phenomena is nothing over and above the material they provide this narrator, and narrators in general, for constructing a work that is ultimately at least partly about them. Coherence, unity, and meaning are generated through the proliferation of surfaces, not through the discovery of a single principle that underlies them. The steeples are important, significant, or meaningful because they are being written about, not because writing reveals something about or behind them.

How is this different picture of interpretation connected to the author figure with which my discussion began? The author now emerges as the agent postulated in order to account for construing a text as the product of an action. In Neitzsche's terms, the author is the ultimate "more extensive process," which contains the original text as its part—which is not to say, of course, that this process can ever be finally captured and displayed. In construing a text as an action, we necessarily see it as the partial expression or manifestation of a character: the author is that character. Different parts of a text may generate different or even inconsistent agents or characters. Different texts by the same writer may also do the same. But interpretation proceeds upon the principle that a more consistent narrative of these (perhaps inconsistent) actions can always be devised.[18] Consistency is achieved, not by finding a single meaning underlying all the differences and changes in a work, but by constructing a consistent account of such changes.

We are thus confronted with the following sequence. Writers produce texts. Some texts are subject to interpretation: understanding them involves seeing them as the products of idiosyncratic agents. Interpretation construes texts as works. Works generate the figure of the author, a character manifested, though not represented in them. We cannot know in advance whether a particular text is or is not suited for interpretation. And, as is always the case with character and action, the relationship between author and work involves them in a process of mutual adjustment which cannot, in the nature of the case, ever end.

Both work and author, therefore, are constructs. Both are situated toward the notional end of interpretation and not at its actual beginning. The most we can assume in interpreting a text is that it constitutes a work, not that we know what that work is: to establish that is the very goal of interpretation. And it is a defeasible goal; in actual fact, we often fail to generate a work out of a particular text.

Foucault, we must notice, doubts seriously that the notion of a work can be given a general and useful articulation (143–44). He sees very clearly that the concepts of work and author are deeply interrelated. He sees that once the author was banished, the work emerged instead as a means of justifying the practice of traditional criticism. That is, given the close connection between the two, the unity the author had been intended to represent now came to be attributed to the work itself. But, Foucault argues, such an appeal is bound to fail. Though "intended to replace the privileged position of the author," the work, he claims, cannot possibly fulfill that role (143). Foucault gives two reasons for being suspicious of this notion. First, he wonders whether we are at all entitled to speak of an individual's work if that individual is not an author. Second, he writes that even when an author is in fact involved, we have no general principle for deciding whether something that author wrote does or does not form part of his work: "How can one define a work among the millions of traces left by someone after his death? A theory of the work does not exist." Therefore, "it is not enough to declare that we should do without the writer and study the work itself. The word 'work' and the unity that it designates are probably as problematic as the status of the author's individuality" (144).

It seems to me undeniable that a general "theory of the work" does not exist. Such a theory would have to be a universal account of everything that is (and isn't) relevant to interpretation. It would have to specify in general terms exactly which features are responsible for a text being construed as a work. Is the fact that we lack such a theory unfortunate? More specifically, does this lack prevent us from being able to engage in interpretation and to construe particular texts as works of authors?

It is ironic that Foucault's view exhibits the form of argument a whole generation of scholars put in Socrates' mouth in his fruitless search for the nature of virtue in Plato's early dialogues. The argument is that we can never recognize, say, a particular instance of courage if we don't already know what courage is, if we lack its definition. But since what we are looking for in the first place is the very definition of courage, the search is bound to fail: it cannot even begin. This argument has been named "the Socratic Fallacy." And though it is a fallacy, Socrates never committed it.[19] But the argument that constitutes it is not very different from the claim that we cannot decide whether a particular text is or is not a work unless we already possess a general theory, a definition of what a work is.

Interpretation does not seem to me to require any such theory or definition. It is not, as its proponents often grant its opponents, a two-step process. It does not begin with a clear idea of what the work is that is to be interpreted and conclude when it has established its meaning. On the contrary, a text's status as a work and its meaning are essentially interconnected. To take a text as a work in the first place is already to have construed it, at least partly, as the product of a particular action: this is just to have formulated at least a partial interpretation of it. Just as we lack a general theory explaining which of the indefinitely many movements in which we engage constitute the actions we perform, so we lack a general account articulating which of the many texts with which we are confronted constitute the literary works we produce. And just as we construe as actions those movements of the significance of which we have at least a rudimentary intentional account, so we construe as works those texts of which we have at least minimal interpretations.

This is also why there is no theoretical account that distinguishes authored texts from texts that are merely written. Some texts explicitly place themselves within the literary tradition; one way of doing this, as we have seen, is to display obvious obedience or disobedience to acknowledged convention. Such texts demand to be interpreted, but there is no guarantee that their demand will be met, that their writers will turn out to be authors. Criticism can be defined, if one is interested in such definitions, only in uninformative terms: texts that are subject to criticism are texts that can be interpreted, that is, texts that have authors. The circle is small. It is a fruitless task, which some might call "metaphysical" in a pejorative sense, to try to determine the nature of a discipline independently of its actual practice and in the hope that this nature will itself determine the practice. We can tell that a particular text is a work only when we can actually criticize it: which texts are works will depend on what counts as criticism, and what counts as criticism will depend on which texts have been considered as works. Is "the notation of a meeting, or of an address, or a laundry list" found among Nietzsche's papers, Foucault asks, part of his work? But how could we answer this question just on such information? There is, and there can be, no a priori answer. Such texts may turn out to be parts of Nietzsche's work if, for example, they can be suitably connected to other texts of his, if they can be used to support or contradict them, to illuminate them or make them more obscure than before: if, that is, in conjunction with those other texts they can generate a different "extensive process," a slightly different author. Should notations of meetings, addresses, or laundry lists, Foucault asks, be included in editions of Nietzsche's works? The question is urgent, but it can be given no general answer. The editors of Nietzsche, like all editors, will have to answer each specific question as it arises for each particular text.

Texts, then, are works if they generate an author; the author is therefore the product of interpretation, not an object that exists independently in the world.

But if this is true, it may now appear that the figure of the author is seriously arbitrary. If this figure refers to whatever character is manifested in a text when it is construed as a work, and if each text can be interpreted, as it is often claimed, in different and even incompatible ways, then the author appears to collapse into fragments. Each interpretation generates its own author, and each text can give rise to many different and even inconsistent authors.

No part of the argument of this essay prevents a critic from following out the implications of this objection. I can think of no logical reason that shows that the innovation with which Borges ironically credits Pierre Menard cannot be adopted as a conscious policy. This, of course, is the "technique . . . of the deliberate anachronism and the erroneous attribution. This technique . . . prompts us to go through the *Odyssey* as if it were posterior to the *Aeneid* and the Book *Le Jardin du Centaure* of Madame Henri Bachelier as if it were by Madame Henri Bachelier . . . to attribute the *Imitatio Christi* to Louis Ferdinand Celine or to James Joyce."[20] If the author is our product, why not produce anyone we like out of any particular text?

We could, indeed, try to read the *Imitatio Christi* as if it were by James Joyce and not by Thomas à Kempis. But James Joyce is, among many other things, the Irish Catholic author of *Ulysses*. In reading the *Imitatio Christi* as Joyce's work we would have to read it as the work of the Irish Catholic author of *Ulysses*. We would have no choice about it: this is just what it is to read this as the work of Joyce. In doing so, we would have to bring the *Imitatio* into some sort of relationship with *Ulysses* and therefore change in many ways our interpretation of both works. We would thus begin to fit them into a new, more extensive process. This would now involve not only their reinterpretation but also a new reading of *A Portrait of the Artist as a Young Man*, which would in turn reflect on our interpretation of the first two works. We would also have to read anew Joyce's other works and letters, and probably some of Pound's poems and some of Beckett's early work as well, and much else (that is, everything) besides. Whether, of course, we actually did this or not does not affect the logical point: we would remain committed to this extreme revisionist approach. No argument can show that we would be wrong to try to revise the history of literature. But in order to show that the author is an arbitrary figure, we would actually have to produce such a revision, as well as a number of others, involving different but equally plausible rearrangements of the canon and even new canons. To say that this can always be done is very different from doing it. And only this latter, if it is successful and convincing, can show that the author is arbitrary.[21]

In general, the author is to be construed as a plausible historical variant of the writer, as a character the writer could have been.[22] The author actually means what the writer could have meant, even if the writer never did. In producing texts, writers are immersed in a system with an independent life of its own. Many of its institutional or linguistic features, many of its values or connections to other systems, are beyond the most unconscious grasp of any writer. For all we know, many texts would have been radically different had their writers been aware of some of those features. But the author, who is the joint product of writer and text, of critic and interpretation, who is not a person but a character, is everything the work shows it to be and what it is can in turn determine what the text shows. The author has no depth.

The objection may now be raised that the very principle that the author be a writer's plausible historical variant is itself arbitrary. And so it is, if we take everything that is supported by less than demonstrative argument as arbitrary. But this is not a useful conception of the arbitrary. To show that a well-established practice is arbitrary entails showing that at least one alternative practice, truly distinct from it, actually exists and makes a claim to being followed. Yet the critics who do not commit themselves to the author as construed here, whether they pursue their new technique in jest (as Borges does) or not, seem to me to confine themselves to partial interpretations of parts of texts. Such readings often are interesting and important. But, once again, saying that such anachronistic readings can be produced is very different from actually producing them. Only a consistent effort to read an entire text in a thoroughly anachronistic manner, an effort that would involve nothing less than reading the entire history of the literary tradition in this manner, would show that the figure of the author is arbitrary in an important or harmful sense. The mere possibility of alternatives never shows that actuality is dispensable.

The figure of the author, in contrast to that of the writer, allows us, however, to avoid the view that to understand a text is to re-create or replicate a state of mind which someone else has already undergone, and which, if I understand him correctly, is Foucault's ultimate target. Such states of mind, whatever their relation to the meaning of a text, belong to writers but not to authors. Though instrumentally important, perhaps, they have of themselves no critical significance. Authors, not being persons, do not have psychological states that might determine in advance what a text means. We can thus even accept E.D. Hirsch's view that a "determinate verbal meaning requires a determining will . . . since unless one particular complex of meaning is *willed* (no matter how 'rich' and 'various' it might be) there would be no distinction between what an author does mean by a word sequence and what he could mean by it," and turn it around.[23] It is only the latter and not, as Hirsch's argument is intended to show, the former that is the object of critical attention. We can therefore also refuse to accept the view, expressed by Erwin Panofsky but influential far beyond the disciplinary limits of art history, that "the humanist has . . . mentally to re-enact the actions and to re-create the creations of the past . . . meaning can only be apprehended by re-producing, and thereby, quite literally, 'realizing,' the thoughts that one finds expressed in . . . books and in the artistic conceptions that manifest themselves" in artworks.[24] There is nothing there, if my view is correct, for us to *re*-create.

Being a construct, the author is not a historical person whose states of mind we can ever hope, or even want, to recapture. In interpreting a text, we form a hypothesis about the character manifested in it. We thus come—always tentatively, of course—to understand that character better. But this is not to re-create and make our own someone else's experiences and thoughts. We do not need to become a character (we don't, that is, need to assume it) in order to understand it. After all, having a certain character is sometimes the most crucial obstacle to understanding it.

In a passage of *The Archaeology of Knowledge* Foucault writes:

If a proposition, a group of signs, can be called "statement" [*sic*], it is not . . . because, one day someone happened to speak them or to put them in some concrete form of writing: it is because the position of the subject can be assigned. To describe a formulation *qua* statement does not consist in analyzing the relations between the author [i.e., in our terms, the writer] and what he says (or wanted to say, or said without wanting to) but in determining what position can and must be occupied by any individual if he is to be the subject of it.[25]

In interpreting a text, in construing it as an action, we want to know what *any* individual who can be its subject must be like. We want to know, that is, what sort of person, what character, is manifested in it. And to know this is simply to know what other actions that character can engage in, what relations it bears to other texts and to the characters manifested in them. To interpret a text, on this model, is not to go underneath it, into a meaning covert within it, but to connect it to other texts and to their authors, to see what texts have made is possible and what texts it, in turn, has made possible itself. This is the literal analogue of the metaphors of breadth and spreading to which I appealed earlier. Interpretation is an activity that relates texts, or their parts, to one another. But to do this, we must construe those texts as works, and to construe them as works we must see them as actions exemplifying a certain character. Again, to understand a character is not to become identical with it, though nothing prevents us as readers from trying, in addition, to make that character at least part of our own. Nevertheless, to understand the character manifested in *Remembrance of Things Past*, to the extent that this is something (as it is not) that can be fully accomplished, is not to become identified with Marcel Proust, even for a moment. Rather, it is to formulate a series of hypotheses about the actions which we must attribute to the author Proust in order to account for the features of this work. It is, to return to the origin of our circle, to offer an interpretation of the text.

If this is so, then the figure of the author does not constitute the repressive principle with which both Barthes and Foucault identify it. The unity the author represents, in the view I have offered, is not a unity that must be assumed to be there at first but a unity that may be possibly captured at last. The charge of repressiveness is much more appropriate against the use of the historical writer as an independent principle by means of which any interpretation of a text is to be judged. Yet Foucault, though he himself makes this distinction, does not attack the writer. On the contrary, he writes that it is the *author* who provides the means

by which one impedes the free circulation, the free manipulation, the free composition, decomposition and recomposition of fiction. In fact, if we are accustomed to presenting the author as a genius, as a perpetual surging of invention, it is because, in reality, we make him function in exactly the opposite function. One can say that the author is an ideological product, since we represent him as the opposite of his historically real function. ("What Is an Author?," 159)

It could be that Foucault believes that we wrongly confuse writer with author, and that we therefore fail to realize the greater freedom the author figure allows us. Yet he does not attack this identification; instead, he attacks the figure of the author itself. He considers as "pure romanticism" the hope that doing away with the author, as he urges us to do, will enable us to treat fiction without any constraints whatever (160). He cannot, of course, predict what those constraints will be, but he thinks that they will have to be preferable to those provided by the author, whom he sees as the sign under which a psychological construal of reading and interpretation has been victorious.[26]

Foucault's essay ends with an echo of Beckett: "What difference does it make who is speaking?" I have been arguing that the question asked about the author is not, Who *is* speaking?, but, Who *can be* speaking? Even the free circulation, manipulation, composition, decomposition, and recomposition of fiction is committed to asking this second question. Even partial, anachronistic, or consciously perverse readings of texts generate an author for them. Such readings generate a character to whom these texts, construed (partially, anachronistically, or perversely) as works, can be assigned. A text, though it usually has one writer, need never have (that is, generate) a single author. But not every author is as acceptable as any other, and the mere possibility of having many authors does not show that the author is dispensable.

My own view is that Foucault himself has fallen prey to the illegitimate identification of author with writer against which he so elegantly warns. We have seen that he believes that the author emerged only during the Enlightenment, and that there are reasons to doubt this claim. I have suggested that the history of the author is longer and more complex than Foucault believes. What may have occurred during the Enlightenment is the identification of the role of the author, which has appeared through history in many guises, with the actual historical agent who is causally and legally responsible for the text. But this has been only a moment—though important and long—in this history. Foucault identifies this moment with the history of which it is only a part.

What leads us to believe that a complex conscious or unconscious mental state, an intention or experience, lies at the origin of every text, constituting the text's meaning, and that to understand a text is to recapture that mental state, is the view that to understand a text is to understand its writer. But the ownership with which my discussion began changes radically as we move from writer to author. Foucault's joint attack on these two notions depends, I think, on over-looking that difference. Writers own their texts as one owns one's property. Though legally their own (*eigen*), texts can be taken away from their writers and still leave them who they are. Authors, by contrast, own their works as one owns one's actions. Their works are authentically their own (*eigentlich*). They cannot be taken away (that is, reinterpreted) without changing their authors, without making the characters manifested in them different or even unrecogniz-able. Authors cannot be taken apart from their works.

Precisely because of this, because both author and work emerge through the interpretation of a text, neither stands at the text's origin, imparting a preexisting significance to it. The author is therefore not an independent constraint, forbid-ding in an a priori manner desired but unlawful interpretations or extensions. Construing the author as I have done here puts the very distinction between interpretation and extension, understanding and use, into question. In "Prison Talk," Foucault accepts this distinction when he claims that he wants to "utilize" the writers he likes. "The only valid tribute to thought such as Nietzsche's," he writes, "is precisely to use it, to deform it, to make it groan and protest."[27] But can we use Nietzsche's thought without understanding it? Can one remain en-gaged with an author, make that author's thought groan and protest without, at the very same time, being in the process of interpreting it? Isn't this just what I have been doing with Foucault himself, trying to take some of his own views but using them against him, connecting them with other views, his own, and those of Barthes and Booth, and mine? Haven't I been interpreting and at the same time using him? There is, in my opinion, no clear line between these two. But to insist that criticism must engage only in interpretation and to claim that it must abandon interpretation altogether in favor of extension is to believe that such a line can be drawn. And this belief, in turn, presupposes that the author is identical with the writer and therefore also with the writer's own self-understanding. This identification, which ultimately also identifies the foes and the defenders of pure interpretation, has been the subject of my attack.

In writing to Malcolm Cowley, Faulkner once remarked:

It is my ambition to be as an individual abolished and voided from history, leaving it markless, no refuse except the printed books . . . It is my aim and every effort bent, that the sum and history of my life, which in the same sentence is my obit and epitaph too, shall be then both: He wrote the books and he died.[28]

There is irony in the fact that this passage was quoted in a review of one of Faulkner's numerous biographies. But there may be even more irony in the fact that whatever we know about Faulkner's books is also something we know about their author. And though we may not ever know what Faulkner, the writer, really was, we may come close to knowing who he could have been. Having no private property, authors also have no privacy to protect.[29]

NOTES

1. Brian Silverman and David Torode, *The Material Word* (London: Routledge & Kegan Paul, 1980), 227–44, argue that a similar view can be found in John Locke's "Of Property."

2. Roland Barthes, "The Death of the Author," in *Image, Music, Text*, trans. Stephen Heath (New York: Hill & Wang, 1977), 142–43 [p. 4].

3. Michel Foucault, "What is an Author?" in Josué V. Harari, ed., *Textual Strategies* (Ithaca: Cornell University Press, 1979), 149. Parenthetical page references to Foucault in the main text will all be to this essay [p. 14].

4. William Cain, "Authors and Authority in Interpretation," *Georgia Review* 34 (1980): 819.

5. This view can also be found in Foucault's "Discourse on Language," in *The Archaeology of Knowledge*, trans. A.M. Sheridan (New York: Harper & Row, 1972), 222–23.

6. Foucault also makes this point in "The Discourse on Language," 223. St. Jerome discusses authorship in these sections, among others: 1.7. 9–11, v. 12. 1–3, xxv. 26. 15–17, xxxiv. 86. 24–25, xlii. 90. 13–17, lxvi. 98. 24–27. The first of these passages actually suggests that attributions of authorship were already common by Jerome's time: "Scripsit Simon Petrus duas epistulas, quae catholicae nominantur; quandum secunda *plerisque* eius negatur propter stili cum priore dissonantiam" (emphasis added).

7. Part of this history, in connection with modern literature, is given by Patrick Crutwell in "Makers and Persons," *Hudson Review* 12 (1959–60): 486–507.

8. An important though sketchy discussion of social roles can be found in Alasdair MacIntyre's *After Virtue* (South Bend, Ind.: University of Notre Dame Press, 1981). MacIntyre believes that every age conceives of itself in terms of certain privileged social roles, which he calls "characters."

9. J. Hillis Miller, "Ariadne's Broken Woof," *Georgia Review* 31 (1977): 59.

10. John Sturrock, *Paper Tigers: The Ideal Fictions of Jorge Luis Borges* (Oxford: Oxford University Press, 1977), 183.

11. Wayne Booth, *The Rhetoric of Fiction* (Chicago: University of Chicago Press, 1961), 71.

12. Though this expression is intended to allude to the views Stanley Fish expresses in *Is There a Text in This Class?* (Cambridge: Harvard University Press, 1980), I also want to emphasize the multiplicity of the communities to which each person belongs. It is precisely this fact that makes it possible to criticize the conventions accepted by each community and to provide rational alternatives to them.

13. Susan Horton, *Interpreting Interpreting: Interpreting Dickens's "Dombey"* (Baltimore: Johns Hopkins University Press, 1979), 7.

14. Friedrich Nietzsche, *The Will to Power*, trans. Walter Kaufmann and R.J. Hollingdale (New York: Random House, 1968), sec. 672.

15. *Will to Power*, sec. 485.

16. Marcel Proust, *Remembrance of Things Past*, trans. C.K. Scott Moncrieff and Terence Kilmartin (New York: Random House, 1982), 1:138–39.

17. Representative of the extensive literature on this passage is George Poulet, "L'espace proustien," *Entretiens sur Marcel Proust*, ed. George Cattaui and Philip Kolb (Paris: Mouton, 1966), 75–94.

18. I discuss the problem of interpretation in general, and apply this discussion to one particular figure, in *Nietzsche: Life as Literature* (Cambridge: Harvard University Press, 1985).

19. This term was first used by Peter Geach in "Plato's *Euthyphro*: An Analysis and Commentary," *Monist* 50 (1966): 369–82. I have disputed Geach's claim in "Confusing Universals and Particulars in Plato's Early Dialogues," *Review of Metaphysics* 29 (1975): 287–306, and discuss the issue more fully in "Socratic Intellectualism," forthcoming in *Proceedings of the Boston Area Colloqium for Ancient Philosophy* 2 (1986).

20. Jorge Luis Borges, "Pierre Menard, Author of the *Quixote*," in *Labyrinths*, trans. and ed. Donald A. Yates and James E. Irby (New York: New Directions, 1962), 36–44.

21. This argument is made in detail in *Nietzsche: Life as Literature*, 62–73.

22. I have discussed this view in detail in "The Postulated Author: Critical Monism as a Regulative Ideal," *Critical Inquiry* 8 (1981): 131–49.

23. E.D. Hirsch, *Validity in Interpretation* (New Haven: Yale University Press, 1967), 46–47.

24. Erwin Panofsky, "Art History as a Humanistic Discipline," in *Meaning in the Visual Arts* (New York: Doubleday, 1955), 14. Despite his insistence on a "transcendental" author, George Poulet still believes that successful reading involves such a meeting of two minds: "What is this mind who all alone by himself occupies my consciousness?" "The Phenomenology of Reading," *New Literary History* 1 (1969): 57. It is for this reason that I do not try to align my position with his.

25. Foucault, *Archaeology of Knowledge*, 95–96.

26. Barthes also rejects the author as a constraint on interpretation and instead appeals to a "reader . . . without history, biography, psychology . . . simply that *someone* who holds together in a single field all the traces by which a written work is constituted" ("Death of the Author," 148). But can there be such a "someone"? And what single field can such a someone occupy? [p. 7].

27. Foucault, "Prison Talk," in *Power/Knowledge*, ed. Colin Gordon (New York: Pantheon Books, 1980), 93–94.

28. Quoted in the *New York Times Book Review*, 22 Feb. 1981, 9.

29. I am grateful to W.J.T. Mitchell for his comments on an earlier version of this essay.

CHAPTER 8

Authorship and Authority

Nickolas Pappas

According to an old story whose point I have forgotten, the following practice was once common among editors of Soviet periodicals: if a book appeared that criticized communism or the Soviet government, the editors would write a lengthy and ideologically sound excoriation of it—one, however, in which they quoted the book's central argumentative points and summarized its position. To this they added clumsy refutations, with the actual aim of getting the book's point across to their readers. Anyone could see from such a review that the refutations were bad, and that the book's point was well taken. That is, such a reader saw through the refutation.

Of course, something like this occurs in every country. Soviet readers are not the only ones to consider the source of what they read. An American movie critic's reviews, for instance, commonly are translated by each reader into a more reliable judgment, depending on that reader's history of agreements and disagreements with that critic. If a certain critic says that a movie is funny, I know that it's silly; if well-paced, that it's contrived; if warm, that it's senti-mental. Nothing could be less remarkable than this adjustment for someone else's judgment.

What is the difference between these two cases? Everything: the Soviet re-viewers were hoping for their readers to draw the further conclusion, while the American reviewers certainly were not. This difference is seen from the point

Nickolas Pappas, "Authorship and Authority," *The Journal of Aesthetics and Art Criticism* 47:4 (Fall 1989), pp. 325–32. Reprinted by permission of *The Journal of Aesthetics and Art Criticism*, Temple University.

of view of the author. But from the reader's point of view there is not much difference. In practice the Soviet example could not be distinguished from an identical case in which the editor was just sincerely clumsy (which is the point of writing like that).

What the reader does in these cases therefore renders the author's intention irrelevant. The author's desires drop out of the picture—not because they cannot be known, but because the author's desires or intentions do not determine the outcome of this sort of reading. These readers have gone over the authors' heads (or behind their backs); the most interesting question has ceased to be the authors' intentions.

Such a reading procedure shows us, by contrast, the normal function of the author as our goal in reading: the American example seems unfair or unsatisfying, because the right way to read is the way which leads us—by plan or not—to the author. We may call this the pull of the author's person. It's not so much that we believe the author knows best what the work is about, as that what matters most about the work is what the author thinks it means. What we want most to know is what the author said.

I call this typical attitude an attitude toward authority, because it draws us to behave (in this case, to read) in one way rather than another, out of an interest in pleasing the authority. I am interested less in what the author is like as an entity, than in how we behave toward that entity. For this reason I find the most useful analysis of authorship in an essay of Michel Foucault's, "What Is an Author?"[1] Foucault's argument builds toward a question of the "ideological" status of the author: "The author is the principle of thrift in the proliferation of meaning."[2] The author "is a certain functional principle by which, in our culture, one limits, excludes, and chooses; in short, by which one impedes the free circulation, the free manipulation, the free composition, decomposition, and recomposition of fiction."[3]

Foucault is describing a certain structure of power. It is nevertheless easy to misconstrue his essay, for two reasons. First, the literary-theoretic question of whether the author's intentions can be known is often superimposed on a question like Foucault's, which is actually quite distinct from it. Secondly, Foucault seems to call for (or at least desire), but never describes, alternatives to the obedient sort of reading he wants to undermine. Thus his objections look more purely hypothetical than I think they need to be.

Although this is not an essay about Foucault, my aim is to explicate a sense of the author's authority by overcoming these two obstacles to understanding Foucault. First, I will describe a *normative* question of possible relationships to the author which is distinct from the *epistemological* question that is typically asked—namely, the question of whether (and how) the author's mind may be known. Secondly, I want to go beyond what Foucault says by offering illustrations of unauthoritative readings—specifically, of readings whose success depends on their avoidance of the author-figure. By seeing what some works by Nietzsche and Proust do to their authors, we may be able to identify more clearly what hold authors have had on us, and why we might want to subvert that hold. The exceptional cases can cast light on our ordinary behavior.

I

Perhaps because deconstruction, and Foucault in particular, are centrally concerned with the classic opposition between appearance and reality, Alexander Nehamas takes that opposition to be the principal issue in this essay too. In "What an Author Is," Nehamas argues against Foucault's picture of the author by denying that our attachment to the author-figure is as insidious as Foucault thinks, or indeed anything ideological at all.[4] But he argues in ontological terms—concentrating on what the author is, instead of what our attachment to the author is like—and as a result fails to avoid Foucault's critique of authorship.

Nehamas distinguishes between the author and the writer, the latter being the actual historical human who wrote the words we read. The former, though, should not be thought of as a person, and is therefore not a locus of authority. On the contrary, for Nehamas the author is merely a postulated entity implied by every act of interpretation.[5] "To say that a text is authored, therefore, is just to say that it can be given a literary interpretation."[6] This does not mean that the interpretation is conceived of as digging beneath the surface of the work, to find the buried form of the author; Nehamas considers metaphors of depth and concealment largely disposable features of interpretation. What really matters is not a real, as opposed to an apparent, reading, so much as a complete one, a reading which coherently describes all the author's words taken together. Interpretations do not plumb the author's depths, but spread out over the surface of all the author's work. "In interpretation strictly conceived we account for an object's features by appealing to the features of an unusual, original agent who is manifested in it. We construe it as an event, characteristic of such an agent but not of many, or any, others."[7] Then the author is present in every detail of the work, but not visible until those details have all been looked at together.

Nehamas thinks that Foucault's criticisms will not apply once the author is seen for the theoretical (and almost empty) posit it is. "To take a text as an action is to undertake to relate it to other actions, to account for its features by appealing to theirs, and for their features in turn by appealing to its own."[8] Somewhat like an earthquake's epicenter, which is not hidden or disguised, nor is an occult explanatory object, but unifies a set of scattered tremors under a single description (once the tremors have been identified and measured and looked at together on a map)—in this way too, Nehamas's author is made to seem just a sensible part of a literary description: "This author is the agent postulated to account for construing a text as an action."[9] It is therefore not a repressive principle.[10] The fact that the text in question has an author makes no difference to the content of the interpretation we develop. "No reading can fail to generate an author," because to attribute a meaning to the author is to add nothing to that meaning: it is merely to append the tag, "Joyce says," to whatever interpretation we come up with.[11] What can be repressive about such a formal gesture?

If Foucault were making an epistemological point, in the tradition of denials that we can know an author, Nehamas's distinction between author and writer would have more purchase. But Foucault has already insisted that an author is not simply the historical writer, but in some larger and more nebulous sense a social construct. It is of this social construct that he asks, What sort of subject is it?—meaning, What sorts of power does it wield? To answer, as Nehamas does, that the author is not a subject just by virtue of not being the human writer is to beg the question of how a non-human social posit can wield power.

More generally, the issue of authority has not been addressed with Nehamas's transformation of the author. His reassuring picture of a broad description of the literary phenomena organized around a single explanatory entity leads, as surely as any old picture of the author, to a repression of interpretations. If the author is, as Foucault says, "a certain functional principle by which, in our culture, one limits, excludes, and chooses," then Nehamas has described, not denied, the activity of limitation and exclusion.[12] If I try to coordinate my reading of *Ulysses* with my readings of Joyce's other works, and with the historical context in which it arose, then I am compelled to rule out a number of readings. But this coordination of readings of texts is, Nehamas says, the point of postulating an author. Therefore, even the postulated author is a repressive principle—which is to say, an authority.

Foucault has not, after all, distinguished historically between author and writer merely in order to call the former unknowable; rather, he wants to expose the various powers that the author's person wields. The artificiality of the author reveals it to be a social construct. But what matters more is that we have been, all along, deferring to this construct as to a human authority. Nehamas's model of interpretation thus at best fits into Foucault's analysis as one more example of how that deference works.

The question is what to do next, given this state of things. Consistent with his general attitude toward power, Foucault identifies the nature of the authority implicit in interpretation, but is reluctant either to describe or prescribe any act which may subvert it. He calls for a new attitude toward reading only in the sense that he thinks such an attitude will emerge after the next social upheaval. A new attitude toward texts will not arise just because he asked for it, nor just because some people choose consciously to read in a new way; at most he predicts that, "as our society changes . . . the author function will disappear, and in such a manner that fiction and its polysemous texts will once again function according to another mode."[13]

Nevertheless, I think we may use Foucault to define a normative question about authorship, because he has focused on our practices, as opposed to the transcendental question of some truth of the matter about authors. He says that the author figure has—in some sense arbitrarily—served to restrict the activity of reading. If reading is not, then, bound essentially to an author's mind, we may ask in certain instances, not whether or not we can know that mind, but whether or not we should care about it.

The normative question stands independent of the epistemological one.[14] On the one hand, the matter has not been settled if it turns out that intentions cannot be known. Even if it is impossible to know an author's intentions, it is not hugely and obviously impossible. It is more like my running a mile in five minutes than running it [in] one: both are impossible, but I can try to do the former. I rest beforehand, eat at exactly the right time, run indoors on a good track with enormous concentration, and so on. But as for running the mile in one minute, what would count as my trying? Resting even longer? Concentrating harder? All my added efforts would legitimately be seen as misguided, even comic. The author's intention does not strike me as so clearly unreachable that the normative issue I have raised makes no sense, or is funny, like running a mile in a minute.

Nor is the discussion over if, with Nehamas, we say that every interpretation automatically does lead to the figure of an author. This position might seem to rule out the normative question I raise, since every reading already looks for an author, and the desire to stop looking for that figure is doomed to go unfulfilled. We must recognize, however, the extent to which Nehamas may be right. At most it may be true that everything we now call an interpretation presupposes some real or fictitious person as the source of the interpreted work. But that is just to name the problem, not to answer it: the problem is that this is how we have been reading. Indeed, Foucault anticipates this response when he acknowledges attempts to replace talk of the author with talk of "the work."[15] He says, "A certain number of notions that are intended to replace the privileged position of the author actually seem to preserve that privilege and suppress the real meaning of his disappearance."[16] So far a demythologized analysis of the author has not freed us from our old deference to authority.

Perhaps what accounts for a reaction like Nehamas's is our usual picture of a reading. Reading is a more general matter than interpreting. To interpret is always to read; but I may, in the most ordinary sense of the word, read without interpreting. I do not interpret my shopping list when I read it (though I may interpret yours, for instance by inferring that you eat no meat). Not every story or poem that is read is also interpreted, and certainly few more trivial texts are ever subjected to interpretation: billboards, road signs and personal checks pass before my eyes in uninterpreted innocence, although I do read them.

The difference between reading and interpretation need not imply the greater depth of the latter. But in most discussions an interpretation is understood as an act which, rightly or wrongly, aims at a further statement that the text is making. This further statement may then also be the author's, in which case we say that all interpretations look for authorial intentions.

But if a reading need not be an interpretation, perhaps there exist responses to written works—recognizably readings—which do not aim at revealing some other statements in those works. These are the responses I am looking for. A subversive reading will release the reader from the power of the author as seen symbolically in such legal structures as copyright laws, but experienced more intimately as limitations upon the creation of meanings.

II

. So far, then, everyone has talked about writing, but no one has done anything about it. If the normative issue of authorship is to make sense, I need to describe readings which leave the author aside.

This must mean more, of course, than the claim that some uses of a text ignore the author—for that is trivially true, and says nothing about authorship. No one has ever denied that things may be done to written works which bypass their authors' plans for them: whenever a book is used for a doorstop it is presumably being treated in a way that ignores its author's intent. And if I assign sentences out of *Gulliver's Travels* in a logic course, to be paraphrased into logical terms, surely I am doing something to the work—something which even requires one sort of careful reading—which cannot be called a search for Swift's intentions, or mind, or thoughts. But these cases threaten no one. Surely the decomposition and recomposition of fictions ought to amount to more than that; for what I have described is not even a reading (certainly not an interpretation). So what if *that* bypasses the author? Not reading the book at all does too, and proves nothing.

To keep what I am saying from sounding trivial, then, I need to find a recognizably real reading in the course of which the author's person is set aside. Perhaps one way to make a reading look real is to show that it is called for in, or suggested by, the author's words themselves. Very simply, the author's own words lead us to ignore the author.

Now that point, put so simply, may sound mysterious. If left in such abstract terms it does promise to turn into a silly sort of paradox: the author gives me the command, "Don't follow my commands," in which case my obedience is disobedience and vice versa.

But when the point is given content that air of paradoxicality disappears. A king instructs his guards to ask everyone for a password, since people are disguising themselves as him; but then the king comes home and has forgotten the password. That's not a paradox at all, even if it is ungracefully ironic. A president appoints an independent prosecutor to investigate scandals in his administration, but the prosecutor's work leads him to suspect the president. In my logic class I teach my students how to test an argument's validity, and one of them finds a contradiction in something I have said. None of these examples looks even remotely paradoxical.

What the examples do show is authority unseated by some means which the authority made possible in the first place. If the authority behind a text is its author, then unseating the authority will mean carrying on some activity the author has instigated, to a point at which it no longer is relevant to ask about the author's own desires.

By an activity the author has instigated I mean something like an implicit instruction for reading the text. In *Ulysses*, Leopold Bloom's meditation on a pun of Molly's may be taken this way. "She used to say Ben Dollard had a base barreltone voice."[17] Bloom takes the joke apart to show how many meanings are packed into it: legs like barrels, a voice like someone singing into a barrel, a drinker of Bass ("Barrel of Bass, See? it all works out," Bloom thinks). As Harry Blamires has pointed out, "Bloom shows us ... how wide awake we need to be when reading *Ulysses*."[18] The novel's readers are being told to pay attention to all its other plays on words. Now naturally such an instruction cannot guarantee that all plays on words have been likewise authored; the point is that that no longer matters. I am shown how to take apart "base barreltone" and I move on to another neologism. I do not say either that this new pun was or wasn't meant; I say instead that now that I've learned what to do, I don't need Joyce any more.

Some process like this one, of going on from the work in some way appropriate to it, but in some other way contrary to its author's person, becomes especially interesting in the following examples. I offer these not as thumbnail interpretations, but as directions I think readings of the books may take. I may be wrong about both of these works but still right about some such common feature occurring, either here or in other books.

Proust's *Remembrance of Things Past* is significantly a long book. Its length is important not mainly as a means to fitting all of its narrator Marcel's life into it, but because, if I may be so plain, it takes a long time to read. Its length enables the novel to mimic the lost time it repeatedly describes: thus the earliest pages of *Swann's Way* seem, by the end of the whole, as deeply buried in the reader's past as the narrator's childhood is in his own. Proust's novel emphasizes the associative powers of memory: the madeleine is only the most famous example. As I understand *Remembrance*, the time required for reading the novel makes for associations between the novel's episodes and the reader's own life. Thus, when Marcel evokes his childhood, the reader will presumably not only think about the episode in question but actively remember it—that is to say, call it up with all its old associations. Because the novel's symbols, as Beckett has pointed out, are not allegorical—they conjure up not some external, previously available meaning, but derive all their meaning from occurrences in the narrative—they are left especially open to these new associations.[19] Marcel's childhood in Combray is no more intrinsically tied to the taste of madeleine than to the hot sun on the roof of my apartment building in Cambridge, where I read *Swann's Way*. That hot sun surfaced in my memory when I reached *Timed Regained* almost a year later, and read Marcel's evocation of his childhood: the word "madeleine" at the novel's end, itself like a ghostly madeleine, arouses the reader's associations with the circumstances under which the novel was read.

I take it that this is how Proust ought to be read. Otherwise involuntary memory cannot be explained. But this means that Proust's novel cannot be understood (that is, read) unless its symbols are given meanings independently of Proust's, or his text's, imprimatur. This is a decomposition and recomposition of the fiction, in Foucault's words, and moreover an activity legitimately called reading.

A similar escape from the author may occur when reading Nietzsche's *On the Genealogy of Morals*. I have always been struck by the end of the book's first essay, at which Nietzsche poses a question, in the form of an essay competition, about the histories of our ethical terms: "What light does linguistics, and especially the study of etymology, throw on the history of the evolution of moral concepts?"[20] The problem is just that Essay 1 has been, to all appearances, an answer to exactly this question. Why does Nietzsche ask the very question he's just answered, aside from wanting to remind us that he deserves a prize for all the writings he has given us? Maybe the question admits of several answers, all compatible with the etymological data but incompatible with each other. I take Nietzsche's question to suggest (and its new answer by the reader to prove) that the genealogy of morals could have been otherwise, i.e., that our ethical terms may be invested with quite different meanings from both the ones they have now, and the ones they aboriginally had. The genealogy of morals has not been completed; it is not even authoritative, because it cannot be completed.[21]

The point is not that ethical terms have different meanings for different readers, but rather that by themselves they reveal *no* deep meanings, no true story of our moral practices. We are not liberated because we have seen vestiges of master morality in our words of praise and censure. Instead, the arbitrariness of our bondage to morality is made clear (though not thereby escaped) by the recognition that our moral practices and words by themselves can be given other and incompatible interpretations—that is, can be shown to serve entirely other purposes. The reusability of moral practices is part of what commonly is called Nietzsche's perspectivism. Thus his perspectivism cannot be understood until the question that concludes Essay 1 is read neither rhetorically, nor as a hint to Nietzsche's view, but as a starting point from which one may come to find Nietzsche's own genealogies of morals inadequate.

Why are these readings not simply more elaborate searches for the author? They are not *only* that, because whatever the reader's motivation at first, eventually the author is left behind. Not just because the results of the reading seem to be too far-fetched to be attributed to the author in question (too trifling a worry to raise), but because their attribution to the author would be a sign of the reader's failure. In these cases, to persist in unearthing the author's intention is not to do something impossible but rather something wrong. Looking for an intention is wrong because it is an undue deference to authority.

(And concerning the common objection that authors ought to be respected, and therefore interpreted in accordance with their intentions, I only want to say that respect takes many forms. Although respect by itself sounds unproblematically attractive, deference to authority [one form respect may take] does not.)

In turning now from Nietzsche and Proust to Plato, I may be accused of illegitimately extending this discussion. Is the author's role the same for a literary author as for a clearly philosophical one?[22] Certainly there is a presumption that one reads philosophers to learn immediately what they say, while the author of a novel stands in a more nebulous relationship to its reader. (I leave aside questions of the ambiguous status of Plato's writings in particular.) Still, similar issues of authority do arise in both cases. For novelists to get distinctly different treatment from philosophers, there would have to be no point or precedent to asking what the former mean in their novels. It would have to sound like nonsense to ask what Proust is saying; but the very existence of the question of intentionality shows that it does not.

Plato obviously does stand apart, though, from Proust and Nietzsche. I cannot claim him to have been motivated, as they were, by modernist attitudes about authorship. Nevertheless one effect of his writings is the same: most of Plato's shorter, Socratic dialogues, which end indecisively, seem to call for a further activity by the reader which is not conventional interpretation, and which does not aim at understanding Plato's intent.[23] Typically, dialogues like *Charmides, Laches, Lysis, Euthyphro* and *Protagoras* all show Socrates and his interlocutors looking for a definition of a virtue or other ethical concept. They find none— indeed, Socrates normally emphasizes at the end that they have been unsuccessful—but do specify a number of questions relevant to that definition, and agree on the rules of definition (for instance, on the difference between a definition and an example). If, as is often said, the purpose of such a dialogue is to arouse the reader to inquiry as Socrates aroused his interlocutors, then the goal of the reader's activity may be one of several possible definitions of, say, courage, none of which is officially endorsed by the dialogue. Moreover, one test of fruitful reading activity will be that it does not appeal to Plato as guarantor of the definition; for to justify a conclusion with an appeal to authority is patently, from Socrates' point of view, not to justify it at all.

As I said, Plato's is not a modernist concern with the inflated Romantic influence of the author. Still, he does see a danger in the way his contemporaries are drawn into the person of the poet: one of Plato's strongest and most repeated charges against poets is that, as long as our concern is with their person (i.e., with what an individual is saying to us), we will be seduced away from abstract inquiry.[24] Contra Foucault, some notion of an author was already present in antiquity, as the individual source and explanation of the literary text.[25] And in any case, Plato's apparent alternative to the customs of reading, in which the reader begins with the written word and uses it in order to get to a good definition, strikes me as exactly the free composition, decomposition and recomposition that Foucault wants. Plato's speech is, as Foucault says *authored* speech is not, "something that is immediately consumable."[26]

III

My point in describing such reading methods has been to shift attention from the author's intention to the reader's motivation for trying to know it. Somehow that motivation has not often been addressed, as if the desire to know something never needed to be explained. In tying the attitude toward an author to the attitude toward an authority, I was able to suggest what the motivation might be. And therefore, perhaps, what motivation a reader might have for turning away from the author. The image of an authority matters all the more now that the author is conceived of as distinct from the writer; for that distinction implies clearly that the socially produced subject that is the author is a construct made to bend the reader in one direction rather than another—namely, in the direction of less freedom in reading.

An analogy may show more specifically why we should want to subvert the author's hold upon us: The authority customarily projected upon the text's source may be said to work like the transference associated with psychoanalysis.[27] Like transference, the appeal of the author might serve a purpose at one point in the investigation—call this a motivational or inspirational purpose. But analysis fails if transference is allowed to flower into too strong a new relationship, which is to say a relationship the patient does not perceive as transference.

The problem with extreme positive transference is not that I have made some factual mistake (just as the problem with aiming at the author is not, as a point of simple fact, that the author cannot be known). The analyst may really know the truth about me. But my reliance on the analyst to transmit that truth to me signals an unsatisfactory analysis, as Freud comments in "An Outline of Psycho-Analysis." In the course of describing the benefits of transference, he insists on cautioning against it too. "However much the analyst may be tempted to become a teacher, model and ideal for other people and to create men in his own image" (that is, to act like an Author), such inclinations need to be suppressed.[28] If the analyst enters into that kind of relationship, Freud says, "he will only be repeating a mistake of the parents who crushed their child's independence by their influence, and he will only be replacing the patient's earlier dependence by a new one."[29] In analysis this threat of an authoritative relationship is to be fended off by the analyst. "It is the analyst's task constantly to tear the patient out of his menacing illusion and to show him again and again that what he takes to be new real life is a reflection of the past."[30] This does not make the avoidance of transference any less the patient's action; it only means that as things stand some patients need to be helped along. In my examples of new readings, by analogy, I have suggested a consciousness in some texts of a procedure they are vulnerable to, which will lead the reader to reject, the person of the author. Works like *Remembrance of Things Past* and *On the Genealogy of Morals* point the way to a complete understanding of themselves which turns out to frustrate our usual attempts to hang a meaning on the author's name. Their goal is the same as the analyst's goal. Certain things (about the past, for example, or our relationships to our past) cannot be known unless the one who seems to be telling us about them is left behind. To see that is to see why the author's personal presence (whether or not the author is a human being) is one more idol to be overturned.

NOTES

1. Michel Foucault, "What Is an Author?" in *The Foucault Reader*, ed. Paul Rabinow, trans. Josue V. Harari (New York: Pantheon Books, 1984), pp. 101–120 [pp. 9–22].

2. Ibid., p. 118 [p. 21].

3. Ibid., p. 119 [p. 21].

4. Alexander Nehamas, "What an Author Is," *The Journal of Philosophy* 83 (1986): 685–691.

5. For the details of Nehamas's view see his "The Postulated Author: Critical Monism as a Regulative Ideal," *Critical Inquiry* 8 (1981): 131–149. See also, for a similar position, Steven Knapp and Walter Benn Michaels, "Against Theory," *Critical Inquiry* 8 (1982): 723–742.

6. Nehamas, "What an Author Is," p. 686.

7. Ibid., p. 687

8. Ibid., pp. 687–688.

9. Ibid., p. 688.

10. Ibid., p. 690.

11. Ibid.

12. Foucault, "What Is an Author?" p. 119 [p. 21].

13. Ibid.

14. Denis Dutton has drawn another sort of distinction, between what he calls epistemic and metaphysical critiques of intentionality. See "Why Intentionalism Won't Go Away," in *Literature and the Question of Philosophy*, ed. A.J. Cascardi (Johns Hopkins University Press, 1987), pp. 194–209. The latter, which Dutton attributes mainly to Derrida, is "the line of argument which holds that it is the very concept of an intention itself, some purposing or designing mental state, which is in doubt" (p. 197). In lumping both these critiques together as epistemological, I do not mean to deny anything Dutton says; I merely want to distinguish between such critiques considered together, and the practical (in a Kantian sense of that word) critique, which stands apart from both.

15. Foucault, "What Is an Author?" pp. 103–105 [pp. 10–12].

16. Ibid., p. 103 [p. 10].

17. James Joyce, *Ulysses* (New York: Random House, 1961), p. 154.

18. Harry Blamires, *The Bloomsday Book* (London: Methuen, 1966), p. 61.

19. Samuel Beckett, *Proust* (New York: Grove Press, 1931), p. 60.

20. Friedrich Nietzsche, *On the Genealogy of Morals*, trans. Walter Kaufmann and R.J. Hollingdale (New York: Vintage Books, 1967), p. 55.

21. My attitude toward Nietzsche in what follows has been much inspired and informed by conversations with Randall Havas.

22. This objection was pressed by an anonymous reader for *The Journal of Aesthetics and Art Criticism*.

23. In my dissertation, *Plato's Thoughts and Literature* (Harvard, 1986), I argue that this model for reading the dialogues may provide an alternative to literary interpretations of Plato, as well as to the unreflective treatment of his dialogues as merely decorated treatises.

24. I have argued for this analysis of Plato's position, especially concerning the *Ion* and *Protagoras*, in "Plato's *Ion*: The Problem of the Author," *Philosophy* 64 (1989): 1–9, and "Socrates' Charitable Treatment of Poetry," *Philosophy and Literature* (forthcoming).

25. Certainly one of the hermeneutical attitudes by which Foucault identifies our modern conception of the author—as a posit of unity underlying all of that author's works (p. 111)—is already explicit as early as the Hellenistic period: "Another matter for which the ancients, especially Aristarchus, deserve praise is the development of the critical principle that the best guide to an author's usage is the corpus of his own writings, and therefore difficulties ought to be explained wherever possible by reference to other passages in the same author." L.D. Reynolds and N.G. Wilson, *Scribes and Scholars: A Guide to the Transmission of Greek and Latin Literature* (Oxford University Press, 1968), p. 13.

26. Foucault, What Is an Author?" p. 107 [p. 13].

27. My analogy has its roots in Stanley Cavell's suggestion, made in his "Freud and Literature" seminars (Harvard, 1985–86), that rather than speaking of our psychoanalysis of a text, it might be more fruitful to think of the text as analysing *us*. See Cavell's "Psychoanalysis and Cinema: The Melodrama of the Unknown Woman," *The Trial(s) of Psychoanalysis*, ed. Francoise Meltzer (The University of Chicago Press, 1987), p. 258 n29.

28. Sigmund Freud, "An Outline of Psycho-Analysis," in *The Standard Edition of the Complete Psychological Works of Sigmund Freud*, trans. James Strachey, vol. 23 (London: The Hogarth Press, 1964), p. 175.

29. Ibid.

30 Ibid., p. 177.

CHAPTER 9

Apparent, Implied, and Postulated Authors

Robert Stecker

"Things inanimate cannot be authors . . ."

Thomas Hobbes

A number of writers have recently revived a suggestion of Wayne Booth that we distinguish, not only between the writer of a work of fiction and its narrator, but distinguish both of these from something else variously called the apparent, implied, or postulated author (or artist). What motivates making this further distinction? Does the motivation justify the distinction, i.e., establish that there really is a need for it? These are the questions I want to answer in this article.

I

Kendall Walton makes the distinction not only with respect to literature but across the arts.[1] For him, speaking of apparent artists and their apparent acts is merely a convenient way of referring to what appears to be the case with or in a work of art. However, not every way a work appears makes it appropriate to speak of an apparent artist. That a painting happens to appear green under certain unusual conditions of light need not make appropriate talk of an apparent artist. It *is* appropriate to speak of an apparent artist when a work appears to be made in a certain way or with a certain intention, or under the influence of certain beliefs and emotions—in short, whenever acts or states of a maker of the work appear to manifest themselves in the work.

Given this usage, it is certain that there is often license for speaking of apparent artists. Works of art do often appear to be made in certain ways with certain intentions, and so forth. Often, we are not tempted to attribute such acts of making to the narrator (if any) of the work. Sometimes they do not, in fact, belong to the real artist. While Walton's usage gives us formal license to speak of apparent artists, it does not so far give us good reason to. We would have a good reason to so speak only if the appearances picked out by such talk were important for understanding or appreciating works of art.

If we are concerned with appearances simply as our initial estimate of reality and if the focus of critical inquiry is the way a work really is, the intentions an artist really had, etc., then Walton's usage will prove more cumbersome than useful. On the other hand, if the focus of critical inquiry is or ought to be on the appearances themselves, then Walton's usage will help us maintain that focus and not confuse it with the alternative just mentioned. Walton indeed thinks that it is the latter focus that is correct. "From the point of view of art criticism and appreciation, how works appear to have come about is important for its own sake, and not as an indication of how it did come about" (p. 65). It is this claim that really justifies talk of the apparent artist. The question now becomes whether Walton's claim about what is important is itself correct.

One point that might be regarded in its favor is that it preserves the widely held view that a proper appreciation of a work of art ought to find its source in the direct experience of it. (Call this "the direct experience requirement.") Appearances are well suited to such appreciation while "external facts," like the way the work is actually made and the real author's actual intentions, seem not to be. On the other hand, the range of appearances usually recognized is extended by speaking of the way the work appears to be made and of apparent intentions in such a way as to acknowledge that we see works of art as essentially made, essentially the product of intentional acts.

In the following passage, Walton appeals to the direct experience requirement:

One must examine "The Love Song of J. Alfred Prufrock" to ascertain that in it Eliot portrayed the hero compassionately. But if Eliot did not write the poem, he did not perform this act, no matter what the poem is like; and if the poem was "written" by a computer . . . , no one performed the act of portraying the character compassionately. The words of the poem are, to be sure, good evidence that someone wrote it, but it is conceivable that other evidence ("external" evidence) should show no one wrote it. (p. 53)

Walton's point, I take it, is that if what is really important were the acts and intentions of the real artist, we would not rest content with our experience of the poem. Since we do rest content with our experience in deciding whether Prufrock is compassionately portrayed, it is the appearance of compassionate portrayal that is important.

I find unconvincing both Walton's claim about what is important for under-standing/appreciating works of art and the reason given in support of the claim. Let us begin with his remarks about "Prufrock." I believe that we might often rest content with our experience of the poem to find out how a character is portrayed. *This*, however, does not show that we are not interested in how the real author portrayed the character. Certainly this is not shown by pointing out that it is conceivable that Eliot did not write "Prufrock" and the words of the poem might still exist having been produced in the right order by a computer, or by a monkey or by the action of waves on a cliff face. Though these possi-bilities are conceivable, they are not possibilities we have to dispose of before attributing the act of portrayal to Eliot because none of these are possibilities there is any reason to take seriously. We know who wrote "Prufrock" so we can take for granted that the words of the poem are evidence of his acts and intentions.

Walton claims that there is more direct evidence of these things which we would be expected to seek if we were really concerned to discover the acts and intentions of the real artist. However, this is false on a number of counts. First, a work often provides as good evidence of the artist's acts and intentions as possible. A record of how Eliot felt or what he was thinking before, during and after writing "Prufrock," or of a general disposition to compassion or lack thereof, would not be better evidence of how he portrayed Prufrock than the evidence of the text. It would in fact be worse evidence. We cannot, with equal confidence, say the same about how Eliot *intended* to portray Prufrock, but it remains true that professions of intention are not necessarily better evidence of intentions than products of intention. In the case of arts like painting and sculp-ture, there *can* be better evidence of how a work is made than the work itself, e.g., a photographic record of the work being made. But this would not give us more direct access to other artistic acts performed by the artist or to his inten-tions.

Second, even if more direct evidence is conceivable, it may be felt that the work provides *adequate* evidence or that, although such evidence is conceivable, it is unavailable.

It may be thought that all this misses Walton's point in introducing the pos-sibility that the words of "Prufrock" have a nonhuman source. Perhaps he is suggesting that the way Prufrock appears to be portrayed would be the same whatever the cause of the "poem" and that our interest would remain fixed on this appearance. It is *this* that shows only the appearance is important.

However, it is not clear that the appearance would remain the same if we knew of the poem's strange genesis nor is it Walton's view that it would. "Even when what is relevant to criticism is merely with what intention a work appears to have been made or how . . . it seems to have come about, it still may be crucial to consider the actual historical context in which a work was created" (p. 56). So it is not true, in general, that the work itself is all we need for understanding it or that the way it appears is independent of external fact. Walton, like other proponents of apparent artists, discriminates between those appearances that give us a correct perception of a work and those that do not. He claims that considering historical context is among the ways of pinning down the former class of appearances. However, once we discriminate among appearances in this way, the claim that only appearances are important to criticism collapses. We will see that, not only does it collapse, but we are driven to regarding the acts and intentions of actual artists as important. We can see this by looking at an example Walton uses to illustrate the importance of historical context in altering appearances.

The example is an imaginary one borrowed from Borges's story, "Pierre Menard, the author of *Don Quixote*." Menard, in Borges's story, writing in the early twentieth century, produced a text that is identical in wording with certain chapters of Cervantes' *Don Quixote*. The narrator of the story suggests that, although the words are identical, their interpretation will be radically different due to the difference in historical context in which the words were produced. Thus the words, "truth, whose mother is history . . ." are mere historical eulogy to history coming from Cervantes's pen, but are an expression of the pragmatic theory of truth coming from the pen of Menard, a contemporary of William James. Walton approves of the interpretation of the narrator with the proviso that it should be taken to state how the words appear to a reader aware of the two historical contexts rather than as an account of what the real Cervantes and the "real" Menard had in mind.

But exactly why does the historical context create these differing appearances and why should we want to view a work from the perspective of its historical context? Walton does not have a satisfactory answer to either question.

First, why does historical context create different appearances? "The information that makes Cervantes's *Don Quixote* seem not to have been written with pragmatism in mind is . . . that . . . it was written . . . long before William James, and hence that it is unlikely that its author would have had in mind the doctrines of pragmatism" (p. 64). By parity of reasoning, one would expect Menard's *Quixote* to give the impression that it was written with pragmatism in mind because historical context makes it likely that the author had it in mind. Walton surprisingly denies this. "If Menard's text . . . seems to have pragmatism in mind, it does so in a sense that does not provide the slightest support for the claim that Menard . . . did have pragmatism in mind." (p. 65). If historical context (combined perhaps with Menard's words in his *Quixote*) made it *likely* that he had pragmatism in mind, it would provide not slight but strong support for the claim he *did* have it in mind. On the other hand, if Walton is right, and it provides no support for this claim, we have been given no reason, comparable to the one given for Cervantes's text, for saying that Menard appears to have had pragmatism in mind. So Walton has no satisfactory explanation why placing a text in its historical context creates different impressions. Or rather, he does suggest such an explanation (in his remarks about Cervantes), viz., that historical context makes attributions to the real author probable or improbable, but he recoils from it because it not only makes important for criticism historical context but the acts and intention of real artists.

Second, why do we want to view a work from its historical perspective? According to Walton, "I think we can agree that it is correct . . . to read Cervantes's *Don Quixote* as a seventeenth-century work, since it was in fact written in the seventeenth century; to construe it as a product of the twentieth century would be to misconstrue it . . ." (pp. 57–58). Walton tries to *justify* a historical perspective by citing the (external) fact that works are produced in a historical context. In the same way we can justify the importance of the artist's acts and intentions by citing the fact that works are produced by such acts and intentions. We can also point out that if ignorance of historical context leads to misconstrual, there is as much reason to suppose that ignorance of the historical author does so as well. To return to Menard's *Quixote*, we should stop pretending that historical context alone could make it likely or produce the appearance that the author had pragmatism in mind. Such a context would only give us an array of early twentieth-century philosophies. It is only by linking *Menard* to one of these (either through his text or otherwise) that we would make it likely to produce the appearance that he had pragmatism in mind. To take another example, suppose we discover a manuscript by an Irishman from the eighteenth century. That the Irishman is Berkeley would lead us to interpret it one way, that he is Swift would lead us in quite a different direction.

The argument so far only shows that Walton gives no reason for being concerned with historical context that is not also a reason for being concerned with historical author. There may still be a way of showing why we should regard the former but not the latter as important for criticism. I will look at another attempt to do so in the next section. It may be worth pointing out now the implausibility of any such attempt. Walton unintentionally pinpointed why we would ordinarily be interested in historical context. Since it is the context in which the artist worked, information about the historical context renders probable or improbable hypotheses about what the artist was doing, or intending to do, in a work. Cutting off an interest in historical context from an interest in historical author not only arbitrarily confines a critic to only some historical information out of the total information, but deprives him of an obvious reason for being interested in historical information.

II

According to Alexander Nehamas, the object of critical understanding is the *postulated* author, an agent hypothesized to explain the features of a text.[2] According to Nehamas, this agent is not the historical writer. Nevertheless, the postulated author has to be understood as occupying the historical context of the historical writer. So far this sounds just like Walton's apparent artist but the postulated author is a rather different creature. In constructing the postulated author, we are by no means confined to how a text appears to us against a background of common historical knowledge. All sorts of information, including biographical information about the writer, no matter how esoteric, can be relevant to the enterprise which Nehamas compares to the construction of a scientific theory to explain natural phenomena.

I find Nehamas's conception of the enterprise of interpretation attractive. I agree that much interpretation consists in forming and defending hypotheses about what the author meant, though some interpretation consists in accounting for divergences between what the author evidently did and what he might have meant.

I find puzzling, however, Nehamas's distinction between the postulated author and historical writer. Nehamas's description of the enterprise—"to construct . . . a complete, historically plausible author" ("PA," p. 147)—*sounds* like it is concerned with the actual writer. In Nehamas's first article on the subject, "The Postulated Author," he only offers a few hints of his motivation. Unfortunately none of these really justifies the distinction.

At one point, Nehamas distinguishes the postulated author from the actual writer's *self-understanding*. As Nehamas says, such self-understanding (e.g., of the writer's intentions) is fragmentary. If we were to identify the actual writer with his self-understanding, we could see how the former could be distinguished from the postulated author. But of course, such an identification is incorrect. The intentions that a writer is unaware of or misconstrues are still his.

The other hint we are given is this: "The author is postulated as the agent whose actions account for the text's features; he is a character, a hypothesis which is accepted provisionally, guides the interpretation, and is in turn modified in its light. The author, unlike the writer, is not a text's efficient cause, but, so to speak, its formal cause, manifested in though not identical with it" ("PA," p. 145). The formal cause of a thing is its essence, and, since a text is essentially a production of someone, I do not see how the efficient/formal distinction is supposed to work here. Earlier in the passage the postulated author is identified with a hypothesis which the actual writer certainly is not. But the identification cannot plausibly be taken literally, or else it conflicts with the characterization of the postulated author as an agent. "Hypothesis" must be loose for "hypothetical agent." Taking "hypothesis" this way, the passage goes on to suggest that the identity of this agent is constantly changing (while the real writer does not change with every change in our interpretation). However, our changing hypotheses are more plausibly construed as changes in belief about the author rather than changes in the identity of the author. In that case they can be construed as hypotheses about the actual writer.

Nehamas has recently made a more elaborate attempt to justify the distinction between postulated author and historical writer.[3] The background of this attempt is Foucault's critique of the author in "What is an Author?" Nehamas accepts two points that Foucault makes: (A) Rather than a person, the author is a figure, function or role which implies the appropriateness of certain questions about the text and the expectation of certain answers. (B) The author has been a repressive principle used to force texts to undergo certain operations and to exclude others. I will return to B at the end of this section. For the time being I will concentrate on A.

Let us first examine Nehamas's main argument for distinguishing writers and authors. It is found in the following passage which harks back to and clarifies the passage in "The Postulated Author" distinguishing the efficient and formal cause of a work:

Writers are extrinsically related to their texts. This is reflected in the possibility that Henri Beyle, for example, never wrote the works that are commonly attributed to him. . . . It is, so to speak, not necessary for Henri Beyle . . . have been Stendhal. But notice how we must construe the expression "to have been Stendhal" in this context: it is not a reference . . . to the actual person. This, in turn, reflects the essential connection between Stendhal and the texts of which, necessarily, he is the author. Stendhal is whoever can be understood as the author of these texts. ("WTAW," p. 272)

The argument of this passage can be stated as follows: (1) it is not necessary that H.B. wrote S.'s works. (2) Therefore, H.B. is only contingently related to S.'s works. (3) S. is whoever can be understood as the author of these texts. (4) Therefore, S. is essentially (noncontingently) related to these texts. (5) Therefore, S. is not H.B. (6) Therefore, the author is not the writer.

I think we can admit that there are at least two senses in which it is not necessary that H.B. wrote S.'s works. First, it is logically or metaphysically possible that H.B. did not write them: it is not contradictory to assert he did not, and we can imagine a possible world in which someone else wrote them. Second, it is epistemically possible that H.B. did not write them: we might discover that someone else wrote them. I am also willing to grant that (2) follows from (1) and that (3) is true except that I find obscure the phrase "can be understood as" in (3). What I certainly would accept is: (3') S. is whoever is the author of these texts.

The argument goes wrong at the next step. It seems to me that (3') can be construed in two ways, neither one of which implies (4). On one construal of (3'), "whoever" is a pronoun that refers to the person who wrote the texts without specifying who that person is. On this construal, (4) not only does not follow, but, since (3') would mean that S. is the writer, whoever he may be, who wrote these texts, (3') in conjunction with (2) would imply not (4). On the other construal, "whoever" is a variable, and the expression "whoever is the author of these texts" would be a predicate or open sentence. On this construal, "whoever" does not refer to the writer. Nehamas may have inferred (4) because, construing (3')—or (3)—this way, he supposed that "whoever" still referred to something and that whatever is referred to is essentially related to the text. However, on this construal of (3'), "whoever" does not refer to anything. (3') would mean that the predicate "x is the author of these texts" is true of S. This too does not imply (4). I know of no way of construing (3')—or (3)—on which (4) does follow. So I conclude that Nehamas's argument is invalid.

Furthermore, when Nehamas specifies the questions that the author figure invites, it becomes as puzzling as it was in his earlier article on why the author is not the historical writer. According to Nehamas, to interpret a work (which for him is the same as supposing it to have an author) is to construe it as the product of action by an agent and to ask questions appropriate to the understanding of actions and products of agents ("WTWA," p. 277). If this is what interpretation is, why in the world is it not concerned with the writer? He *is* the agent whose actions brought about the product we are interpreting *as* the product of actions of an agent! What else could we be talking about?

Nehamas answers this question in many ways: (A) "the agent postulated . . . to account for construing a text as the product of an action" (p. 281); (B) "a plausible historical variant of the writer" (p. 285); (C) "a character the writer could have been" (p. 285); (D) "what any individual who [produced the text] must be like" (p. 286).

Not all these come to the same things. (A) is precisely where we began and would normally be construed to refer to the writer, the actual agent. (D) surely implies that we are describing the writer; he did produce the text and so, if anyone who produced the text must answer to our description, the writer must. (C) at least leaves open that the writer coincides with the author. Only (B) seems to imply that we are not talking about the writer. However, even (B) can be accommodated with the identification of author and writer. After all, our hypotheses about what the agent (i.e., the writer) was doing in producing a text will usually be just that: hypotheses rather than highly confirmed theories. To that extent, it is likely that the agent we describe will be a plausible variant of the actual agent. That is simply a way of saying that our hypotheses will fall short of the truth. As in his original article, it is not clear why Nehamas prefers to think of hypotheses as constructing characters rather than imperfectly characterizing the writer.

There are other things Nehamas says about authors which do clearly distinguish them from writers, but at the same time they undermine his account of interpretation. One (crucial) example will have to suffice here. "Authors, not being persons, do not have psychological states that might determine in advance what texts mean" ("WTWA," p. 286). If this is so, authors are indeed not writers, but it is not clear how they can be regarded as the agents postulated to explain the features of a text. Agents do have psychological states and it is precisely in terms of such states as intention, desire and belief that the actions of agents are understood.

Finally, I return to Foucault's claim that the author is a repressive principle. This is a claim that Nehamas takes very seriously. Another motive that he has in distinguishing between writers and authors is to avoid the accusation involved in the claim. However, I do not think that Nehamas's author figure would escape Foucault's condemnation. What Foucault was condemning was a conception of reading texts which forces texts to undergo some operations and exclude others. Nehamas's conception of interpretation certainly does this.

On the other hand, the author, even construed as the writer, needn't be invoked as a repressive principle. It would be repressive if regarded as the only principle that determines legitimate interpretations. However, the project of constructing hypotheses about what a writer is doing in a work, can be regarded as one of many possible projects all equally deserving the name "interpretation." To so regard it would be to abandon the critical monism it was Nehamas's original purpose to defend, but given the state of contemporary criticism, I believe that such monism has to be abandoned.

III

It seems wrong to think of the acts and intentions of actual authors as unimportant for criticism. It may still be true that the apparent author should be important too. While I don't want categorically to deny this, I do want to argue that apparent authors are harder to come by than is commonly thought. The reason for this is that it is harder to find room for the apparent author between the narrator and the real author.

Wayne Booth tries to make room with his notion of an implied author.[4] This notion is harder to pin down than that of Walton's apparent artist and Nehamas's postulated author though it has more affinities with the former. The basic idea seems to be this. A novel has an ethical, emotional, intellectual perspective. In fact, a novel may have many such perspectives belonging to the various characters including narrators. But there will be a more fundamental perspective that may not belong to anyone in the novel. It is from this perspective that the novel can be said to pass, or refuse to pass, judgment on its characters. The perspective determines how much knowledge characters have of themselves, others, and the world. It determines the moral significance, or lack thereof, of the situations of the novel, and characteristic ways of reacting to them. It proposes, or refuses to propose, an attitude toward these reactions.

According to Booth, this perspective is created by the actual writer, but it is not necessarily his. It *is* necessarily the implied author's. This claim is compatible with what I have been arguing: that the actual writer's acts and intentions are important in understanding a work including the perspective of the implied author, but it claims that we still need the implied author to attribute this perspective to. While I do not deny that such perspectives exist in novels, I question whether we need any categories other than narrator and actual writer to account for such perspectives.

Very often, the role of implied author is filled by the narrator of a work. Booth acknowledges this is so whenever the narrator is undramatized, i.e., stands wholly outside the world of the fiction. Such are the narrators of *Emma* and of *Anna Karenina*. (Actually, if an undramatized narrator turns out to be unreliable, and I do not see why this is impossible, we would *not* identify his perspective with the perspective of the novel.) Booth suggests, however, that whenever we have a dramatized narrator, the implied author should be distinguished from the narrator. His practice, unfortunately, does not follow this suggestion. For a class of narrators, called "reliable spokesmen for the implied author" (p. 211) such as the narrator of *Tom Jones*, Booth's practice is to constantly shift between maintaining and ignoring the distinction.[5] Since his substantive remarks ignore the distinction—necessarily, since whatever can be said of the implied author can be said of the reliable spokesman—I infer that once again the category of narrator does all the work.

If there is reason to introduce a new category—the implied author—it ought to be found in those works with a narrator or narrators who are not reliable "spokesmen." Such narrators need not be unreliable; they may also include narrators whose perspective is more limited than the author's. In such works, we are particularly anxious to find a perspective that transcends that of the narrator, but why shouldn't we say that the one we are looking for is simply the actual writer's?

I have already mentioned one reason Booth gives to think otherwise. Though the perspective we seek is created by the author, it is not necessarily held by him. Thus one follower of Booth has suggested, "however querulous and intolerant the actual Tolstoy may have been, the implied author of *Anna Karenina* is full of compassionate understanding."[6] Booth himself has suggested that there is some doubt whether the actual Fielding held some of the moral beliefs that are part of the perspective of *Tom Jones*. (Ignore the fact that neither of these works contains an unreliable narrator.)

A minor point about such claims is that they are often simpleminded, as is the one just given about Tolstoy. Just because someone has a tendency toward intolerance does not mean that he is not also full of compassionate understanding. When understanding is acute, a person often vacillates between compassion and intolerance. There is much evidence that Tolstoy was just such a person and even his novels display both tendencies, though in these they are directed to different characters, the tendency to intolerance usually only to minor ones.

The main problem with such claims is that, even if the perspective of a novel is not the actual writer's, in the sense that he firmly holds every belief and has every disposition constituting it, it is not necessary to posit an implicit author who does. Such perspectives can exist and guide the reader's judgment of the narrator and the events he narrates without it being anyone's in this sense and without the reader attributing it to anyone. In another sense, however, the perspective is the actual author's.

Let me try to explain these two senses. Just as the world of the novel is not asserted by its actual author to be the real world (no matter how much resemblance it bears to the real world) but is presented as something to be entertained in the imagination, so the perspective a novelist adopts in presenting this world may itself only be entertained. From the point of view of a certain moral perspective, say, characters are judged, situations are given ethical significance, and so forth. It is the real author who is doing this; it is in this sense that the perspective is his, not an implied author's. But the moral perspective from which the writer judges characters, etc., is one he may not unequivocally affirm (though he can unequivocally be said to present it to us). The writer may be exploring it, trying to imagine what it would be like to actually hold it, but he does not hold it. This is the sense in which the perspective is not the writer's, but in this sense it does not have to be anyone's in or out of the novel.

This is not to say that perspectives are not sometimes held in the strong sense of affirmed by writers or that it is never worth asking whether a perspective is affirmed or merely entertained by its writer. It may be part of understanding a work to understand this.

IV

It may be that the idea of an apparent or implied artist does not have a useful general application, but it may still have an application in certain special cases. Walton provides several special cases where this is plausible. For example, Mozart's "Musical Joke" at one level appears to be written by an incompetent composer, though at a deeper level it appears, and in fact is, written by a composer of genius. And Jackson Pollock's paintings at one level appear to be painted in a haphazard and spontaneous manner, though at a deeper level they appear, and in fact are, carefully planned and executed. I think it is significant that these examples come from arts other than literature. If a novel appeared to be written incompetently "at one level" but not at a deeper level, the incompetence would probably be attributable to the novel's narrator. Similarly if it appeared to be produced in a haphazard and spontaneous manner at one level but not at a deeper level.

I am inclined to think that the notion of an apparent artist has genuine, significant application in these cases. In the "Musical Joke," Mozart establishes the fiction that the piece was composed by an incompetent composer just as novelists can establish the fiction that a story is written by an incompetent writer. But while we already have the notion of a narrator to handle the latter case, we need some other notion like that of apparent artist to handle the "Musical Joke." I would be less inclined to say that Pollock establishes a fiction, but no less inclined to endorse the usefulness of the notion of apparent artist in understanding his paintings, at least if Walton's account of them is correct.

Whether the notion of apparent artist has any useful application to literature—the art to which it was thought to have the most obvious application—I do not know.

NOTES

1. Kendall Walton, "Style and the Products and Processes of Art," in *The Concept of Style*, ed. Berel Lang (Philadelphia: University of Pennsylvania Press, 1979).

2. Alexander Nehamas, "The Postulated Author: Critical Monism as a Regulative Ideal," *Critical Inquiry* 8 (1981): 133–149; hereafter abbreviated "PA."

3. Alexander Nehamas, "Writer, Text, Author, Work," in *Literature and the Question of Philosophy*, ed. A.J. Cascardi (Baltimore: Johns Hopkins University Press, 1987), pp. 267–91 [pp. 95–115]; hereafter abbreviated "WTAW."

4. Wayne Booth, *The Rhetoric of Fiction* (Chicago: University of Chicago Press, 1961).

5. Ibid.; see especially pp. 71–73 for a passage where the distinction is ignored.

6. Jenefer Robinson, "Style and Personality in the Literary Work," *The Philosophical Review* 94 (1985): 234. It may be noted that philosophers are particularly fond of finding compassion in implied authors.

———— CHAPTER 10 ————

Feminist Literary Criticism and the Author

Cheryl Walker

In the late 1960s French theorists began to take account of the phenomenon we now know familiarly as "the death of the author." Writers like Michel Foucault raised startling questions about the voice or voices in a text, asking, "What difference does it make who is speaking?"[1] In the days of author criticism, the author was thought to be the speaker whose presence behind the text signaled his (or her, though usually his) capacity as originator. Textual interpretations often alluded to this historical personage as a genius whose subjectivity, once understood, provided a set of principles for discovering the underlying unity of a great work of literature.

According to Foucault, in his essay "What Is an Author?" (1969), this authorial presence has disappeared. In the modern period the author is an effacement, an absence of the personal, who writes him- or herself out of the text through the strategies of fictive composition. Nonetheless, we still have what Foucault calls "the author function," which allows us to classify "a Woolf novel," for instance, as a different kind of entity than a novel by Jane Austen. The author-function is not a subjective presence but a signature, in which "the author's name serves to characterize a certain mode of being of discourse" ("WIA," p. 107).

Though the death of the author may be variously traced to certain nineteenth-century writers like Stéphane Mallarmé and Friedrich Nietzsche, today some of us associate it more often with the theoretical moves of French critics like Fou-

Cheryl Walker, "Feminist Literary Criticism and the Author," *Critical Inquiry* 16 (Spring 1990), pp. 551–71. Published by The University of Chicago. © 1990 by The University of Chicago. 0095–1896/90/1603–0011$01.00. All rights reserved.

cault, Roland Barthes, or Jacques Derrida who have questioned the whole notion of the unified subject, the center, the self.[2] Individuals cannot be authors, in part, because there is no such center or integrated core from which one can say a piece of literature issues. The binary oppositions between self and other, inside and outside, are two of the many dualities Derrida has powerfully deconstructed. The self is a structuring mechanism, not a godlike creator. Unlike the deity, we do not originate; we only translate among various given languages of feeling: "the writer can only imitate a gesture that is always anterior, never original. His only power is to mix writings, to counter the ones with the others, in such a way as never to rest on any one of them," Barthes says ("DA," p. 146).

In 1969 Foucault is less extreme than Barthes or Derrida in the sense that he believes "it would be pure romanticism . . . to imagine a culture in which the fictive would operate in an absolutely free state, in which fiction would be put at the disposal of everyone and would develop without passing through something like a necessary or constraining figure" ("WIA," p. 119). Thus he does not at that time propose that texts be construed as fields of discourse without *any* boundaries (authorial or otherwise) to limit the free play of the signifier, as Barthes and Derrida do. Instead, he diverts our attention from the intentions of the text to "the modes of circulation, valorization, attribution, and appropriation of discourses" ("WIA," p. 117) or, in other words, to the reception of texts according to the modes of distribution established by power relations. However, he also considers significant "the subject's [the author's?] points of insertion, modes of functioning, and system of dependencies" within culture ("WIA," p. 118), a point to which I will return later.

The issues that Foucault raises about reception and reading are certainly part of the contemporary discussion of literature. However, they are not the only issues with which we, as today's readers, are concerned. Discussions about the role of the author persist and so we continue to have recourse to the notion of authorship.

For instance, in her recent book *Sexual/Textual Politics* (1985), the feminist critic Toril Moi feels called on to return to these twenty-year-old issues in French theory to tell us what it *has meant* to speak of the author, when she says: "For the patriarchal critic, the author is the source, origin and meaning of the text. If we are to undo this patriarchal practice of *authority*, we must take one further step and proclaim with Roland Barthes the death of the author."[3]

In the course of this essay I wish to reopen the (never fully closed) question of whether it is advisable to speak of the author, *or* of what Foucault calls "the author function," when querying a text, and I wish to reopen it precisely at the site where feminist criticism and post-structuralism are presently engaged in dialogue. Here in particular we might expect that reasons for rejecting author erasure would appear. However, theoretically informed feminist critics have recently found themselves tempted to agree with Barthes, Foucault, and the Edward Said of *Beginnings* that the authorial presence is best set aside in order to liberate the text for multiple uses.[4]

I wish to examine the ways in which feminist critics have moved away from what some would call the old-fashioned assumption that what we do when we read is try to decipher the intentions of the text in terms of what we assume to be the author's deepest self. I also wish to make a further argument for reanimating the author, preserving author-function not only in terms of reception theory, as Foucault would seem at one point to advocate, but also in terms of a politics of author recognition.

1

A mild form of author questioning can be found in two recent anthologies of feminist theory. In their 1985 *Making a Difference: Feminist Literary Criticism*, Gayle Greene and Coppélia Kahn advise feminist critics to pay attention to those theorists who "in liberating the text 'from the authority of a presence behind it,' released it 'from the constraints of a single and univocal reading,' making it 'available for production, plural, contradictory, capable of change . . . unfixed, a process.' "[5]

Though the postmodern feminist critic is almost certain to practice her trade in defiance of *authority*, often proceeding polyvocally herself and rarely claiming that a unified, coherent, and transcendental subjectivity lies behind the text, nevertheless the author has never quite disappeared from our practice. The above quotation from Greene and Kahn, for instance, is less doctrinaire than Barthes, suggesting not that we refuse all attempts at deciphering a text's meaning but that a single referent be replaced by an interactive model of the text as inviting interpretation through a process of multiple readings and references.

This quotation itself is drawn from a double authorship where we do not know which of the two voices (Greene's or Kahn's) is speaking in any given phrase. Furthermore, there is a third presence (or absence) in the interpolated quotations from Catherine Belsey, who is herself quoting Derrida. Clearly, there are many voices speaking in this text. But the ascription to Belsey suggests as much as anything that we are unwilling to do away with the author entirely, though it should be noted that when Foucault speaks of the author, he does not mean simply the proper name of the writer but a system of limiting meaning that allies the proper name with a whole series of assumptions about what belongs to it. (A "Woolf novel" is not simply one written by Virginia Woolf.) The author's name is not, for Foucault, just a proper name like the rest. Still, Greene and Kahn feel obliged to mention Belsey as the "author" of the quoted remarks. What are the implications of this gesture? Foucault suggests that such an act may be a consequence of bourgeois ideology because it signifies that the text "belongs" to an individual like a piece of private property. My own instincts tell me that Greene and Kahn's attribution may involve the notion that texts function like property, but textual property, they imply, has special attributes: it is alienable and inalienable at the same time.[6]

From one point of view, they are joining *with* Belsey, thus, in a sense, making a communal statement in which there is no need to divide up authorship like property. From another viewpoint, of course, proper ascription is necessary in order not to be caught in an act of misappropriation, an act of stealing. However, this politics need not be simply one of guilt (stealing is sinful) nor one of fear (stealing is punishable); it can also be one of respect (we wish you to have the credit for configuring this semantic sequence that we are appropriating for our own purposes). In all three cases, the author remains in some form.

This is not, however, the same thing as suggesting, as Steven Knapp and Walter Benn Michaels have done in their essays "Against Theory" and "Against Theory 2," that the meaning of a text is always and only what its author intends.[7] It is, to the contrary, a position *neither* consonant with Barthes's belief that the most revolutionary form of criticism requires refusing to discover the author in a space of writing *nor* synonymous with the proposition (à la Knapp and Michaels) that the author provides the only locus in which meaning can properly be ascribed. What we are often seeking as feminists, it seems, is a third position.

So far the discussions within feminist criticism concerning the implications of post-structural theory for the positioning of the author have generally proceeded from theory to practice. (There continues to be much practice, of course, in which the theoretical issues are not even raised.) The theorists, however, reasonably wonder: should we valorize the author if such a position necessarily implies the same kind of repression we associate with patriarchy?

It is well to remember Foucault's caution here that the author-function implies a convergence of many indicators given status within a particular context. "As a result, we could say that in a civilization like our own there are a certain number of discourses that are endowed with the 'author function,' while others are deprived of it" ("WIA," p. 107). Though Foucault's examples of deprivation concern private letters and contracts that, he says, do not have authors in this sense, we might also remember the way the canon guarantees authorship to certain privileged writers while others are degraded to the level of mere literary names, which only a Trivial Pursuit–minded individual would think it necessary to "know" in the kind of detail that, we are told, a literate person should know, say, Dostoyevski.[8]

My second example of recent author discussion concerns Nancy K. Miller's "Changing the Subject: Authorship, Writing, and the Reader." Miller returns to the question of authorship, hoping to keep several balls in the air at the same time: post-structuralism's assault on the author and feminism's productive attention to the writing subjectivities of women.[9] Miller finds useful for feminism some aspects of the ideology of "the death of the author." She reminds us that "it is, after all, the Author, canonized, anthologized, and institutionalized, who excludes the less-known works of women and minority writers from the canon, and who by his authority justifies the exclusion" ("CS," p. 104). Yet Miller is suspicious of applying the same version of author erasure to women writers since our relation to subjectivity formation has been different.

The postmodernist decision that the Author is dead, and subjective agency along with him, does not necessarily work for women and prematurely forecloses the question of identity for them. Because women have not had the same historical relation of identity to origin, institution, production, that men have had, women have not, I think, (collectively) felt burdened by too much Self, Ego, Cogito, etc. ("CS," p. 106)

Miller leaves open the possibility of retaining a reconceived author-function in the case of women writers. However, she does indeed "change the subject" as her title implies by concentrating primarily on women as readers (a position she like Barthes believes to be "the necessary counterpoint to the death of the Author" ["CS," p. 104]). Furthermore, she backs away from post-structuralism as an ontology (perhaps a deontology) that denies meaning to coherent subjectivity and to the author (any author, male or female) as the originator of discourse. Her argument seems to imply that the notion of the death of the author arises because men feel overburdened by ego, self, and so on rather than, as Foucault would have it, that the author is a function created entirely by the writing itself and unlocatable outside of it. Foucault says, "In short, it is a matter of depriving the subject (or its substitute) of its role as originator, and of analyzing the subject as a variable and complex function of discourse" ("WIA," p. 118).

If authors only emerge from the written texts, then the question of how these texts were written in the first place attempts to go "behind" the writing in a way rendered illegitimate by critics like Barthes, whom Miller seems to wish not to attack. Identity formation may have different structural patterns for women, but these are irrelevant to the question of whether women can, under such poststructural theories of textuality, operate as the authors of their own works. Miller says that we must pay attention to the *asymmetrical demands generated by different writing identities, male and female, or, perhaps more usefully, canonical or hegemonic and noncanonical or marginal*" ("CS," p. 105). But this is surely a different perspective than that of Foucault and Barthes, as it implies that women (or noncanonical and marginal writers) can be authors whereas men (or canonical and hegemonic writers) cannot. The question remains, how can an absence generate a demand?

Moi's is probably the most radical feminist borrowing of French male theory in its insistence on a feminist proclamation of the death of the author. Moi's *Sexual/Textual Politics* has had very wide circulation, and so it seems worthwhile to look more closely now at what she does with this notion in her own work. To begin with, she discounts the tendency in Anglo-American feminist criticism to supply biographical material about an author (in her case, Woolf) when writing about literary texts. Dismissing as "emotionalist" and irrelevant Jane Marcus's notation that Woolf trembled as she wrote, Moi asks: "does it really matter whether or not Woolf was in the habit of trembling at her desk?" (*STP*, p. 17).

Presumably it doesn't matter, if the author is "dead" as a reference point for the meaning of the text. Yet in terms of some of Moi's other critical assumptions, her position on this issue seems contradictory. When Foucault asked "What difference does it make who is speaking?" he may have been suggesting that we reveal our own epistemological assumptions and our own politics of interpretation by our insistence on a certain notion of subjectivity as speaking. It can never be shown that the treatment of the author as speaking makes *no* difference, since every way of constructing the text makes *some* difference. The point is to consider what difference such a difference makes.

Similarly, nothing can be proven irrelevant to a text unless some principles controlling relevance (that is, restricting potential hermeneutic strategies) are posited, a position problematic for those who, like Moi, are committed to radical open-endedness. If the text cannot be closed to effects previously considered extrinsic to it, effects like its reception, the history of its conventions, the sociopolitical context of its composition, and so on, it also cannot be closed to the biographical contexts of its writing.

The second way in which Moi's argument seems to me problematic is in its radical distinction between fictional writing and critical writing. Moi's own textual politics involves an extended dialogue with authors who are critics. These critics operate in terms of the "author function" Foucault describes so well. That is, Moi ascribes to these critic/authors certain unified positions that categorize them as speakers. Their works are not read by Moi as indeterminate, contradictory, elusive; she assumes that we can sum them up, know what they are saying, and place them in terms of the way their arguments are made. Information about their sociohistorical relations is important to her classifications. An Anglo-American heritage is different from a French one.

In short, Moi preserves the notion of authorship when reading critics while advising we dispense with it when reading literature, presumably following Foucault's notion that the author-function does not affect all discourses in a uniform and constant way. Though recently we have come to know a good deal more about the biographical circumstances of critics like Sandra Gilbert and Susan Gubar than used to be typical outside the rumor mill of academy insiders, Moi implies we read criticism differently. We don't try to locate autobiographical traces in the work of discursive writers; we simply use the proper names as a shorthand for identifying the theory. We do not concern ourselves with the sociological conditions of composition.

Or do we? Certainly the recent brouhaha over the publications of Paul de Man in the Nazi-oriented journal *Le Soir* during the early 1940s has spawned a rereading of his critical works by both detractors and sympathizers. In fact, in what seems to be a radical reversal of earlier positions, Derrida has recently recommended such a rereading in order to understand the historical personage Paul de Man.[10] In Moi's own case, her close association with British Marxist critic Terry Eagleton during the historical moment of *Sexual/Textual Politics* has led some readers to say privately that the book was either overdetermined by Eagleton's own thinking or, conversely, an extended argument with Eagleton's brand of feminism. My point here is certainly not to make an argument against Moi *ad feminam* but to question her separation between fictional and critical texts.

It seems to me that the assumptions operating here are deeply problematic even within the context of post-structuralism. It is possible to deconstruct Moi's argument by remembering with it the contemporary presentation of all culture as discourse and Derrida's proposition, in particular, that there is nothing outside the text. The false dichotomy Moi offers is that of assuming *only* an old-fashioned, author-centered critical practice based on a unified, coherent, bourgeois notion of self *or* a contradictory, open-ended, free plane of discourse on which critics range over a space of writing " 'ceaselessly posit[ing] meaning ceaselessly to evaporate it,' " as she suggests, using Barthes's words (*STP*, p. 63).[11] Like the distinctions between critical and creative writing, and those between historical circumstances and literary texts, this dichotomy somehow forgets other propositions that belong to the very forms of critical practice—feminism, post-structuralism—Moi herself claims to be interested in bringing to bear.

As I have tried to suggest above, it is not true that we read criticism and fiction in diametrically opposed ways, limiting the importance of the author's subjectivity in one while exalting it in the other. Furthermore, the reversal of these positions (erasing the author of fictive work while preserving the author of criticism) also seems misguided.

In terms of post-structuralism, it is worth paying attention to the attack made by Hayden White and others on the old division between creative and critical discourse.[12] White and Dominick LaCapra have both argued that this division will not bear scrutiny. They have been at pains to show that analytical history uses the same rhetorical techniques, the same tropes, the same narrative strategies as literature. Narrative history, narrative criticism, and narrative literature all use the formulae of narrativity.

Presumably Moi would argue that she is not writing narrative criticism. Yet all of the critical texts Moi engages tell a story. In fact, it is precisely because Moi doesn't like the story that Gilbert and Gubar tell that she reminds us that telling a story "can in itself be constructed as an autocratic gesture" (*STP*, p. 68). Does Moi believe she herself is doing anything else? Is her text not an elegant story about the way female critics, connected to one another like characters in a Woolf novel, engage in gestures of mutual recognition and respect while at the same time seeking to escape the party to find room for solitary reflection and independence? Doesn't her book have a clearly identifiable beginning, middle, and end at which the defiant figure of Julia Kristeva emerges somewhat battered but victorious nonetheless, repeating a pattern with roots as ancient as storytelling itself?

Second, the distinction between history and literature (reanimated where Moi dismisses biographical circumstances in favor of the texts themselves) somehow

assumes that the process of juxtaposing historical information with literary artifacts is something other than what some post-structuralists assume it is, an
experience of intertextuality to be valued no more and no less than any other
intertextual exercise for the illumination, the sparks of recognition, it produces.
In his chapter "History and the Novel" in *History and Criticism* (1985), LaCapra
advises historians and literary critics to engage the past through such a process
of intertextual dialogue:

A move in a desirable direction is, I think, made when texts are understood as variable
uses of language that come to terms with—or "inscribe"—contexts in various ways—
ways that engage the interpreter as historian *and* critic in an exchange with the past
through a reading of texts.
    Contexts of interpretation are at least three-fold; those of writing, reception, and critical
reading.
    Contexts of writing include the intentions of the author as well as more immediate
biographical, sociocultural, and political situations with their ideologies and discourses.
They also involve discursive institutions such as traditions and genres.[13]

Like LaCapra's advice to the critic, Derrida's famous statement that there is
nothing outside the text implies that we are free to develop intertextual dialogues
by juxtaposing biography with literature, history with criticism, medical handbooks with political treatises, and so forth. The life of the author is not a privileged content, since it, too, is a set of texts (Gilbert has called it "the life-text"),
but the question remains as to why such texts should be denied or repressed, as
they appear in Moi's argument.
    Most disturbing for me, however, are what I feel to be the antifeminist
implications of Moi's insistence that we joyfully proclaim the death of the author. Miller usefully reminds us that "the removal of the Author has not so
much made room for a revision of the concept of authorship as it has,
through a variety of rhetorical moves, repressed and inhibited discussion of any
writing identity in favor of the (new) monolith of anonymous textuality" ("CS,"
p. 104). What Miller points to here are the limitations of some applications of
post-structuralism in meeting the needs of current feminism. In fact, what we
need, instead of a theory of the death of the author, is a new concept of authorship that does not naively assert that the writer is an originating genius,
creating aesthetic objects outside of history, but does not diminish the importance of difference and agency in the responses of women writers to historical
formations. The loss of the writer runs us the risk of losing many stories important to our history. Radical freedom, of the sort Moi seems to advocate, may
in the end leave us without the tools necessary to consider the way biography
and fiction *are* in dialogue with one another and provide a critique of patriarchy as well as, in some cases, models of resistance. Barthes's form of textual
response (though not Foucault's) would leave us with no literary history whatsoever.

2

Here it may be useful to examine briefly the way contemporary feminist critics, more or less theoretical, are using the author-function in literary criticism of the late 1980s. I will take my examples from the field I know best, criticism concerned with women poets. Though my examples are in no way meant to represent all contemporary positions on authorship among feminist critics, they are instructive both in the way one (Paula Bennett) suggests the problems of ignoring the attack on the author and in the way the others (Alicia Ostriker, Jan Montefiore, and Cora Kaplan) adhere to a revised concept of authorship.

Bennett's *My Life A Loaded Gun: Female Creativity and Feminist Poetics*, Kaplan's *Sea Changes: Essays on Culture and Feminism*, and Ostriker's *Stealing the Language: The Emergence of Women's Poetry in America* were all published in 1986. Montefiore's *Feminism and Poetry: Language, Experience, Identity in Women's Writing* appeared in 1987.[14] Two of these critics are American (Bennett and Ostriker); the other two write in England (though Kaplan is American by birth). It seems to me roughly true that it is still possible to be an American feminist literary critic without taking into consideration recent French theory; it is less possible to be a British one.

This might in part explain the almost total exclusion of French theory from Bennett's book. (There is one footnote listing several sources on French feminism.) *My Life A Loaded Gun* explores the lives and work of three women poets—Emily Dickinson, Sylvia Plath, and Adrienne Rich—and takes the point of view, now familiar from Gilbert and Gubar, that the critical content of women's art is female rage. Bennett assumes no disjunction between poet and speaker and repeatedly reads the poems as though they provide information about the author. Furthermore, the essence of successful authority seems to be integrity, that unified self so inconceivable to postmodernism. Dickinson, Plath, and Rich all wore "self-alienating masks" during some portion of their lives, claims Bennett, "but all finally learned how to discard the mask and speak directly from the unacceptable core of their beings, to claim their loaded guns."[15]

Bennett is not a stupid critic, and I did find many of her insights fascinating. Furthermore, she does not always ascribe conscious intentions to her poets (she does not make Dickinson a feminist, for instance). She is alert to their inconsistencies and sensitive about the influence of cultural context. However, she does fall into many of the traps exposed by French theory. The author is the meaning of the text, a personal, autobiographical personage who has a "true self" that can be embodied relatively transparently in language. The true self has a singular project: the expression of that "constant, never-changing *feminist rage*," which Moi says "manages to transform *all* texts written by women into feminist texts" in American criticism influenced by Gilbert and Gubar of *The Madwoman in the Attic* (*STP*, p. 62).

Ostriker provides another brand of American criticism in *Stealing the Language*. She is much more savvy about theory than Bennett, a fact made abundantly clear from the beginning of her book where she discusses her own eclectic methodology. Furthermore, Ostriker avoids many of the traps that Bennett falls into by arranging her poems thematically (after the first chapter) rather than reading them in terms of their relation to single authors.

Still, Ostriker wishes to preserve the author as speaker in the text.

A warning is therefore appropriate here for readers who were trained, as I was, not to mistake the "I" in a poem for a real person. The training has its uses, but also its limitations. For most of the poems in this book, academic distinctions between the self and what we in the classroom call the "persona" move to vanishing point. When a woman poet today says "I," she is likely to mean herself, as intensely as her verbal skills permit, much as Wordsworth or Keats did, or Blake, or Milton, or John Donne of the Holy Sonnets, before Eliot's "extinction of personality" became the mandatory twentieth-century initiation ritual for young American poets, and before the death of the author became a popular critical fiction. (*SL*, p. 12)

Ostriker takes the intentions of her poets seriously; the poem may not, and often does not for Ostriker, add up to only what the poet intended. Yet the author is also on stage in the poem. This does not, however, mean—as it does for Bennett's most approved models—that in the best poems women have discarded their masks. Neither does it mean that the best women poets—in a Barthesian mode of playfulness—exploit the freedom of knowing the inevitability of masking. Ostriker says, "When masks and disguises govern the poems, . . . it is not to entertain us but because the mask has grown into the flesh." Furthermore, for Ostriker there is no true self or core of identity to which we can refer the final meaning of a poem. "The split selves in women's poems are both true, both false" (*SL*, pp. 12, 84).

However, rather than locating multiplicity as inevitable in all subjective and literary spaces, she implies that this is a special disadvantage of the feminine: "the division reflects and is reinforced by our culture's limited images of feminine personality" (*SL*, p. 84). For my part, I think it important to accept the notion of all authorial subjectivities as plural while at the same time disentangling the modes of subjectivity available to different groups at different times. For me, the personae that function in the first-person pronouns of John Milton and John Donne must differ from those of William Blake and John Keats, because subjectivity in the seventeenth century meant something different from what it meant in the nineteenth century or means in our own day. Furthermore, I think we still need to explore an individual poem's connections to its cultural setting, its invocation of conventions, and projection of an illusion of self. Though I admire Ostriker's work a great deal, I am perhaps more of a Foucauldian than she.

In what amounts to an attack on male author-centered critics of the mid-twentieth century, Montefiore assigns to romanticism the notion that the author/poet is "a transcendent subject representing the 'human spirit,' " but she finds such romanticism also broadly represented in American women poets like Edna St. Vincent Millay and Adrienne Rich. Millay's conception of the poetic is "that poetry is the articulation of a straightforward subjectivity ('the expression of profoundly felt personal experience')" (*FP*, p. 124). Criticizing Millay as romantic also means that Montefiore parts company with those feminist critics who have attempted to trace the role of literary expressions in bringing to consciousness conflicts buried in the poet's psyche, critics like Bennett, Ostriker, Gilbert and Gubar, and myself. "To begin with a literary-critical point, the assumption that the significance of a poem is to be identified with the experience and consciousness of the poet is always debatable, because it is the poems which are available to us, not the poet's mind" (*FP*, p. 5). She refers us to that old chestnut, "The Intentional Fallacy" by W.K. Wimsatt and Monroe C. Beardsley, and also to Barthes's essay, "The Death of the Author."[16]

Feminism and Poetry is, in fact, an extended argument against author-centered criticism involving a number of points. First, Montefiore says that such criticism often ignores the specific linguistic characteristics of poems. "No other kind of writing holds its own words up to the light as poetry does." Second, she finds such criticism narrow: "criticism based on the assumption that what makes a poem valuable and interesting is its author's awareness, enacted within it, of her own dilemma as a woman (which in practice generally means her sexual/domestic life) risks reducing everything to the personal" (*FP*, pp. 6, 5). Finally, Montefiore believes that such criticism ignores many problematic aspects of poems, their ambiguity, contradictoriness, open-endedness, complicity with patriarchy, though why persons should be less ambiguous, contradictory, or open-ended than poems remains obscure.

But in paying little attention to biographical or historical contexts, since they "would explain some of the causes of the poems, not their textual effects" (*FP*, p. 134), Montefiore falls into another trap: that of assuming that the poems are "available to us" (that is, are texts) while the cultures and poets themselves remain unavailable (that is, are something other than texts). A critic whose practice is committed to many sets of textual juxtapositions (biographical, cultural, historical) may find Montefiore's work limited in scope and naive about its own formalistic assumptions.

Still, Montefiore, like Margaret Homans whom she admires, is adept at investigating ideological contradictions and linguistic ambiguities.[17] Her stance gives her a certain latitude [*sic*] within feminism not shared by others. She can admire a poem (like Sylvia Townsend Warner's "Drawing you, heavy with sleep to draw closer") that does not transcend the assumptions of patriarchy. She can appreciate Dickinson's range of poems, calling them "too ambiguous and contradictory to be read as purely woman-centered texts" (*FP*, p. 175). Even more interesting, she can relentlessly attack Rich's statements and intentions while clearly (because consistently) preferring her above all contemporary others. In a reading of "Twenty-One Love Poems," Montefiore writes, "Like many of Rich's best poems, this purports to re-create experience straightforwardly, but actually creates a fable" (*FP*, p. 163). So much for the author's intentions and for the poet's experience as the locus of the poem.

On its own ground, Montefiore's criticism is very shrewd. Where she uses French theory, as she frequently does, to critique essentialist assumptions and the notion of a female space outside history, I find her work quite convincing. However, there are many aspects of the relation between author and text that her critical practice will not illuminate, like the multiple contexts of reading and writing that LaCapra does such a good job of enumerating.

Kaplan, a feminist Marxist critic, comes much closer to my own brand of cultural criticism in her insistence on reading women's work as statements about actual women's experiences in history while not sliding over the contradictoriness and opacity of such works as information about the writer's psyche. Kaplan says:

Women's fiction and poetry is a site where women [have] actively structured the meaning of sexual difference in their society, especially and powerfully as it [has] applied to difference between women. . . . [T]hese writings properly considered undermine the programmatic way in which bourgeois ideology is used as a shorthand by male marxist critics for a unified, genderless, hegemonic system of ideas. (*SC*, p. 3)

Kaplan constantly interrogates her own political ideologies—Marxist and feminist—illustrating the gaps and contradictions in the ways these ideologies are currently structured. She finds that literature has a lot to say to politics, about the need to reconceptualize Marxism, for instance. Her authors are present and active, intervening in culture though often drawn back into collusion with oppressive cultural practices.[18]

For Kaplan, the engagement of feminism with theory has had considerable effect on critical practice and has been one of the principal factors preventing French structuralist, psychoanalytic, linguistic, and political analysis from being entirely transformed and depoliticized outside of France. However, the usefulness of theory does not mean advocating the death of the author.

Kaplan does not specifically address the idea of the death of the author. Nevertheless, implicit in her analyses is a revised conception of author-function. She applauds Ellen Moers as a critic because "she does not attempt to prove anything about Christina Rossetti's individual experience" (*SC*, p. 104). Writers have intentions ("these complex lyrics of Rossetti and Dickinson were designed to circumvent the resistance of writer and reader" [*SC*, p. 114]), but poems are not reducible to intentionality. Indeed, as Anne Sexton (and Elinor Wylie) proclaimed, the writer may not *want* to know exactly what she is saying in a poem.[19]

Addressing Elizabeth Barrett Browning's *Aurora Leigh*, Kaplan is perfectly ready to say that the poem memorializes Browning's own troubled history, but the point of Kaplan's argument is not to heroinize Browning as much as it is to revise a whole strand of feminist criticism. Kaplan argues that the text suggests that "daughters cannot be constructed wholly as social and psychic victims of their fathers or their fathers as wholly unregenerate villains." Furthermore, "the family romance woven through *Aurora Leigh* is only one strand of this rich poem" (*SC*, pp. 211, 210).

The essential components of Kaplan's view of authorship are the following: (1) Literary texts *have* (rather than *are*) authors. (2) Authors are never full subjective presences because of the fluid nature of subjectivity. (3) Both psychoanalysis and sociopolitical criticism that engages the author's experience in culture can be useful in interpreting texts, though texts are not reducible to such interpretations. (4) One important function of criticism is to see how ideology emerges in the context of a specific historical text *or* subjectivity, which is simultaneously social and psychic. (5) None of Barthes's so-called hypostases (author, society, history, psyche) are unified or totalizing in their effects, and we can understand more clearly the complexity of culture and psyche by reading literature. A fine summary of Kaplan's position may be found in her presentation of one of the values of fiction.

Literary texts give these simultaneous inscriptions narrative form, pointing towards and opening up the fragmentary nature of social and psychic identity, drawing out the ways in which social meaning is psychically represented. . . . Literary texts tell us more about the intersection of class and gender than we can learn from duly noting the material circumstances and social constraints of characters and authors. (*SC*, p. 167)

3

At this point it may seem unnecessary, given my evident admiration for Kaplan's approach to authorship, to proceed any further. However, I have two reasons for wanting to do so. First, since Kaplan does not directly engage "the death of the author," it seems to me worthwhile to formulate the dialogue between postmodernism and feminism emergent from her work. Second, I wish to expand Kaplan's implicit argument for retaining the author-function by adding my own theoretical response to Foucault's question: "What difference does it make who is speaking?"

To return to my introductory summary of post-structuralism's position on the death of the author given in Barthes and Foucault, we might usefully ask: what precisely was killed off in the late 1960s when the death of the author was first articulated by French theorists? For Barthes, it was any attempt "to impose a limit on that text, to furnish it with a final signified, to close the writing." Pondering a sentence in Balzac, Barthes insists: "No one, no 'person', says it: its source, its voice, is not the true place of the writing, which is reading." But in theory the reader is without attributes: "yet this destination cannot any longer be personal: the reader is without history, biography, psychology; he is simply that *someone* who holds together in a single field all the traces by which the given text is constituted" ("DA," pp. 147, 148).

For Barthes, then, what is killed off with the author is any specific historical subjectivity *as a determining factor* in textuality. Let us not fall into the trap of misunderstanding his purpose, however. Barthes does not deny that there are authors (he calls them scriptors); he does not insist that real readers have no personalities or historical circumstances. Such assertions would obviously be absurd. What he is claiming is that a proper theory of the text does not make its meaning *depend* on authors as unified subjectivities or on readers given individual characteristics. Readers make unities out of texts but a text itself is "made up of multiple writings, drawn from many cultures and entering into mutual relations of dialogue, parody, contestation" ("DA," p. 148). In terms of a theory of the text, its unity emerges in readings and can always be reinterpreted.

This is, in fact, far less radical or objectionable than it has been interpreted to be. It simply has the limitations of many theoretical statements. It doesn't address a whole range of issues one may well feel are worth addressing. What it does address is a certain authoritarian critical climate in which "the real meaning" of a text was deciphered either in terms of a unified conception of the author's subjectivity or in terms of a specific kind of reader.

Barthes's essay is short and pithy. Foucault clearly felt it worthwhile the following year to expand on it. To my mind, Foucault's essay is both more and less satisfying than Barthes's. Foucault agrees with Barthes on all the basic issues except that Barthes implies that there is no point in talking about authors at all while Foucault preserves the author-function as characteristic of a historical present in criticism though a critical function in need of interrogation. Though in Foucault, "one has already called back into question the absolute character and founding role of the subject" as author, he goes on to say: "Still, perhaps one must return to this question, not in order to reestablish the theme of an originating subject, but to grasp the subject's points of insertion, modes of functioning, and system of dependencies" ("WIA," p. 118). This will lead to a new set of questions, questions that involve, as we might expect in Foucault, politics and power relations. "What are the modes of existence of this discourse? Where has it been used, how can it circulate, and who can appropriate it for himself? What are the places in it where there is room for possible subjects? Who can assume these various subject functions?" ("WIA," p. 120).

These are important questions, I would argue, and ones that do not emerge from Barthes's discussion. However, Barthes does not provide hermeneutic guidelines but merely offers a theory about the way writing functions as text. Even Barthes says we can follow up leads in disentangling a text—"the structure can be followed, 'run' (like the thread of a stocking) at every point and at every level, but there is nothing beneath" ("DA," p. 147). Foucault actually says that textuality is political but then seems, in his last words, to deny the significance of politics: "And behind all these questions, we would hear hardly anything but the stirring of an indifference: What difference does it make who is speaking?" ("WIA," p. 120).

Kaplan, in her implicit dialogue with Barthes and Foucault, seems to agree with some points and disagree with others. Authors do not originate texts in the sense that God originates ex nihilo. Still, authors are possible subjectivities whom we may consider as contradictory, fluctuating presences in the text, which she calls significantly a "site." Kaplan is open about her political project as a Marxist critic. She therefore tells us that she is reading not for ultimate meaning but for positional meanings. Feminism and Marxism are alike in fostering such readings.

Kaplan retains all of Foucault's questions about the relevance of author-function to understanding culture. Yet it remains possible in Kaplan's practice to talk about authors as historical agents of cultural criticism and change. The author does exist outside of the writing, has a life (as Browning has a family). It seems to me important to say, as many seem unwilling to do, that this cannot be reconciled with a certain brand of deconstructive criticism that would leave no significant place for authors as functional particularities.[20]

This leads me to my own position on author-function, which I feel supplements Kaplan's in important ways. My problems with Barthes and Foucault certainly do not have to do with the notion that we cannot fix an ultimate meaning through interpretation. Few would dispute that. However, a small point turns into a big point concerning the masculine pronoun used everywhere as representative in their work. Authors and readers are both masculine for Barthes and Foucault.

To Barthes I would want to say, writing is not "the destruction of every voice" but *the proliferation of possibilities of hearing*. I intend this statement as a feminist reversal of Barthes, as Nelle Morton writes that feminist practice involves "hearing one another to speech."[21] To say this, it seems to me, is a way of calling into question the impersonality of Barthes at both the level of his abstract formulations and the level of his linguistic practice, his generic masculine pronouns that obscure the differences among writers and readers.

In Foucault I puzzle over the following statement: "Using all the contrivances that he sets up between himself and what he writes, the writing subject cancels out the signs of his particular individuality. As a result, the mark of the writer is reduced to nothing more than the singularity of his absence; he must assume the role of the dead man in the game of writing" ("WIA," pp. 102–3). Does this work equally well with all writers? Here it seems to me the difference between writing subjectivities is crucial. For H.D., for instance, writing does not place her in the position of the dead man for "she herself is the writing," as she said in one work, and the choice for her is to "write, write or die,"[22] not to write *and* die, as Foucault says is now customary.

Postmodernism has certainly made us aware that we cannot locate full presence anywhere, whether in the psyche, in history, in culture, or in the text. However, presence must be distinguished from what has replaced it. Though there is no presence behind a text, there is an infinite number of presences, or traces, in a given text. One of these presences is the author, about whom we cannot know everything (whose mind is not fully available to us, as Montefiore says). But the text is not present to us outside of interpretation either. There are always questions remaining about any complex text and many "texts" to consider. The success of our intertextual tracings of author in relation to literature will be determined by our readers. Some readers are not interested in the sociological contexts of text construction, but many are, as a recent issue of *Critical Inquiry* devoted to the sociology of literature attests.

In this issue, Robert Weimann makes a valuable (though somewhat impacted) statement at the beginning of his article, "Text, Author-Function, and Appropriation in Modern Narrative: Toward a Sociology of Representation." He says, in effect, that in order to explore the contradictions between textual performance and what might seem to be its determining factors (psyche, history, society, culture), we need a multileveled exploration of textual history, looking "not only on the level of what is represented (which would reduce this project to some genealogy of the signified) but also on the level of who or what is representing." The interdependence of these various levels as well as the disjunction between them is significant to a sociological study of representation.[23]

If it makes sense to ask who or what is representing, under what conditions, with what set of concerns, and so on, it also makes sense to consider how the relation between author and reader differs under different social circumstances. Miller quotes Jonathan Culler on this issue: " '*For a woman to read as a woman is not to repeat an identity or an experience that is given but to play a role she constructs with reference to her identity as a woman, which is also a construct, so that the series can continue: a woman reading as a woman reading as a woman*' " ("CS," p. 108).[24]

Third-world women and lesbians have been especially articulate about the importance of reading the work of authors who belong to disenfranchised groups with which they identify. Biddy Martin and Chandra Talpade Mohanty, for instance, raise the issue of author-function in their article "Feminist Politics: What's Home Got to Do with It?"[25] They acknowledge that their experience of reading Minnie Bruce Pratt, the subject of their essay, violates what they call "deconstructive" assumptions about reading and authorship. Pratt's text is conventional in that it collapses the distance between author and narrator, it conveys explicit author intentionality, and it claims personal and political authenticity. Having said this, however, Martin and Mohanty go on to say:

Our reading of Pratt's narrative contends that a so-called conventional narrative such as Pratt's is not only useful but essential in addressing the politically and theoretically urgent questions surrounding identity politics. Just as Pratt refuses the methodological imperative to distinguish between herself as actual biographical referent and her narrator, we have at points allowed ourselves to let our reading of the text speak for us.[26]

A leftist politics, as opposed to a theory, of reading should involve the sense of a legitimate relationship between author and reader as it does, for instance, in essays by Alice Walker, Sherley Anne Williams, Adrienne Rich, and Judy

Grahn.[27] This does not, of course, establish the author as precisely and uniformly the subjective presence her readers take her to be any more than it establishes the text's meaning as only the one assigned to it by such readers. Though I may not wish to treat texts as the private property of their authors, I am unwilling to lose the sense of vital links between women that only a practice which preserves authors in some form can provide.

My own brand of *persona criticism* assumes that to erase a woman poet as the author of her poems in favor of an abstract indeterminacy is an act of oppression. However, every version of the persona will be a mask of the author we cannot lightly remove. When one discovers the proliferation of a certain kind of mask in a given poet (the mask of the passionate virgin in Sara Teasdale, for instance), it is interesting to me to ask: What social configurations of the feminine might have led to this mask? Why did so many women readers of the 1920s delight in it? How representative is this mask and what contradicts it? How can I use my insights about the way masks function in women poets to illuminate previously obscure dimensions of women's history and women's relation to language, authorship, creativity, identity?

We all know that many voices are speaking simultaneously in the poems we read. When I read I am, in a sense, rewriting the poem to suit my own political agenda, but that doesn't necessarily mean that I will construct the poem to duplicate my politics; I may be as likely to hear a patriarchal voice as a feminist one. Or I may feel the poem is interesting precisely because it attempts to evade political analysis.

Ideology will also govern our construction of the author, especially but not only if the author becomes *un sujet à aimer*, a someone to love. Yes, I want to ask like Foucault "What difference does it make who is speaking?" But I want to answer, the difference it makes, in terms of the voices I can persuade you are speaking, occupies a crucial position in the ongoing discussion of difference itself.

NOTES

For advice on this essay, I wish to thank Francés McConnel, John Peavoy, Elizabeth Minnich, and Marilyn Edelstein. I also owe a debt of gratitude to Walter Benn Michaels, who started me down this path by forcing me to rethink my own naive assumptions about authors.

1. Michel Foucault, "What Is an Author?" trans. Josué V. Harari, in *The Foucault Reader*, ed. Paul Rabinow (New York, 1984), p. 120 [p. 22]; hereafter abbreviated "WIA."

2. See Roland Barthes, "The Death of the Author," *Image, Music, Text*, trans. Stephen Heath (New York, 1977), pp. 142–48 [pp. 3–7]; hereafter abbreviated "DA." For Jacques Derrida's conception of the role of the subject, see his *Of Grammatology*, trans. Gayatri Chakravorty Spivak (Baltimore, 1976); "Structure, Sign and Play in the Discourse of the Human Sciences," trans. Alan Bass, in *Critical Theory Since 1965*, ed. Hazard Adams and Leroy Searle (Tallahassee, Fla., 1986), pp. 83–94; and *Limited Inc* (Evanston, Ill., 1988).

3. Toril Moi, *Sexual/Textual Politics: Feminist Literary Theory* (London and New York, 1985), pp. 62–63; hereafter abbreviated *STP*.

4. See Edward W. Said, *Beginnings: Intention and Method* (New York, 1975), p. 162.

5. Gayle Greene and Coppélia Kahn, "Feminist Scholarship and the Social Construction of Woman," in *Making a Difference: Feminist Literary Criticism*, ed. Greene and Kahn (London and New York, 1985), p. 25; also see pp. 27–28. The interpolated statements are from Catherine Belsey, *Critical Practice* (London and New York, 1980), pp. 136, 134.

6. Nancy K. Miller disagrees with Foucault about the possibility of finding a language site outside bourgeois ideology. Since she appears to agree with Barthes that no such site exists, she finds appealing certain metaphors of stealing and disguise in order to suggest the need for reforming the dominant text. See Miller, "Changing the Subject: Authorship, Writing, and the Reader," in *Feminist Studies/Critical Studies*, ed. Teresa de Lauretis (Bloomington, Ind., 1986), pp. 102–20, esp. p. 111; hereafter abbreviated "CS."

7. See Steven Knapp and Walter Benn Michaels, "Against Theory," in *Against Theory: Literary Studies and the New Pragmatism*, ed. W.J.T. Mitchell (Chicago, 1985), pp. 11–30, and Knapp and Michaels, "Against Theory 2: Hermeneutics and Deconstruction," *Critical Inquiry* 14 (Autumn 1987): 49–68. Knapp and Michaels make a radical argument that a text has only one meaning, the meaning its author intends, and that that meaning never changes. The only point of literary criticism is to figure out what the author intended.

8. Moi's argument is different. Since she believes that author-critics have engaged in an imperialist attempt to repress, undermine, overwhelm, or otherwise colonize the freedom of interpretation, we must get rid of all versions of the author, male or female.

9. De Lauretis makes an interesting assessment of Miller in her introduction to *Feminist Studies/Critical Studies* where she says that Miller is a keen observer of the "double temporality of intellectual history, which unfolds concurrently—and discontinuously—in 'women's time' of feminist criticism and in 'the Eastern Standard time' of traditional scholarship" (de Lauretis, "Feminist Studies/Critical Studies: Issues, Terms, and Contexts," in *Feminist Studies/Critical Studies*, p. 16).

10. See Derrida, "Like the Sound of the Sea Deep within a Shell: Paul de Man's War," trans. Peggy Kamuf, *Critical Inquiry* 14 (Spring 1988): 590–652. The Summer 1989 issue of *Critical Inquiry* contains responses to this essay.

11. See "DA," p. 147.

12. See Hayden White, *Metahistory: The Historical Imagination in Nineteenth-Century Europe* (Baltimore, 1973). See also Dominick LaCapra, *History and Criticism* (Ithaca, N.Y., 1985), and his more recent *History, Politics, and the Novel* (Ithaca, N.Y., 1987).

13. LaCapra, "History and the Novel," *History and Criticism*, p. 127.

14. See Paula Bennett, *My Life A Loaded Gun: Female Creativity and Feminist Poetics* (Boston, 1986); Cora Kaplan, *Sea Changes: Essays on Culture and Feminism* (London, 1986), hereafter abbreviated *SC*; Alicia Suskin Ostriker, *Stealing the Language: The Emergence of Women's Poetry in America* (Boston, 1986), hereafter abbreviated *SL*; and Jan Montefiore, *Feminism and Poetry: Language, Experience, Identity in Women's Writing* (London and New York, 1987), hereafter abbreviated *FP*. For another comparison of Bennett and Ostriker, see my review of these two books in *Signs: Journal of Women in Culture and Society* 14 (Autumn 1988): 220–22.

15. Bennett, *My Life A Loaded Gun*, p. 11.

16. See W.K. Wimsatt, "The Intentional Fallacy," *The Verbal Icon: Studies in the Meaning of Poetry* (Lexington, Ky., 1954), pp. 3–18.

17. See Margaret Homans, *Women Writers and Poetic Identity: Dorothy Wordsworth, Emily Brontë, and Emily Dickinson* (Princeton, N.J., 1980), esp. pp. 216–18. Both Homans and Montefiore find the whole question of how women's experience becomes embodied in fictive language so perplexing that they prefer not to discuss any autobiographical traces in women's poems.

18. The most delightful aspects of *Sea Changes* for an American reader like me are the way the book embodies energies usefully deployed, the respect it pays to the successful agency of women writers, and the constant sense of Kaplan herself as peripatetic writer, teacher, cultural critic, and political activist. Such work can make one believe that literary criticism and the writing of poetry can *be* political practices in England, which one is rarely able to believe in the United States.

19. Kaplan quotes Anne Sexton as saying that her poems sometimes had a meaning so deep that she didn't want to know what it was (*SC*, p. 114). Similarly, Elinor Wylie saw in fictive language a way to avoid " 'the bitterness of being understood,' " but also "the bitterness of understanding" (Wylie, "Symbols in Literature," *Collected Prose of Elinor Wylie* [New York, 1933], pp. 878, 879).

20. Miller also makes some of these points but seems straining to prevent an open break with French theory. I have tried to be clearer about where I agree and disagree.

21. Nelle Morton, "A Word We Cannot Yet Speak," *The Journey Is Home* (Boston, 1985), p. 99. See "DA," p. 142.

22. These quotations, widely taken as representative of H.D.'s conception of authorship, are from *Helen in Egypt* (New York, 1961), p. 22, and *Hermetic Definition* (New York, 1972), p. 7.

23. See Robert Weimann, "Text, Author-Function, and Appropriation in Modern Narrative: Toward a Sociology of Representation," *Critical Inquiry* 14 (Spring 1988): 432.

24. The reference is to Jonathan Culler, *On Deconstruction: Theory and Criticism after Structuralism* (Ithaca, N.Y., 1982), p. 64.

25. See Biddy Martin and Chandra Talpade Mohanty, "Feminist Politics: What's Home Got to Do with It?" in *Feminist Studies/Critical Studies*, pp. 191–212.

26. Ibid., p. 194.

27. For examples of impassioned readings, see Alice Walker's *In Search of Our Mother's Gardens* (San Diego, 1983), and her dedication and afterword to *I Love Myself When I Am Laughing . . . And Then Again When I Am Looking Mean and Impressive: A Zora Neale Hurston Reader* (Old Westbury, N.Y., 1979); Sherley Anne Williams's foreword to Hurston's *Their Eyes Were Watching God* (Urbana, Ill., 1978); Adrienne Rich's essay about reading Judy Grahn, "Power and Danger: Works of a Common Woman," *On Lies, Secrets, and Silence: Selected Prose 1966–1978* (New York, 1979), pp. 247–58; and Judy Grahn, *The Highest Apple: Sappho and the Lesbian Poetic Tradition* (San Francisco, 1985), esp. pp. xvi and xxi.

CHAPTER 11

A Theory of the Author

Jorge J.E. Gracia

I. FUNCTION OF THE AUTHOR

A. Function of the Historical Author

The *historical author* is the subject who produced the historical text, that is, the historical artifact we call a text and that consists in certain entities used as signs and intended to convey a specific meaning to an audience in a certain context.[1]

The task of the historical author is to select and arrange the signs that compose a text to convey a specific meaning to an audience in a certain context. At least two important elements must be considered for the understanding of the function of a historical author. The first is the activity in which the author engages; the second is the object toward which that activity is directed.

Beginning with the second, we know that a text is a group of entities, used as signs, selected and arranged by an author to convey a specific meaning to an audience. We also know that the meaning is not the signs that are selected and arranged to express it. Finally, we know that the connection between the entities used as a text and the meaning of the text is conventional. So we may ask, For which of these is the historical author responsible? Is he responsible for the meaning? Is he responsible for the entities that compose the text? Is he responsible for the connection between entities and meaning? Or should we say that he is responsible for two of the three or for all three? With respect to the first, we may ask, What is entailed by the "selection and arrangement" of the signs and how is this to be related to the creativity generally attributed to historical authors? Our inquiry in fact amounts to the identification of what makes someone a historical author, that is, the necessary and sufficient conditions of a historical author, and thus entails further unpacking the general description that we have been using thus far of a historical author. Moreover, since the notion of historical author is a functional one, vis-à-vis texts, our inquiry will be restricted to a functional interpretation of that notion.

Let me begin with the notion of creation. This notion has been and still is much contested and discussed in philosophy.[2] Within the Judaeo-Christian theological context that stands behind Western discussions of this notion, creation is generally understood to involve both the production of something separate (*ad extra*) and also the production of something from nothing (*ex nihilo*). In the Western tradition, only the divinity is regarded as being able to create in this way. Human authors of texts, then, could not be taken to be creators in this sense. But there is also a secondary and less stringent understanding of creation. In this sense, to create is simply to produce something new (*de novo*) and separate, even if the production involves pre-existing materials. It is in the sense of creation *de novo* and *ad extra*, but not *ex nihilo*, that artists are said to create art objects; and it is in this sense that an author can be said to create a text. The historical author of a text produces something new and separate out of pre-existing materials.

That a text is something separate from the historical author appears to pose no serious difficulties at the outset. Most texts are objects that enjoy an existence independent of their historical authors and often exist long after their historical authors have ceased to exist. There is a category of texts, however, whose separateness is not as clear; namely, mental texts. Mental texts appear to depend on the author for their existence, and furthermore, they seem to be part of the author in some way.

I would like to argue, however, that in spite of the relation of dependence a mental text may have on the mind of the historical author or anyone else who might be able to think it, it also has an objective status that distinguishes it from the author's mind and thus may be considered separate from it in this sense. Historical authors are related to texts, including texts that have never left their minds, as subjects are related to objects, and as such texts are something other than subjects even if they depend on subjects for their existence. This is all that is needed to maintain that a text is separate from its historical author and thus that it is produced *ad extra*. For, although there may not be any physical separation between the two—indeed if we are dealing with a mind and a mental text there could not be one—a text and its historical author are still distinct entities. That this is so may be easily illustrated by considering that one can imagine the transference of a mental text from one mind into another. If we think of minds as TV monitors and of mental texts as the images they reproduce, it is obvious that several minds can have the same image simultaneously or at different times.[3]

The novelty of a text is more difficult to explain than its separateness. The first thing that needs to be said is that, although there may be some merit in the view that creation *ex nihilo* entails creation *de novo*, there is no merit in the contrary position: Novelty does not require production out of nothing. But if creation *de novo* does not entail creation *ex nihilo*, what does it entail? It need entail no more than the creation of something different from what was already there, so that novelty involves a kind of difference.[4]

Differences come in a wide variety and not all of them need be regarded as pertinent to the novelty of a text. Only some of them are sufficient for a text not to be the same as some other text. Moreover, the ways in which difference is measured depend in turn on whether the text in question is universal, say, the universal text of *Don Quixote*, or instances of that universal, say, copies of the text of *Don Quixote*. The differences that count as far as the universal text is concerned are differences of meaning, syntactical arrangement, and type-sign composition. Some changes in audience and author are sufficiently significant to allow us to speak of "a new text." But these modifications have to be of the sort that change the meaning of the text.[5]

The differences that count as far as an individual text is concerned are the differences relevant for the universal text of which the individual is an instance in addition to conditions of individuality and continuous existence. A new individual text is either one belonging to a different type from that of all other individual texts, or one that belongs to the same type as others but does not fulfill the condition of continuous existence.

Having established the conditions that make a text different and, therefore, new, we can now see in what sense a historical author is the creator of a text: To create a text is to produce a new text; thus a historical author is a creator of a text insofar as he produces a different text according to the specified ways.[6]

Strictly speaking, to be an author of a text entails that the author has created a new universal or a new individual text, but the element of novelty can appear in various areas.[7] In the case of universal texts, it is in the meaning, syntactical arrangement of the signs which compose the text, and the type-sign composition. In the case of individual texts, it is in those mentioned with regard to universal texts and those that affect individual identities such as individuality and continuous existence. An author may create a new universal text by giving new meaning to signs and arrangements already in use or by expressing an already known meaning with new signs or the new arrangements of signs already in use. This entails that the author of a text need not be regarded as creator of the meaning of a text or even of the relation between that meaning and the entities that constitute the text. Qua author, he need be considered creator only insofar as he is responsible for a text that is different from all other texts. Thus, an author of a text understood in the sense of creator of the text need not be considered the author of the work in cases where the meaning of the text is a work.[8] The work may be something already known. In this sense, for example, translators are the authors of the texts we call translations because they put together signs in new arrangements even though they express meanings already expressed by other signs. What has been said concerning universal texts and their relation to authors applies, *mutatis mutandis*, to individual texts.

At this point we encounter a difficulty, for we have been speaking of universal texts as well as their instances and of novelty in both. But, if universal texts neither exist nor are located in time or space, as I have argued elsewhere,[9] it is not clear how historical authors can function as creators of universal texts. It would seem to make sense to speak of historical authors as creators of individual texts, for both are historical entities that exist in a temporal or spatial dimension. But, does it make sense to speak of historical authors as creators of universal texts that are neither historical nor spatio-temporal in any sense? Yet, we do want to say, for example, that Cervantes created the text of *Don Quixote*, even though that text can be multiply instantiated and thus must be considered universal. The same problem arises with artistic and culinary creations; we want to say that a chef created a new soup if he created a new kind of soup or recipe for a soup.[10]

To answer this question we must note that a universal text, that is, the universal of the instances of a text, is not an entity distinct in reality from those instances. A universal and an instance of it are not two distinct things that require two distinct authors. The question of the authorship of a universal text as distinct from that of its instances should not come up if one keeps in mind the ontological character of universals. There is only one author of a text—of the universal and of its instances. There is one complication, however, for it is not the author of every instance of a text that is considered to be the author of a text. Indeed, if that were so there would be many authors of the same text, because different people may produce different instances of it. Only the agent who produced the first historical instance of a text (more on this later) is considered its author. The notion of historical author is a historical designation that refers to the relation of one historical phenomenon to other historical phenomena. There is a distinction between the agent who first produces an instance of a universal text and those agents who produce subsequent instances, and this distinction gives rise to the view that universal texts have historical authors. In this sense, a historical author is the author of a universal text when he is the first one who considered the type of text of which he produced an instance. The others are not historical authors, because they are reproducing what someone else had already considered.[11]

Having stated that historical authors create texts *de novo* and *ad extra*, but not *ex nihilo*, and that authors create universal texts only insofar as they produce instances of them, one may want to ask whether in fact historical authors should be described as discoverers rather than creators of universal texts. Is their function not in fact to find something that was in a sense available all the time but that had never been noticed before? In this sense the author is only a person who reveals or discloses what was hidden or had gone unnoticed.

This conclusion does not follow from the understanding of authorship that has been presented here. It is true that considered from my position universal texts are neither created nor not created, because temporality, location, existence, and their contraries are not categories that apply to them. It makes no sense to speak of the creation of something that neither can exist nor cannot exist, and likewise with the other categories mentioned, for creation involves the notion of causing to exist at a certain time or location. In that sense historical authors cannot be creators of universal texts. But in that sense they cannot be discoverers of texts either, for the notion of discovery, just like the notion of creation, involves the notions of existence, temporality, and location. To discover something is to make known or display at a particular time or place something that already existed. But according to the view I hold, these categories do not apply to universal texts considered in themselves, so it makes as little sense to say that authors discover them as it does to say that authors create them. From this standpoint, universal texts do not seem to be created or discovered.

From another standpoint, however, matters look different. I have already argued that universal texts have authors and can be considered to be the creation of authors insofar as their instances have authors and have been created by them. So our question amounts to the question of whether the authors of the instances of universal texts are better described as discoverers rather than as creators. Hence, we need to determine which categories apply to those authors.

The situation with respect to instances of universal texts is quite different from the situation with respect to universal texts, for the categories of existence, temporality, and location apply to all of them, except mental texts, to which only the first two apply. In principle, individual texts can, therefore, be created and discovered insofar as the categories mentioned apply to them. The question, then, is whether their historical authors are best described as their creators or discoverers. To say that they are their creators is to say that they have produced something different that did not exist as such before; to say that they are discoverers is to say that they have uncovered something that existed before but was not known. The argument for discovery is based on the fact that individual texts are instances of universals and thus are preceded by them. But existence and temporality do not apply to universal texts and thus the precedence in question cannot be temporal or existential. It is not possible to argue that the existence of individual texts is preceded by the existence of the universal texts of which they are instances. Under these conditions the only alternative is to hold that the first historical instance of a universal text has not been discovered but, rather, has been created by its historical author. Now we can go back to universal texts and see that they too cannot be described as being discovered, for their instances are not discovered.

The understanding of the function of historical authors presented here makes room for the important distinction between author and user. To explain this distinction, let me go back to the main point of the discussion and note that the historical author of a text is the person responsible for the features that make a text different from other texts. The historical author creates a text insofar as he produces a textual artifact that is different from other textual artifacts either in meaning, syntactical arrangement, or sign-type composition. By contrast, those persons who use the text are not responsible for the features that make it different from other texts. The user of a text does not create a different text, but merely employs a text of which there is, or there has been, at least one previous instance.

Historical authors may also be users, since they are responsible for the differences in texts precisely because they wish to use the texts to convey some meaning. Very often texts are created and used simultaneously, as when someone uses an expression for the first time; but it is not the case that the creation of a text implies its use. Someone may, for example, create a text and not use it, as when a woman writes a poem for the man she loves and never gives it to him. Authors may also at times use texts after they have produced them, say, that the woman does after all give the poem to her lover. Finally, authors may be considered partial users insofar as most times the texts they produce are composed of linguistic signs and formulas already in use. A long novel may be composed of sentences and expressions, many of which are commonly used, even though the complete text of the novel is different from all other texts produced until the time such a text was created. Clearly, historical authors may be, and often are, users, but users need not be historical authors.

Note that I have restricted the discussion of author vs. user to universal texts, but something similar can be said concerning individual texts. Nothing philosophically interesting results from such a discussion, so I have omitted it.

Some philosophers want to reserve the notion of author of a text for those persons who also produce works, thus eliminating the creators of clever phrases and the like from the category.[12] I find this unacceptable, because the matter of what is or is not a work is a purely historical affair dependent on cultural conventions, and authorial creativity can be evident as much in a text of a work as in one that does not have a work.

It is also misleading to identify what I have called here the *historical author* with the *writer* of a text.[13] The notion of writer, like the notions of speaker and imaginer, are closer to the notion of user than to the notion of author. A writer is simply someone who produces a written text, and this need not imply that the text is original in any sense and therefore that the writer is its author. And the same can be said of speakers or imaginers of texts. At the same time, it is not the case that writers, speakers, and imaginers need be merely users, since the production of an original written text implies an author. The scrambling of these categories so typical of some of the literature on textuality is unfortunate, often resulting in confusion rather than enlightenment. Let me go back now to authors.

There is the possibility that more than one person may create instances of the same text, either simultaneously or at different times, independently of each other. In such a case, the question arises as to whether each of the persons in question is to be considered a historical author or only one of them, the others being users. Let me separate the two and restrict the number of persons and instances of texts to two for the sake of simplicity, although the principles involved may also apply, with appropriate modifications, to cases of more than two instances and persons.

Case 1. Two and only two instances of the same text are produced, and they are produced simultaneously by two persons independent of each other.

Case 2. Two and only two instances of the same text are produced, and they are produced at two different times by two persons independent of each other.

In Case 1 both persons fulfill the criteria of authorship; they have created a different and therefore new text. Both persons are authors of the text and both of them are equally and rightly so. This is not very different from what happens with scientific discoveries made simultaneously by scientists working independently of each other.[14] This means that in principle there can be many historical authors of the same text. By the "same" text is meant, of course, the "same type" of text, for the individual texts or instances are numerically different in each case. The condition of there being more than one author of the same text is that the authors in question be the first ones to have selected and arranged the group of signs that constitute the text to convey the specific meaning in question to the same type of audience in the same type of context. I say the "same type" of audience and context because it is sameness of type and not numerical sameness in these categories that is relevant for the preservation of meaning.

Thus, it is possible in principle, for example, that there be many historical authors of the text of *Don Quixote*, and I do not mean many collectively, in the way in which the American Declaration of Independence has many authors, but many authors distributively, in the way in which Cervantes is the historical author of the text of *Don Quixote* and Shakespeare is the author of the text of *Hamlet*. But this possibility is merely logical. If it were to be realized, there would have to be not only sameness of signs and syntactical arrangement, but also sameness of type of context and audience insofar as these may affect the meaning of the text, and the fulfillment of all these conditions does not seem likely. Indeed, the different historical authors who would compose the text of *Don Quixote*, for example, would themselves most likely have different features that might affect the way they view the meaning of the text they compose. For different persons to be authors of the same type of text, they would have to have the same relevant types of features themselves as well as be placed in the same types of circumstances, even though they would not have to be numerically the same. And such requirements seem to be very difficult—indeed impossible from the practical standpoint—to meet. For all intents and purposes, then, it would seem that each text has only one historical author, although this applies only to long and complicated texts. The possibility of having many authors of the same text increases proportionally as their length and complexity decrease. It is altogether possible that many instances of the text "Please do not smoke" were first produced independently by many historical authors at the same time. Several persons may have reacted that way at the English Court when someone first brought tobacco to England from the Americas via Spain.

Case 1 suggests the logical possibility of there being more than one simultaneous historical author of a text, but our discussion illustrates the difficulties of actualizing such a possibility. Case 2 raises a similar point but in a situation where the production of the text by two different authors working independently of each other is not simultaneous. Do we have one or two authors, then? If two persons at two different times produce two instances of the same text independently and the text is different from all other texts, it would seem reasonable to conclude that they both are authors of the same text. Indeed, if this is possible for all texts and even likely for short and simple ones (as in Case 1), it would seem even more obvious in Case 2, where the persons in question work separately not only in terms of space but also of time.

Yet, something seems to be wrong with regarding someone as a historical author of a text when another instance of the text has already been produced previously by someone else, even if such production is carried out without knowledge of the existence of that instance. Let us take an example from the arts and suppose that someone, unacquainted with Picasso's *The Old Guitarist*, were to produce a painting exactly like that of Picasso. Would we call the second *The Old Guitarist* an original painting? Would we value it as we value Picasso's painting? Most of us would be inclined to answer negatively. But why, and how are we to reconcile this answer with the claim of authorship by both persons?

The point, of course, is that someone who produces an instance of a text of which other instances have been produced without knowledge of those instances is a creator of the text insofar as he has produced something new within his experience, but cannot be considered its historical author because he has not produced something new within a larger collective experience. Someone else has prior claim to novelty in the larger context. This indicates that authorship is historical and contextual. To be a historical author entails the creation of something new at a certain time in history and within a particular set of circumstances. Novelty, within or without the realm of textuality, is a historical phenomenon.

Moreover, there is another reason on the basis of which one may doubt there can be two authors of the same text under the conditions specified in Case 2: when the text is long and complex. History does not repeat itself and, for as long and as complicated a text to be produced at two different times, such repetition would be required because textual identity would presuppose identity in context, audience, and so on. This does not appear to be logically impossible, but the factual impossibility at least in the case of long and complicated texts appears to be quite an obstacle.

In conclusion, the function of the historical author of a text, qua historical author, is to produce a text that differs, qua text, from all others. There may be more than one historical author of a text distributively, although it is unlikely that long and complicated texts have more than one historical author. On the other hand, there is no reason why the historical author of a text may not be more than one person. Certainly the text of the American Declaration of Independence was the result of the work of several persons who produced it and thus cannot be considered to have only one author. Nor are historical authors prevented from also being users of texts, including those they compose.

A text, indeed, may have many users. Every time we quote a poet or use a cliché we are using texts whose historical authors are other than we. But that is something that does not need further explanation. Perhaps, however, it may be in order to add here the rather obvious point that to use a text does not necessarily imply plagiarism. Plagiarism involves the misrepresentation of ourselves as authors of texts. Users of texts are not plagiarists unless they represent themselves as the historical authors of the texts in question.

Moreover, with respect to quoting, perhaps we should make clear that in some circumstances, quoting involves the kind of creativity characteristic of authors rather than users. If a text is taken out of context and its meaning changed, then the person who quotes the text is acting as an interpretative author rather than as a mere user of the text, for the result is not an instance of the universal historical text but rather an instance of a new text that happens to have in common with the historical text the same type of constituting entities (ECTs).

Finally, let me also draw attention to the distinction between *historical author* and *translator*. This distinction had been generally well respected until recently, when the suggestion has been made that translators are in some sense authors. This view is concordant in many ways with the position I have defended, according to which the historical author of a text is the person responsible for creating a new (universal) text. Thus, translators, insofar as they produce a different composition and arrangement of signs from the original one, even if the meaning of the text is the same, are historical authors. They are historical authors of the translation of the text, which of course is also a text; but they are historical authors neither of the historical text nor of the work. They are not historical authors of the historical text because they are not responsible for the type of artifact used by the historical author to convey the meaning he intended to convey. And they are not historical authors of the work for two reasons: first, because the work is the meaning of the text and that is supposed to be the same for the historical text and its translation; second, because whether the person responsible for that meaning is the author of the historical text or not, the historical author of the translation is not the author of that meaning.

A translation itself is a historical text, for it has a historical author and was produced at some point in time. But the historical text that is the translation should not be confused with the historical text of the work which has been translated.

Translators, then, are historical authors, but only of the translations, not of the historical texts of the works they translate. Moreover, their originality is restricted to the choice and arrangements of the signs they use in place of the signs and arrangements used by the historical author of the historical text of the work they translate, and even there it is limited, for the choice of signs and their arrangements is dictated to a great extent by the meaning that is to be conveyed. Indeed, translators try to communicate meanings and works to persons who cannot understand the texts of historical authors. To that extent, they are in many ways interpreters, and translations are interpretations. Translators are authors to some extent, but they cannot be considered on equal footing with the historical authors of the texts they translate.[15]

[B]. Function of the Pseudo-Historical Author[16]

The *pseudo-historical author* may be understood in two ways. In one way, he is simply a composite of what we know or think we know about a historical author independent of what the historical author wishes others to think concerning the composer of the text.[17] In another way, the pseudo-historical author is the persona whom the historical author wishes others to think composed the text.[18] In either case, the pseudo-historical author, unlike the historical author, never existed as a real person.[19] The pseudo-historical author is the persona an audience believes, or is intended to believe, is the historical author of a text. As such, it is generally mythical, although it may approximate in various ways the historical author.

As a more-or-less accurate view of the historical author, the pseudo-historical author cannot be considered to have created anything in fact, even though he is presented precisely as the creator of the historical text. The function of this author is primarily epistemological. The pseudo-historical author is supposed to help us understand—even if it may just do the opposite in some cases—a text. Knowledge about the identity of an author is meant to aid us to figure out what the text means. The pseudo-historical author does not create anything and is not the cause of a text; he functions rather as one of the causes of the understanding an audience derives from a text insofar as he regulates and influences the understanding an audience derives from it.

There is one exception to this conclusion, however. When the pseudo-historical author is a dramatis persona in the text, his function is more than epistemic insofar as he is one of the factors that determines textual meaning and thus textual identity. Consider the case of Chaucer in *The Canterbury Tales*, where he plays the role of author and pilgrim, creating, reporting, and affecting the tales. In situations such as this, the pseudo-historical author functions both epistemically and ontologically.[20]

II. NEED FOR AN AUTHOR

The question of whether texts have authors has been explicitly raised only recently. Indeed, from a commonsense point of view it would seem that if there is a text there must be or must have been an author that produced it,[21] although the existence of an author is not sufficient to make something a text. We refer to art objects, tools, and other artifacts as well as to thoughts, ideas, and actions as having authors, but these objects are not necessarily texts. If they turn out to be texts, it is not solely in virtue of the fact that they have authors but owing to other factors as well. The view that having an author is not what determines that something be a text, however, is not the one under fire in contemporary circles. Rather, the view that has recently been attacked holds that authors are necessary for texts, that is, that there can be no texts without authors. The attackers fall into two groups. The most radical position argues that texts never have authors.[22] A less radical point of view maintains that, although some texts have authors, not all texts have them.[23]

Various factors have fueled the recent interest in the view that texts, or at least some texts, do not have authors. One such factor is the often noticed point that not only texts but also their meanings are independent of the authors that compose them. Texts have a "life," to use a standard metaphor, and an existence of their own after they are created that has very little to do with those who create them. Their creators may in fact die while the texts remain and continue to exert direct influence on audiences. Most old texts, as opposed to recently produced texts, fall into this category. Also along these lines, it is noted that often we understand the meaning of a text without knowing anything about its author. This is most clearly the case with simple, ordinary texts, such as the "No smoking" sign posted in the classroom where I teach. There are scores of anonymous texts whose meaning is not seriously questioned in spite of our ignorance of who produced them. The text of the epic poem *El Cid*, for example, is one of them. Its language, structure, and nature make it a relatively easy text to understand, even though no one knows who put it together. Finally, there are cases where persons other than the author of a text understand the text better than the author. This is often the case with very complicated texts, for example, where commentators who have devoted their lives to studying these texts are sometimes thought to know more about them and their meanings than the authors who produced them. There can be better Aristotelians than Aristotle, if you like. These considerations fuel the speculation that authors are not necessary for texts. They also lead to another important point that results in the same conclusion; namely, that the meaning of a text has more to do with its audience than with its author. Indeed, some go so far as to say that the meaning of a text has nothing to do with the author but is solely up to the audience; the latter, rather than the author who composed the text, determines the meaning.[24]

More specific reasons can be given for the positions that only certain texts have authors or that no texts have authors. For example, one may wish to argue that it is certainly odd to speak of signs such as the words or letters of natural languages as having authors. And, indeed, it is odd to talk in this way, though the reason is not that the words and letters used in natural languages do not have authors, but rather that their authors are frequently anonymous—we do not know who they are—or these words and letters are the result of collective rather than individual efforts. We generally associate authorship with known persons and with individuals rather than groups. The case of the symbols used in artificial languages should help us see the point, for I doubt anyone would object to calling whoever produced an artificial language its author. If the person in question is not an author, what is he? A maker? A producer? An inventor? A discoverer? None of these terms seem to apply as well.

Similar sorts of reasonings probably are behind the view that notices and simple texts do not have authors. It is difficult to pinpoint the first person who combined the words 'no' and 'smoking' into the text 'No smoking' to convey the request that someone not smoke tobacco. Before tobacco was introduced in Europe, such combination may not have been in use and, if in use, it could not possibly have been used to mean what we mean by it today. Yet, someone must have been the first person (or persons) to have done this, which means that the text has an author in the general sense indicated.

It is not the length of a text, however, that may preclude it from having an author, for some very short texts, such as the Japanese poems known as haiku, are universally accepted as having authors. Earlier I referred to relative simplicity as another reason that may be given for certain texts lacking authors. But again a haiku can be quite simple. So it does not look as if the length, or the degree of complexity, has anything to do with whether a text has an author or not. Is there something, then, that is required of texts that have authors?

Another possibility is that only those texts capable of multiple interpretations have authors.[25] Now, this will not do as it stands, for any text can be the subject of multiple interpretations; even the most simple texts can be understood differently, whether correctly or incorrectly, by different people and in different contexts. The interpretations in question must be, if not correct, at least allowable. A text has an author, then, only if the text is of such a sort that it is legitimate for an audience to understand it in different ways.

Unfortunately, this view has at least one undesirable consequence: It excludes from the category of texts with authors scientific treatises that allow only one legitimate interpretation. I am thinking of such texts as Euclid's *Elements* and Newton's *Principia*. Those who composed these texts wanted to convey a very clear and specific message about the subject matter and not a variety of views about it. And the same can be said concerning shorter texts used in ordinary speech. When I ask my daughter "to open a window to let fresh air into a stuffy room" I mean exactly that I want her to open a window to let fresh air into a stuffy room and for someone else to understand what I say differently is to misunderstand it.

It cannot be, then, that only texts with a substantial range of legitimate interpretations can have authors. So, we are back at square one. It is true that it is quite different in many ways to be the author of the text of *Don Quixote* and the author of "No smoking." But the differences are a matter of degree. Fundamentally, those who produced both texts were engaged in the same kind of activity, the creation of something new. For that reason both texts can have authors.

The confusion associated with the question of whether texts require authors has to do in part with the complexity of the question and in part with what is meant by 'author.' Therefore, to bring some clarity to its discussion, we must examine it in the context of the various authors distinguished earlier.

A. Need for the Historical Author

Two questions having to do with the historical author should be distinguished to prevent confusion. The first asks whether it is possible for texts to exist without causes; the second asks whether it is possible for texts to exist although they do not have persons who intend to convey some specific meaning through them among their causes. The answer to the first question seems quite straightforward. It makes no more sense to hold that texts can exist without causes than that there is rain without something that produces it. No matter what entities are used to make up texts, whether artificial or natural, those entities and the texts they make up must have causes. Unless, like Hume, we are willing to challenge the whole notion of cause and to accept that there are entities with no causes, we must accept that texts too cannot exist without causes that bring them about.

The answer to the second question, by contrast, is not as easily determined. Some may wish to argue that, indeed, some texts are produced without the causal agency of persons who intend to convey some specific meaning through them. Various examples may be cited to support this argument, but I refer to only two.[26] One is the case of "found" texts. Consider the situation in which someone who is walking on the beach finds a group of pebbles arranged in the same way in which an English speaker would put them if he wished to form the text 'No smoking.' Granted, I have not heard of anyone finding such an arrangement of pebbles and, indeed, it seems difficult even to imagine that the arrangement would occur naturally, without the intentional operation of a subject. But it is certainly logically possible for this to happen. A combination of high winds, tides, and so on could in principle produce the arrangement in question. And if that is the case, so goes the argument, then we have an instance of a text in whose production persons have not played a role.[27]

At the outset it appears as if there were only two ways of answering this objection. One is to deny that the arrangement of pebbles on the beach is a text; the other is to find an author for the arrangement. But both of these alternatives run into difficulties. The first alternative has to account for the fact that a person walking on the beach got meaning out of the arrangement. The second has to contend with the problem that no person produced the arrangement. Must we then acknowledge that historical authors are not always necessary for texts?

I would like to propose a different way out of this dilemma, based on the distinction between the entities that constitute a text (ECTS) and a text itself.[28] The entities that constitute a text are whatever is used to convey meaning, considered apart from both the meaning and the fact that the entities convey this meaning. Examples of these entities are the pebbles on a beach about which we have been speaking, or any other physical or mental entities that constitute texts. The text, by contrast, consists of those entities taken as conveyors of certain meanings. Now, since we have two sorts of things, the entities that constitute the text and the text itself, the causes that account for them need not be the same. In our example, the causes that produce the particular pebbles and their arrangement on the beach need not be the same as the causes that produce the text (that is, the pebbles and their arrangement understood as having a certain meaning). The meaning "No smoking" and its connection with the arranged pebbles was not produced by the wind and the tide. The cause of that meaning and its tie to the arranged pebbles is the result of whoever first connected the shapes and arrangement instantiated by the pebbles to the meaning. But then, we may ask, is the person walking on the beach the author of the text on the beach, for she seems to be the first to think of the pebbles and their arrangement as having meaning? Again we must distinguish. For, although she is the first who identified the individual pebbles and their arrangement found on the beach as having meaning, she may not have been the first to have connected the particular sort of arrangement the pebbles display to this particular meaning. If she understood the arrangement of the pebbles to mean "No smoking" because she already knew that this certain arrangement meant "No smoking," then she is not the author of the text. She is not the author of the text insofar as she did not first make the connection in question. She is rather a user, for she uses what is already available.

This case is quite different from cases where a person takes a natural object and uses it as a text by stipulatively connecting it to a meaning. In such a case, the person who makes the connection is obviously the author, and thus this sort of case poses no difficulty for the view I have been defending here. This sort of situation is similar to the case of "found art," where, for example, a piece of driftwood is picked up by someone at the beach. The piece of driftwood is an aesthetic object that, for this reason, attracts the attention of a person who then uses it as an art object by displaying it on the mantelpiece. The artist in this case is the person who picked up the piece of driftwood and displays it, even though it was nature which produced the object that has become art.[29]

In short, we need not deny that the arrangement of pebbles on the beach constitutes a text, nor must we identify the passerby as the author of the text, in order to hold that texts must have authors. For a text is not just the entities of which it is constituted, but rather those entities intended as conveyors of a certain meaning. In the example of the pebbles, the intention to convey a certain meaning with the particular arrangement exemplified by the pebbles belongs to whoever thinks of it first. The passerby need not be the author unless she is in fact the one who first establishes the connection between a particular arrangement of entities and a meaning. But an author there must be, for the connection in question is a matter of convention, not of nature, and conventions require persons to adopt them.[30]

In the case of the pebbles it is not too difficult to envision the passerby as the author of the text. This is so because seeing a text composed of pebbles on a beach involves a "creative" mental selection of what objects, features of objects, and arrangements available on the beach are significant and thus constitute the text. The proof of that process of mental selection is that not everyone may see the text. This is very similar to what happens when someone looks at a cloud and sees a camel or when a person looking at stars sees patterns in them, such as a big dipper. Selection and arrangement do not require physical alteration—remember, some texts are mental. But the passerby is not so easily identifiable as author in other cases.

A second example that may be used to impugn the need for causal agents is the proverbial example of the monkey who, given sufficient time, will eventually type a copy of Shakespeare's *Hamlet* by randomly hitting the keys of a typewriter. This may be taken as a counterexample to the proposed view because the monkey in question knows nothing about the meaning of the text it produces, does not have any knowledge of the signs of which it is composed or the semantic or syntactical significance of their arrangement, and has no intention to convey meaning. And yet, there it is: the magnificent text of *Hamlet*, typed by the monkey.

The very idea that a monkey would be able to produce the text of *Hamlet* is farfetched, and we all know that the probabilities in question are infinitesimal. But this observation will certainly not do away with the counterexample.[31]

Three alternative strategies suggest themselves at the outset to deal with it. The first is to deny that what the monkey has produced is in fact a text,[32] the second is to argue that the monkey is the author of the text,[33] and the third is to hold that whoever first got hold of the monkey's manuscript and understood it as *Hamlet* is the author.[34] But none of these alternatives appears to be *prima facie* satisfactory. The first does not appear to work because the object the monkey produced can be read and understood by anyone who knows English in the way one would read and understand any copy of the text of *Hamlet* produced by a person. The second alternative does not seem satisfactory because the monkey knows nothing about the meaning of what it has typed and, therefore, has no intention of communicating that or any other meaning. And the third does not appear acceptable because the author of *Hamlet* is not the person who found the monkey's typescript but Shakespeare.

Following what was said concerning the case of "found texts," one could try to develop a solution by distinguishing between the entities produced by the monkey and the text of *Hamlet*. The entities produced by the monkey consist of certain marks on a paper, whereas the text is made up of those marks insofar as they are intended to convey meaning. In this respect, the example is very similar to the one of the pebbles on the beach and can be analyzed in the same way. The monkey is the agent that produces the marks (the counterpart of the wind and the tides), the author of the text is Shakespeare, who first connected those marks to the work or meaning that we know as *Hamlet*, and the person who finds the monkey's typescript is merely a user of the text (the counterpart of the walker on the beach).

Some difficulties, however, undermine this solution. For example, it might be argued that the typescript produced by the monkey has meaning, regardless of whether anybody finds it or anyone has authored the text. Suppose, say, that the monkey produced the text of *Hamlet* before Shakespeare existed (or suppose that Shakespeare never existed) and suppose further that no one ever finds the text. Under these circumstances can we say that we have a text, and if we do, who is the author? In this situation we cannot hold that Shakespeare is the author of the text or that the author is the finder, for Shakespeare does not exist and the typescript has not been found by anyone. Yet, we might like to hold all the same that the typescript has meaning. For the typescript is composed of signs belonging to English and arranged in ways that are consistent with the syntactical rules of English grammar in such a way that they could be recognized as meaningful by anyone who knows English. Indeed, if one were to find the typescript after all, one could read it, understand it, and even could pass as the author of *Hamlet* by peddling the manuscript as one's own.[35] Thus we are justified in asking, then, Who is the author in this situation?

One might try to answer this question by saying that the reason why the case of the monkey's typescript raises difficulties is that it is composed of letters and words—artifacts created by persons to convey meaning—that have established meanings; because of this the typescript appears to have meaning even though it has no author.[36] The monkey is using established linguistic signs to produce the typescript, and if these signs make sense at all they do so because they are arranged in accordance with the grammatical rules of the English language. Thus, the connection between the typescript and meaning that results in a text is latent in the accepted meanings of the signs and their arrangement. There is, then, no single person who can be called the author of the text in this example, but rather the persons who developed the language and its rules function as latent authors of the text. There is a person component in the causal complex that is responsible for the monkey's *Hamlet*, and this component is represented by the language in which the text is composed, which is in turn a result of the fact that the monkey types on a machine made by persons to produce linguistic signs. This is quite evident in the case of a short text like 'Fire!' accidentally typed by a monkey, for the author of the text (the counterpart of the text of *Hamlet*) is not the monkey, but whoever connected the shape of the composite 'Fire!' with the meaning the text has in English.

One might also add that, if a monkey strikes the keys of a typewriter, it most likely does this because it has watched humans do so. And this therefore involves a person or persons in an indirect way as well. Imitation, however, is not a necessary condition of the textuality of what the monkey produces, because the monkey could hit the keys whether it had seen anyone do so or not and the monkey has no intention to convey meaning in doing so.

The case of the monkey's typescript, then, does not appear to be exactly like that of the pebbles on the beach, for in the case of the pebbles it is possible to hold that the passerby is the author of the text at least in the unusual case in which she is the first person to attach meaning to the shapes formed by the pebbles. Nor does the case of the monkey's typescript seem exactly like that involved in the identification of cloud formations with animals and the like, which we do occasionally. In this case one could argue that the observer is the author, because she is the one that connects the cloud, say, with a camel or the arrangement of certain stars with a big dipper. But the monkey's typescript is composed of well-established linguistic signs, namely, letters and words, that are not so on the basis of a similarity observed by someone, but on the basis of accepted conventions. The reader of the monkey's typescript cannot be considered to be "creative" in the way the passerby at the beach or the cloud watcher can.

In spite of all that has been said, however, we do not seem to have solved the problem posed by the text of *Hamlet* produced by a monkey, for the cases of the text of *Hamlet* and the text 'Fire!' are different insofar as 'Fire!' is a well-known and frequently used text in English, but the text of *Hamlet* (as produced by the monkey) is an original, new product. Society or whoever invented the text 'Fire!' may take authorial credit for it, but no one seems to deserve authorial credit for the text of *Hamlet*. The monkey cannot take credit for it because it knows nothing about the meaning and has no intention to convey it. Society cannot take the credit because it has not created the particular text of *Hamlet* about which we are speaking, although it has created a language whose possible arrangements include one such as that of the text of *Hamlet*. Moreover, if we were to give authorial credit to society in this case, why could we not give authorial credit to it in the case in which Shakespeare is in fact the person who composed the text? Finally, the finder of the monkey's typescript cannot take authorial credit because she did not create the typescript, the meaning, or the connection between the typescript and the meaning. We seem, then, not to have advanced toward a solution of this case. The typescript of *Hamlet* produced by the monkey is either not a text or, if it is a text, has no historical author.

Let us explore the second alternative first; namely, that the text has no historical author. One could argue that this is possible because a complex set of causes can come together and by chance produce what under normal circumstances only an author can produce. Thus, in the last analysis it would seem to be true that in at least one type of case there can be texts without historical authors, that is, there can be texts without someone who intentionally selects and arranges the signs of which the historical text is composed to convey a specific meaning to an audience in a certain context. But this is an anomaly, an exception, and does not mean that the existence of the text cannot be causally explained even though such a causal explanation includes an element of chance. Moreover, this view must be distinguished from the views described earlier in which texts were considered not to have authors at all, at least not always. For the understanding of what it means to have an author in those views and the one presented here is different.

This alternative may be clarified further by referring to meaning. Textual meaning is related to certain entities that, when considered by a person, can yield understanding of the meaning in the person. Moreover, because texts must have meaning, it appears that understanding by a person is required for textuality. The problem with the cases of the monkey's typescript and "found texts" is that they are understandable to audiences that were not instrumental in producing them and yet they were not understood by the agents or causes that produced them.

Now, in the case of signs and texts that were produced by agents before they were accidentally reproduced by causes unaware of their meaning, it is obvious that their authors are those who first consciously produced them. There is no problem here. Moreover, there is no problem concerning signs that are first regarded as signs by someone other than the causes that produced the entities of which they are constituted. In this case, that someone is the author. The problem arises with texts that are produced by unconscious causes, make sense, and have never been produced before by conscious agents. This would be the case of the text of *Hamlet* produced by a monkey before Shakespeare produced it. One way to dispel any lingering doubts is to argue that in this case there are conscious agents who developed the signs and rules whereby those signs could be arranged. Thus, although no single, overall conscious agent is responsible for the text, there are conscious agents whose intentions make possible the connection between the work *Hamlet* and its text. Indeed, the meaning of texts and therefore the texts themselves are the result of a multiplicity of factors, even when an author can be identified as their producer. So it makes sense to argue that these factors, considered together, make up for the absence of what is required under normal circumstances.

Finally, it could be added that it is precisely the complex nature of texts and the fact that their meaning is in part the result of the meaning of the signs of which they are composed that makes this explanation plausible. If the components of an entity are meaningful and fall into semantically significant arrangements, the entity is bound to be a text even when no subject is responsible for that entity.

Still, the truth of the matter is not only that this alternative violates the conception of texts we have adopted but that it seems to go contrary to some of our most basic intuitions about textuality. The idea that there can be texts without authors who intend to convey some specific meaning through them seems absurd. But, then, can the alternative view, that the monkey's typescript is not a text, be defended? I believe it can because I think that its implausibility stems from an assumption that has gone unquestioned in the discussion so far. The assumption is that the typescript has meaning. But can we really question this assumption? After all, any reader who knows English and reads the monkey's typescript seems to understand it. Moreover, the typescript is composed of words belonging to the English language that appear in arrangements in accordance with the grammatical rules of the language. So, how can anyone possibly argue that the typescript is not a text because it does not have meaning?

If one examines the example more closely, however, it becomes clear that the situation is not that simple. The reason is that the meaning of the signs of which the typescript is composed is not clear, because signs, like texts, are historical entities, the products of conventional uses whose meanings change from time to time. Thus, the meaning of the monkey's typescript in the sixteenth century might be different from its meaning in the eighteenth or the twentieth centuries. Because the monkey is a historically neutral entity (not having an understanding of what it has typed) and the typescript has not been produced in a social context (there is no audience for it), we cannot possibly say that the meaning of the typescript is this rather than that.[37]

Consider another example. Suppose the monkey typed 'Fire!' instead of the typescript of *Hamlet*. Here also we have a situation in which the meaning is undetermined, for there are several possible incompatible meanings that could be attached to it. Does it mean, for example, that someone should pull the trigger of a firearm? Does it mean that a certain building is on fire? Is it merely a report of someone who is learning the use of the English word 'fire'? Clearly, context is essential for meaning and a typescript that lacks context must lack meaning. Note that the point I am making is not epistemic, although epistemology confirms it. We have no way of knowing the meaning of what appears to be a text outside its historical context; texts outside history are silent. The point I am making is ontological, for it concerns the fact that, for entities to acquire meaning and become signs, and for signs to compose texts, they must be picked and endowed with meaning in certain arrangements at some point in history. Otherwise they are no more than the entities they are. Texts outside history are not texts.

Nor is this view affected by the fact that a particular text may have a range of meanings or be open ended in meaning. The determination of the limits of meaning is established ultimately by the cultural function of a text and that cultural function depends on historical circumstances.[38] Thus, such function and historical circumstances are necessary to establish the range of meaning even in cases in which such a range is open ended. What the monkey's typescript lacks precisely is a determinant of the range. So it cannot be argued that the case of the monkey's typescript is the same as the case of a text that has been determined by cultural function to have an open-ended range of meaning.

Our conclusion, then, is that texts do need historical authors, for texts without authors are texts without history and texts without history are texts without meaning; that is, they are not texts. Thus, in spite of what appear to be counterexamples, historical authorship is a necessary condition of textuality.

These considerations open up another possibility for typescripts such as the one produced by the monkey. It is that, after all, the one who finds the typescript for the first time may function as its author. For what that person does is to fix the meaning of the signs of which the typescript seems to be composed in accordance with the usages and conventions of the time. Of course, the originality of this author would be rather limited,[39] but nonetheless there would be an authorial thrust to such activity.

B. Need for the Pseudo-Historical Author

The pseudo-historical author is a mental construct that is believed by an audience—or constructed by someone (sometimes the historical author) to lead an audience to believe it—to be the historical author. The answer to the question whether there can be texts without pseudo-historical authors is easily determined if we compare this question with the questions raised in the previous section concerning the historical author. The reason is that it can be based on empirical evidence. In our everyday experience we are acquainted with scores of texts that have no pseudo-historical authors. For example, I doubt very much whether anyone has an idea about the author of the "No smoking" sign posted in the classroom where I teach on Thursdays. Indeed, signs understood in the sense of notices posted are mostly regarded as not having authors. That does not mean that anyone believes that they are uncaused. Obviously, someone painted the words on the wall, someone ordered them painted, and someone must have been the first person who put the words together to convey the command not to smoke. But no one bothers to think about the persons who did these things. The reason is that the meanings of those signs are so clear and contextually transparent, and the signs in question generally have so little originality and value in themselves, that it is unimportant either for understanding or in terms of proprietary interests who their author is. This is not always so, however, even with relatively simple signs. We are interested in identifying a person who painted a swastika on a tombstone of a Jewish cemetery, for that involves a violation of the law and reveals something about the mind and beliefs of the person who did it.[40] But in general, signs whose meaning is clear and whose import is simple do not elicit a pseudo-historical author. The pseudo-historical author is a construct of an interpreter who wishes to know more about a text or wishes to pass judgment upon its author.

Texts of literary, philosophical, religious, or scientific works, for example, elicit pseudo-historical authors. The reason is that they are subjects of interpretations or present characteristics of originality and value that lead to the development of proprietary interests in them. Even if a text is semantically transparent, it can elicit a pseudo-historical author as a result of its originality, for example. We want to know and have images of the authors of well-known clichés even if their meaning is quite clear.

The identification of pseudo-historical authors with historical authors seems to be the main reason why some philosophers hold the position that texts do not require authors and that some texts do not have authors. For what they really mean is that some texts do not have pseudo-historical authors and do not need them for carrying out their function.[41]

The view that no texts have authors is a reaction to the obvious fact that some texts do not have pseudo-historical authors and that there is no absolutely real demarcating criteria between those that do and those that do not. Those philosophers who adopt this view solve the problem of authorship by holding that only works, which they understand as texts that have been subjected to interpretation, have authors. Texts that have not been subjected to interpretation have no authors (i.e., pseudo-historical authors) but only "writers" (i.e., historical authors).[42]

My objections to this position go not so much against what it maintains concerning the pseudo-historical author but against what it holds about works and texts. I already presented my objections to these aspects of the view elsewhere, so I need not repeat them here.[43] The main merit of the view is that it recognizes the pseudo-historical author as a mental construct, the product of an interpretation of a text.[44]

III. REPRESSIVE CHARACTER OF THE AUTHOR

Another important reason why some recent philosophers have argued against the need or desirability to posit authors of texts is that they see the function of authors as fundamentally repressive.[45] Although views on this matter differ widely, the repression in question is interpreted as a kind of limitation on the parameters within which a text may be understood and as an imposition of a certain understanding of a text on an audience. The figure of the author closes the range of possible understandings of a text. This point has been made in many ways, but it can be easily illustrated by saying that, if a text is identified as having been composed by a particular author, our knowledge and opinion of the author, his views and authority, will impose boundaries on the ways the text may be understood, so that other ways of understanding it may be regarded as spurious or illegitimate. This not only limits the freedom of the audience, subjugating and dominating it in various ways, but also may prevent a deeper and broader understanding of the text, for the text is seen, then, only as an expression of an agent that reveals to us something about that agent.[46] Thus, for example, the so-called *Theology of Aristotle* was believed in the Middle Ages to be a work by Aristotle, and this biased scholastics toward a certain understanding of the text of that work, not only producing historically incorrect interpretations of it but also curtailing the freedom of those who sought to understand it. Now that we know the work does not belong to Aristotle, we have been able to appreciate its strong Neo-Platonic flavor.

The author accused of exercising repression is what I called earlier the pseudo-historical author; it is this author that functions epistemically, influencing the way an audience may understand a text. It makes no sense to speak of the historical author as repressive, because this author is simply the person who produced the historical text, and everything we know about him is part of the pseudo-historical author. The historical author has no epistemic significance; he exists epistemically only through the pseudo-historical author. The historical author is a metaphysical entity, but epistemically he is the author-I-know-not-who.[47]

One need not advocate the extreme view that texts have no historical authors to avoid the repression associated with authorship. A more reasonable approach, easily documented in contemporary literature is that a text should be understood apart from what we know about the historical author, that is, independent of the pseudo-historical author, even though, indeed, one accepts that there is a historical author of the text. The text is supposed to speak to the audience for itself, independent of any relationship that it may have with the pseudo-historical author. For, once a text is seen as belonging to an author, the understanding of the audience is limited in certain ways and channeled in certain directions.

This point of view makes quite a bit of sense in the context of a descriptivist view of proper names. This kind of view of proper names holds that proper names have meaning in addition to reference and thus are no different from definite descriptions.[48] Consider the case of Socrates, for example. According to descriptivists, 'Socrates' refers to Socrates but means, say, "the teacher of Plato." Moreover, they argue that what determines the reference of a proper name is precisely its meaning. 'Socrates' refers to Socrates precisely because it means "the teacher of Plato." If 'Socrates' meant "the most famous disciple of Plato," then it would refer instead to Aristotle. We need not get involved in the intricacies of the descriptivist theory to see that such a theory lends support to the view that the use of the name of an author in connection with a text imposes on the audience of the text certain limitations and leads in certain definite interpretative directions.

One obvious way to argue against the view that the use of the name of the author in connection with a text is repressive is to adopt a referential theory of proper names. The referential view holds that proper names have reference but no meaning or, to put it as some who support this view do, that their meaning is their reference.[49] The meaning of 'Socrates' is simply Socrates and not the sorts of descriptions that descriptivists claim. It is, so referentialists hold, the primary feature of proper names and the one that distinguishes them from common names. Naturally, if the use of a name does not carry with it any kind of descriptive baggage, it becomes very difficult to argue that the attribution of a text to an author somehow limits the audience's understanding of it or directs such an understanding along certain ways.

If either of these theories were accepted, the task of deciding on the repressive character of the author would be easier. The recent literature on proper names, however, has made clear that neither of these theories is unassailable. This has given rise to other views. Among these, the most popular is the so-called Causal Theory of proper names.[50] The main tenets of this theory are three: (1) proper names have reference but no meaning; (2) the reference of proper names is initially fixed through descriptions, but the names are not subsequently or necessarily tied to those or any other descriptions; and (3) after the reference of the proper name has been fixed in an initial act (called by proponents of this view baptism), reference is fixed through a causal chain of communication in which speakers who learn the name must intend to use it to refer to the bearer of the name intended by the person from whom they learned it, all the way back to the original baptism.

Elsewhere I have argued that none of these three theories is acceptable in the form in which it is usually presented.[51] My objection to them is that they tend to emphasize only one aspect of the problem involved in the meaning and reference of proper names, neglecting the others. Because I have already dealt with these matters at some length, it is not necessary for me to dwell on them here. It should suffice to point out that the view I propose, which I call the Threefold View, holds that three questions must be answered in this matter: (1) What is the function of proper names? (2) How are proper names established? (3) How do language users learn to use proper names effectively? The answer to the first is that the function of proper names is to refer. The answer to the second is that proper names are established through a kind of baptism. And the answer to the third is that language users learn to use proper names through descriptions.

When we apply this view to the question of repression concerning the use of the name of an author in connection with a text, we see that, indeed, as with the descriptivist position, there is room for limitation and thus repression. For, although the function of proper names is not to describe but to refer, we learn to use them through descriptions, and memories of those descriptions may color our understanding of texts. This means that I cannot develop an effective argument against those who hold the use of the name of an author in connection with a text to be repressive, based on the theory of proper names I find most acceptable. I must, then, either accept that such use is repressive or adopt a different strategy. Because I am not convinced that we must give in to the theory of repression so easily, I propose to take the second course of action.

My strategy consists in arguing that the theory of the repressive character of the author relies on a faulty assumption, and once this assumption is eliminated the necessity with which those who favor this theory see the author as repressive disappears. The assumption in question is that to limit the range of understanding of texts is somehow necessarily bad because it curtails the creativity of the audience in its effort to understand a text. This assumption is true only if the aim of the audience is exclusively creative, but that is not the aim of the audience in most, let alone all, cases. Although creativity is desirable and must be encouraged, it is certainly not a good thing in every situation. There are good and bad ways to be creative, depending on the goals being pursued. For example, a surgeon who is operating on someone should by all means be encouraged to be creative insofar as the novel procedures introduced are conducive to the well-being and prompt recovery of the patient. A new way to perform the operation that, say, diminishes bleeding should certainly be encouraged. But I do not think anyone would want to encourage the surgeon to be novel and creative in a way that would produce excessive bleeding, thus harming the patient. Unbridled creativity is not necessarily a good thing for surgeons. Indeed, most surgical training is geared to teach surgeons tested procedures to which they should adhere in the practice of their craft. The introduction of experimental procedures is no doubt to be encouraged also, otherwise surgeons would still be operating as they did long ago and no progress in surgery would have been made, but such experimental procedures are to be encouraged only within well-defined boundaries, where goals are clearly stated and pursued.

If we apply what has been said concerning surgeons and operations to audiences and their understanding of texts, it becomes clear that the imposition of limitations on the interpretation of texts is not necessarily nefarious. Whether creativity in understanding is or is not a bad thing will depend on the goal or goals that such an understanding is to achieve. If the goal of such an understanding is to grasp what the author had in mind when he produced the text, or what the audience contemporaneous with the author understood when it understood the text and so on, then it is clear that any limitation that will facilitate the achievement of those goals will be good, whereas those that do not will be bad. If, for example, my aim is to understand how Plato's contemporaries understood the text of the *Timaeus*, it would help to limit the parameters of its meaning by a consideration of the cultural context within which the dialogue was produced. To attempt to understand the dialogue apart from its cultural location would make no historical sense.

Of course, if the goal of my reading of the text of the *Timaeus* is not to understand what Plato meant or was understood by his contemporaries, but rather to test my creativity, to see what I can do with it, then any limitations imposed by a knowledge about the author would hamper that aim and thus be nefarious. The imposition of limitations on the understanding of texts is not necessarily bad and, consequently, neither are the limitations that the consideration of its author may impose.

This conclusion, however, does not entail that the consideration of the author is always beneficial. In some cases the consideration of the author may, indeed, be pernicious in the sense that it promotes understandings and uses of a text that are not conducive to the understanding that is sought. An interesting case of this situation occurred in the Middle Ages. The author of *Fons vitae* was a Jew by the name of Ibn Gabirol. Yet, at the time he was thought to be a Christian, called Avicebron. The result of this confusion was not only that the use of the *Fons vitae* was not objectionable to Christian theologians—indeed, it became quite popular—but the work was understood in Christian terms. The misunderstanding concerning the author of the text made possible its survival, but it also distanced the scholastic understandings of the text from whatever Ibn Gabirol intended or his contemporaneous audience grasped through the text.

I have argued that the function of the use of an author's name and what we know about the historical author, namely, what I call the pseudo-historical author, in connection with a text is neither necessarily repressive nor necessarily beneficial and thus, by implication, that it can be repressive or beneficial, depending on the goals being pursued and the circumstances involved. Those goals and circumstances also determine what aspects of the pseudo-historical author prove repressive or beneficial. For example, if the aim is to understand the philosophical point of view expressed by a text, it would seem both pertinent and beneficial to consider other philosophical texts believed to have been produced by the pseudo-historical author. On the other hand, it might be of no use, and perhaps even pernicious, to consider the personal psychological idiosyncrasies of the author.[52]

There is, therefore, a good deal of sense in the notion that authorship is repressive, but the current balance of opinion has swung too far in that direction. There are both beneficial and nefarious effects of authorship and both have to be taken into account in a sensible theory of texts and their relations to authors and audiences. Needless to say, the nefarious or beneficial effects of authorship depend to a great extent on the accuracy with which the pseudo-historical author known by the audience reflects the historical author as well as on the purposes for which a text is used. Accuracy concerning the pseudo-historical author entails knowledge of the historical author as a subject, and therefore consideration of the author's subjectivity is of the essence.[53]

NOTES

Editor's Note: This selection is an excerpt from Chapter 3, "Author," in *Texts: Ontological Status, Identity, Author, Audience* (Albany: SUNY Press, 1996), pp. 91–140 (hereafter *Texts*). Gracia begins Chapter 3 of *Texts* with an introduction to the topic and with Section I, "The Identity of the Author," pp. 91–104. Gracia starts this section on the function of the author with an overview of the topic, pp. 104–5.

1. The historical author has parallels to what Alexander Nehamas and others call writer. The notion of "writer," however, is too restrictive, for there are authors of both oral and mental texts, for example. See Nehamas, "What an Author Is," *The Journal of Philosophy* 83 (1986), 685–86, and "Writer, Text, Work, Author," in Anthony Cascardi, ed., *Literature and the Question of Philosophy* (Baltimore, MD: Johns Hopkins University Press, 1987), pp. 272ff. [p. 99ff.]; also Gregory Currie, "Work and Text," *Mind* 100 (1991), p. 333. Michael L. Morgan uses the expression 'historical agent' to refer to the historical author in "Authorship and the History of Philosophy," *The Review of Metaphysics* 42, 2 (1988), pp. 331 and 354–55. *Editor's Note*: This paragraph is excerpted from an earlier section of Chapter 3 of *Texts*, p. 93.

2. See, for example, Vincent Tomas, *Creativity in the Arts* (Englewood Cliffs, NJ: Prentice-Hall, 1964).

3. Two qualifications need to be added. First, it should be obvious that my argument rests on the viability of a subject/object, mind/content-of-mind distinction. Second, the understanding of *ad extra* I have provided is different from the understanding of *ad extra* used in Christian theology. In Christian theology the world cannot be a feature of God's mind, *malgré* Berkeley. But a mental text is precisely that, a feature of whoever thinks it.

4. Understood in this way, not all creation *ex nihilo* entails novelty. It is possible in principle for a divinity, for example, to create a duplicate of an entity out of nothing whatever. In this sense, one might want to distinguish newness from novelty, for the duplicate would be new, because it did not exist before, but it would not be novel, because it is a copy of something else. For purposes of our discussion, however, I ignore the distinction between novelty and newness.

5. These conditions are discussed in Chapter 2 of *Texts*.

6. The view that creativity involves the production of something new is widespread. See Tomas, *Creativity in the Arts*, pp. 98ff. But some have proposed a distinction between creating and making.

7. Cf. Nicholas Wolterstorff, "Toward an Ontology of Art Works," *Nous* 9, 2 (1975), pp. 137ff.

8. For the distinction between text and work, see Jorge J.E. Gracia, *A Theory of Textuality: The Logic and Epistemology* (Albany: SUNY Press, 1995), ch. 3.

9. *Texts*, ch. 1.

10. Cf. Jack Glickman, "Creativity in the Arts," in Lars Aagaard-Morgensen, ed., *Culture in Art* (Atlantic Highlands, NJ: Humanities Press, 1976), p. 140; and Joseph Margolis, "The Ontological Peculiarity of Works of Art," *Journal of Aesthetics and Art Criticism* 36, 1 (1977), p. 45.

11. For a different solution to this problem, see Margolis, ibid., pp. 46ff.

12. Cf. Nehamas, "What an Author Is," p. 686.

13. Roland Barthes introduces a distinction between *author* and *scriptor* in "The Death of the Author," in *Image, Music, Text*, trans. Stephen Heath (New York: Hill and Wang, 1975), p. 145 [p. 5], and Nehamas and others also speak of the "writer" in contrast to the "author." See n. 1.

14. Cf. Nelson Goodman and Catherine Z. Elgin, "Interpretation and Identity," in *Reconceptions in Philosophy and Other Arts and Sciences* (London: Routledge, 1988), p. 64, and Wolterstorff, "Toward an Ontology of Art Works," p. 137. In the case of short texts the notion of simultaneous production does not pose serious problems, but in the case of long ones it does. It is not clear, for example, what is required for simultaneity in the production of a text as long as *Don Quixote*, which was not written at once and which the author corrected at various times. This difficulty, however, should not cloud the issue we are addressing.

15. It is possible to imagine cases, however, in which the translator is more original than the historical author of the text she translates. This can occur, for example, when the originality of the historical author is limited, say, to few of the type signs used in the text. In such a case it may turn out that the translator is more original if the type signs she uses display more novelty. Consider, for example, Fitzgerald's translation of Omar Khayyam's *Rubaiyat*.

16. *Editor's Note*: This section originally appears as Section C in *Texts* and is preceded

by Section B, "The Function of the Composite Author," pp. 114–15. Discussion of what Gracia calls the composite author and the interpretative author has been omitted from this selection.

17. The notion of pseudo-historical author understood thus has some parallels to Michel Foucault's and Nehamas' "author." See Foucault's "What Is an Author?" trans. D.F. Bouchard and S. Simon, in D. Bouchard, ed., *Language, Counter-Memory, Practice: Selected Essays and Interview* (Ithaca, NY: Cornell University Press, 1977), pp. 121ff. [cf. p. 12ff.], and Nehamas's "What an Author Is," p. 689, and "Writer, Text, Work, Author." Morgan, in "Authorship and the History of Philosophy," seems further to divide what I have called the *pseudo-historical author* into the surrogate author and the actual author. The *surrogate author* is the author constructed by an interpreter when subjecting a text to analysis; the *actual author* is also constructed by the interpreter, but is rather an ideal of what the author is and has no determinate content (see pp. 342 and 355). Cf. Kendall L. Walton's notion of "apparent artist" in "Style and the Products and Processes of Art," in Berel Lang, ed., *The Concept of Style* (Ithaca, NY: Cornell University Press, 1987), pp. 88ff.

18. In this sense, the pseudo-historical author is a fiction created by the historical author. In art, such authors have been called *fictional creators*. See Walton, "Style and the Products and Processes of Art," p. 82. George Dickie speaks of the dramatic speaker of a work in *Aesthetics: An Introduction* (Indianapolis, IN: Bobbs-Merrill, 1971), p. II 6.

19. *Editor's Note*: The account of the pseudo-historical author up to this point has been excerpted from an earlier section of Chapter 3 of *Texts*, p. 97.

20. *Editor's Note*: A discussion of the function of the interpretative author follows at this point in *Texts*, pp. 116–17.

21. Cf. Plato, *Phaedrus*, 276e. In spite of recent attacks, this view is still defended today. See, for example, E.D. Hirsch, Jr., "Three Dimensions of Hermeneutics," *New Literary History* 3 (1972), pp. 259–60, and P.D. Juhl, "The Appeal to the Text: What Are We Appealing To?" *Journal of Aesthetics and Art Criticism* 36 (1978), 277–87.

22. According to one version of this position, the author is not the person who created the text but "a function" developed by post-Renaissance literary critics. See Foucault, "What Is an Author?" p. 121 [cf. p. 12]. This does not imply, however, that there is no person who puts together the entities that constitute the text, but that person is not the author of the text. William E. Cain makes this point in "Authors and Authority in Interpretation," *Georgia Review* 34 (1980), p. 619. But there are more extreme versions of this view. Barthes, for example, holds that "one never knows if he [i.e., the author] is responsible for what he writes (if there is a subject behind his language); for the very being of writing (the meaning of the labor that constitutes it) is to keep the question Who is speaking? from ever being answered." *S/Z* (Paris: Editions du Seuil, 1970), p. 140. He makes a similar point in "The Death of the Author."

23. Nehamas, "What an Author Is," p. 685, and "Writer, Text, Work, Author," p. 275 [p. 101].

24. Thus, the meaning is said to be "constructed" rather than "discovered" by the audience. See Laurent Stern, "Factual Constraints on Interpreting," *Monist* 73 (1990), p. 205.

25. Nehamas, "What an Author Is," p. 686, and "Writer, Text, Work, Author," pp. 281ff. [pp. 106ff.]. Note that by 'interpretation' is meant understanding in this context.

26. Other examples are the cases of persons who talk in their sleep, are in a trance,

mumble something, or are under hypnosis. Can the sounds these persons utter be considered texts even though there seems to be no intent to convey meaning? The question of sleep, Freudian slips, trances, hypnosis, and the like can be explained in terms of subconscious intentions, but the case in which one makes sounds that are taken as meaning something, even though the utterer does not intend them to do so, cannot be explained in the same way. Another example is that of computer-generated texts. See Dickie, *Aesthetics*, p. 112. Dickie uses this example to argue against intentionalists who wish to identify the meaning of a text with the author's intention. For a different line of argument against intentionalism, see Jerome J. McGann, *The Textual Condition*, ch. 2 (Princeton, NJ: Princeton University Press, 1991), pp. 48ff.

27. Similar examples have been used in the literature. See S. Knapp and W.B. Michaels, "Against Theory," *Critical Inquiry* 8 (1982), pp. 727ff.

28. See *A Theory of Textuality*, ch. 1.

29. Some aestheticians introduce distinctions between different senses of 'art work' or 'art object,' giving primary status to such things as paintings and the like and only a secondary, derivative status to things classifiable as found art. See Dickie, *Art and the Aesthetic: An Institutional Analysis* (Ithaca, NY: Cornell University Press, 1974), pp. 25ff. These distinctions do not affect the point I am making.

30. See P.D. Juhl, "The Appeal to the Text," p. 282, and John R. Searle, *Speech Acts: An Essay in the Philosophy of Language* (Cambridge: Cambridge University Press, 1969), pp. 16ff.

31. A less farfetched case with which most of us are in fact familiar is the utterance of sounds by a parrot. A parrot presumably does not understand what it says, but what it says appears to have meaning. Some scholastics argued that, because the parrot had no understanding of what it says, what it says has no meaning and thus cannot be considered to be signs. Others rejected this view and found the sounds uttered by the parrot to be significant. The first view was defended by Pedro Hurtado de Mendoza, *Logica* 8, 2, 23; the second was defended by Thomas Compton Carleton, *Logica* 42, 3, 10.

32. Juhl, "The Appeal to the Text," p. 284. See also Knapp and Michaels, "Against Theory," p. 728.

33. Goodman and Elgin, "Interpretation and Identity," pp. 63–64.

34. Those who, like Barthes and Stanley Fish, emphasize the audience in the construction of a text, must accept this view. See Barthes, "The Death of the Author," and Fish, "Interpreting the Variorum," *Critical Inquiry* 2 (1976), pp. 465–85.

35. This seems to be Dickie's position with respect to computer-generated texts. *Aesthetics*, p. 112.

36. In the seventeenth century, the words that compose languages were frequently compared to money. Just as money acquires value from the will of the prince and not from those who use it, so words have meaning from those who made them. Cf. Marcelo Dascal, "Language and Money: A Simile and Its Meaning in Seventeenth-Century Philosophy of Language," *Studia Leibnitiana* 8, 2 (1976), pp. 187–218. The metaphor originates in the scholastic discussions of signs going back to the Middle Ages and still persists today in authors like Donald Davidson and Paul Ricoeur. For its use by Ricoeur, see "Creativity in Language: Word, Polysemy, Metaphor," in Charles E. Reagan and David Stuart, eds., *The Philosophy of Paul Ricoeur: An Anthology of His Work* (Boston: Beacon Press, 1978), p. 121.

37. See Joseph Grigely, "The Textual Event," in Philip Cohen, ed., *Devils and Angels:*

Textual Editing and Literary Criticism (Charlottesville and London: University Press of Virginia, 1991), p. 179, and Arthur Danto, *The Transfiguration of the Commonplace: Philosophy of Art* (Cambridge, MA: Harvard University Press, 1981), pp. 35–36.

38. See *A Theory of Textuality*, ch. 4.

39. *Editor's Note*: A brief mention of the interpretative author has been excised here.

40. In this example we are probably talking about a sign rather than a text, but the point applies to both texts and signs.

41. This is behind the often quoted statement of Samuel Beckett, "What matter who's speaking, someone said, what matter who's speaking." See *Texts for Nothing* (London: Cader and Boyars, 1974), p. 16.

42. Cf. Nehamas, "What an Author Is," p. 688, and the references in n. 1.

43. *A Theory of Textuality*, ch. 2.

44. *Editor's Note*: A discussion of the need for the composite and interpretative authors follows at this point in *Texts*, pp. 128–29.

45. See Foucault, "What Is an Author?" pp. 124ff. [cf. pp. xxff.], and Nehamas's exposition of Foucault in "What an Author Is," p. 686. Nehamas in fact argues against the necessarily repressive character of authors in the same article, pp. 690–91, and in "Writer, Text, Work, Author," p. 287 [p. 111]. Barthes accepts and develops a similar view in "The Death of the Author."

46. This point is made clear by Nehamas in his discussion of Foucault, "Writer, Text, Work, Author," p. 271 [p. 98]. See also McGann, *The Textual Condition*, ch. 2.

47. *Editor's Note*: A brief discussion of the composite author has been excised here.

48. See Bertrand Russell, *Human Knowledge: Its Scope and Limits* (New York: Simon and Schuster, 1948), p. 303; and John Searle, *Intentionality: An Essay in the Philosophy of Mind* (Cambridge: Cambridge University Press, 1984), p. 232.

49. See John Stuart Mill, *A System of Logic* (New York: Harper and Brothers, 1850), p. 21; Russell, *Logic and Knowledge: Essays 1901–1950*, ed. R.C. Marsh (London: Allen and Unwin, 1956), pp. 200–1; and Ludwig Wittgenstein, *Tractatus Logico-Philosophicus* 3.203, trans. C.K. Ogden (London: Routledge & Kegan Paul, 1981), p. 47.

50. See K. Donnellan, "Proper Names and Identifying Descriptions," *Synthese* 21 (1970), pp. 335–58, and "Reference and Definite Descriptions," *Philosophical Review* 75 (1966), pp. 281–304; and Saul Kripke, *Naming and Necessity* (Cambridge: Harvard University Press, 1987), pp. 96 and 59 n.22.

51. Gracia, *Individuality: An Essay on the Foundations of Metaphysics* (Albany: SUNY Press, 1988), pp. 216–26.

52. I discuss this issue in the context of philosophical texts in *Philosophy and Its History* (Albany: SUNY Press, 1992), pp. 229–31.

53. *Editor's Note*: Chapter 3 of *Texts* ends with a section on "The Subjectivity of the Author" and a conclusion, pp. 134–40.

CHAPTER 12

Intentionalism and Author Constructs

William Irwin

The term "author construct" refers to a theorist's conception of the author, particularly as this conception applies to interpretation. Although author constructs were at first instrumental in diminishing the role of the author in interpretation, with sustained attention to them, some theorists have moved back in the direction of authorial intent. No actual (as opposed to hypothetical) intentionalist, however, has provided us with an author construct suitable to his or her position. Thus my purpose in this chapter is to offer an intentionalist author construct, the urauthor, and briefly explicate the intentionalism it supplements. It is not my purpose to defend intentionalism against its critics, as I have done elsewhere.[1]

INTENTIONALISTS WITHOUT AUTHOR CONSTRUCTS

Barthes and Foucault consider the author in an effort to move interpretation away from this "repressive" figure. Further considerations of the author by Nehamas and Gracia have led to views somewhat congenial to intentionalism, but no actual intentionalist has articulated an author construct. What I propose is to articulate an author construct suitable for intentionalism. To do so, I shall focus primarily on the seminal intentionalist theories of E.D. Hirsch, Jr., and P.D. Juhl, and turn briefly to the debate between hypothetical and actual intentionalism as presented by Jerrold Levinson and Noël Carroll.

Though Hirsch himself does not develop an author construct, he does, at times, point to one as being implied by his theory.

On the surface it would seem impossible to invoke the author's probable outlook when the author remains unknown, but in this limiting case the interpreter makes his *psychological reconstruction* on the basis of fewer data. Even with anonymous texts it is crucial to posit not simply some author or other, but a particular subjective stance in reference to which the construed text is rendered probable. That is why it is important to date anonymous texts. . . . In this sense all texts including anonymous texts are attributed.[2]

The speaking subject is not, however, identical with the subjectivity of the *author as an actual historical person*; it corresponds, rather, to a very limited and special aspect of the author's total subjectivity; it is, so to speak, that "part" of the author which specifies or determines verbal meaning.[3]

A reconstruction of the historical producer, then, is implied by Hirsch's position, although, except in scarce few instances, he does not make it explicit and never actually develops the details of an author construct. In an article published over three decades after he first took up the subject of interpretation,[4] Hirsch finally declares, "an author function there must be."[5] Even in this later article, however, he does not develop his own account of the author construct. Another indication that Hirsch means to deal with a construct, rather than a historical person, is his assertion that we must concern ourselves with what the author intended and not everything that may have been "going on in his mind" at the time of composition.

Why should anyone with common sense wish to equate an author's textual meaning with all the meanings he happened to entertain when he wrote? Some of these he had no intention of conveying with his words.[6]

If that is the principle [everything present to the mind of the author], all hope for objective interpretation must be abandoned, since in most cases it is impossible (even for the author himself) to determine precisely what he was thinking of at the time or times he composed his text.[7]

The author with whom Hirsch is concerned in interpretation is not the historical person with his innumerable idiosyncratic thoughts but a limited reconstruction of the author—one that is composed only of what the historical person likely intended. Unfortunately, Hirsch himself is not clear about this distinction and so refers to both the historical person and the construct implied in interpretation as "author." Hirsch is clear in his essential point, however. We need only be concerned with what the author intended to convey by his text.[8] Hirsch seems to have resisted the need for an author construct, at least prior to his declaration of "an author function there must be," because such constructs had been used so readily by anti-intentionalists and because he could not yet see the value of and need for an author construct as a supplement to his intentionalism. Speaking against the French legacy of the author construct, Hirsch says, "Those who keep abreast of literary theory know that the communicative model of textual interpretation has come under disdainful attack by Derrida and other influential French writers [Barthes and Foucault], who have made the quasi-metaphysical objection that the author of a text, being absent, does not really exist for inter-pretation. The author is just a construct."[9]

P.D. Juhl similarly resists developing an author construct, identifying such a figure too closely with the anti-intentionalist position he opposed. In arguing against Wayne C. Booth's implied author, Juhl throws the proverbial baby out with the bath water. He gets rid of Booth's implied author and fails to replace it with an intentionalist author construct, leaving us with only the real historical author. He writes, "But what could be the point of giving a name ('implied author' or 'author personality') to those aspects of the author which are relevant to our understanding of his work and another (the 'real author') to those aspects of the author which are not and saying that it is only the former we are con-cerned with?"[10] Juhl does not adequately recognize that an intentionalist needs an author construct because an intentionalist can never even hope to "have" the real historical author. All we ever have is a more or less accurate version of him as related to his text, an author construct. Juhl admits, as does Hirsch, that we do not need to know everything about the historical author: "Few would be inclined to say it matters what the author believed to be the causes of hair loss or tooth decay."[11] In one instance, Juhl hints at some realization of the difference in ontological status between what we consider in interpretation and the real historical author. "I have been arguing that it is our *picture* of the real, historical author which determines how we construe a literary work."[12]

Continuing the pattern of intentionalists without author constructs, Noël Car-roll, in arguing against Jerrold Levinson's hypothetical intentionalism, eschews the author construct. Levinson argues that not necessarily the author's *actual* intentions, but rather what his or her *oeuvre*, historical context, and so forth suggest to the ideal reader were *likely* the author's intentions should concern us in interpretation.[13] Hence Levinson posits an author construct of sorts, what he might call the "hypothetical author." Levinson's hypothetical intentionalism, then, avails itself of all the information actual intentionalism would, with the notable exception of the author's own statements about his or her intentions. While it seems odd to stop just short of actual intentionalism in this way, it is not our task to settle the debate between hypothetical and actual intentionalism here.[14] Our point is to note that "actual intentionalism," as defended by Carroll, shares in common with Hirsch and Juhl the disavowal of an author construct. Carroll draws on Stecker, telling us that "it is difficult to see how this theoretical construct could really explain the features of the text, since this theoretical con-struct could not have causally influenced the text in any way."[15] Carroll makes a very good point in opposing hypothetical intentionalism in its various forms but fails to appreciate the value and necessity of an "actual intentionalist" author construct. Our best understanding of the actual intention of an author involves a construct of the author, which focuses on that person's intentions *as author* rather than *as person.*[16] Actual intentionalism is also "hypothetical" (or theo-retical) in the sense that our beliefs about the author's intention, that is, the construct of the author, remain always open to revision in light of new evidence about the author. Even if, for example, we have a clear public statement of authorial intent, we remain open to the possibility of new evidence that the statement was ironic or deceptive. In this way, the actual intentionalist's author construct does not arbitrarily limit what the actual author *could* intend but helps to focus our attention on what the actual author *did* intend.

URAUTHOR: AN INTENTIONALIST AUTHOR CONSTRUCT

Let us call the intentionalist author construct "urauthor." This designation suggests that we should go back to the origin in forming this figure. We should not form our author construct arbitrarily but rather seek as far as possible to create it in the likeness of the original, the author herself. There is a notable difference in ontological status between the author and the urauthor. The author is, or was, an actual person, whereas the urauthor is a mental construct, and, consequently, the urauthor can never be exactly the same as the author. Bracketing the clear difference in ontological status, however, we can have greater and lesser matches between the two entities. Of course there are practical limitations as to how accurately we reproduce the original, and in some cases the restrictions will be greater than others. We need also to restrict ourselves in forming the urauthor by taking into account only what is relevant for interpretation. It is impossible to say in advance and in precise terms what is relevant in a particular case, but generally speaking we need to take into account all that contributes to the intended communication.

The urauthor is constituted by several elements. In constructing our author figure on the model of the original we need to take into account whatever information is at our disposal, and all of this is to be subsumed under the author construct, urauthor. Relevant biographical information will be very important.[17] Who was the author and how did she think? What likely were her intentions in composing the text?[18] How did she use language in the text itself?[19] What was her historical context, and who was her audience?[20] What attitudes and knowledge did the author presuppose of her readers? What other texts of the author do we have at our disposal?[21] Some of what is written only between the lines, that which is elliptical, is revealed by an analysis of the author's context and audience, and we may, in fact, construct the urauthor of a text, in part, through interpreting other texts by the same author.

The construct of the urauthor, then, will be composed of relevant available biographical information, likely actual intentions, use of language in the text itself, information concerning the author's context and audience, and other texts of the author inasmuch as they inform the other elements of the urauthor. Which elements are most important will vary, depending on the text to be interpreted, but always of greatest importance will be likely actual intentions inasmuch as all other elements of the urauthor are simply clues to those intentions.[22] How much effort we put into constructing the urauthor is a function of how much evidence we have, how clear the text as indicator of authorial intent seems to be, and how concerned we are that our interpretation be faithful.

The detail in which we form the construct varies greatly. At the very least, however, we assume that the author wrote[23] in the language in which we are reading or was read by someone who translated her work into that language. This is not much, but it can be the first thread in the tapestry that is to become the author construct.[24] My point is simply that we do begin to form the author construct immediately, even if only in simple and pre-reflective terms. One way in which we do this is in making assumptions about the language in which the text is written. Another important way is in assuming that the producer of the text was a rational human being using the language in a conventional way.[25] For this reason, the power of the text to determine its own meaning is often overestimated. It is routinely taken for granted that the author was rational and that her word choice and sentence structures were conventional. Such assumptions are of course defeasible, and it is in cases in which they are shown to be false that we come to realize how reliant upon the author we actually are.

The drive or instinct to form the author construct is natural and pervasive. We must fight it when circumstances call for authorial anonymity. Consider the instructions for preparing a manuscript for blind review. In most cases not only is the author's name omitted but also all self-references as well. It is not enough that the author leave her name off the manuscript; if she even leaves a clue as to who she is, the reviewer may be tempted to follow up the clue and identify the author. Such is the interpreter's instinct. Given an anonymous text, he wants to identify the author. Something inside urges him to do so. Consider the grading of essay exams or term papers. Despite the ideal of impartiality, teachers are influenced by the authors of these texts. They may give the benefit of the doubt to a student they consider bright or hard working, or refuse the benefit of the doubt to a student they consider mediocre or lazy. Any teacher who grades without any consideration of the author has gained this ability only through considerable effort.

Some texts seem to be designed to avoid the production of an author construct resembling the author. Kierkegaard, for example, was concerned that his audience not read some of his texts as his, hence the pseudonyms of *Either/Or*.[26] Hume expressed much of his thought on God in dialogue form rather than in the form of a treatise. Even in these cases, however, the author construct is too seductive a temptress to forgo. Has not philosophical scholarship sought to form the author construct Hume, despite the author's efforts to hide? Cannot much the same be said of Kierkegaard?

URINTERPRETATION

We come now to our brief exposition of urinterpretation. This normative theory is actually just a development and refinement of Hirsch's intentionalism. Indeed, it owes much to the tradition of author-based interpretation beginning with Schleiermacher. The starting point of the theory is Hirsch's distinction between meaning and significance as presented in *Validity in Interpretation.*[27] Suffice it to say that by "meaning" we are to understand the author's intended communication.[28] By "significance" we are to understand meaning-as-related-to-anything other than the text itself. Significance is the product of non-urinterpretation, which may be an acceptable and even highly desirable product of reading.[29]

Also essential to urinterpretation is the tenet that there is only one meaning to be sought in interpretation, that of the author (via the urauthor). The text itself is certainly not to be ignored but rather is to be subjected to detailed scrutiny. The text is ordinarily the most important clue we have as to the meaning of the author, but it is not the only clue; all other elements of the urauthor can also be quite important. Recall that the urauthor is composed of relevant available biographical information, likely actual intentions, use of language in the text itself, information concerning the author's context and audience, and other texts of the same author inasmuch as they inform the other elements of the urauthor.

The central question for any normative theory of interpretation is: How do we gain knowledge of the meaning of a text? Urinterpretation owes much to Hirsch's intentionalism in answering this question but differs from Hirsch's theory in its use of the urauthor.[30] The term "urauthor" suggests that we go back to the origins in forming this figure, that we regain as far as possible the original intention of the actual author. The urauthor is not the historical producer of the text but a mental construct resembling the historical producer as closely as possible in all relevant ways.

The urauthor is our vehicle for gaining access to the meaning, the intended communication, of the author himself. And it is this meaning we are ultimately seeking in urinterpretation. There is, however, no certainty that our urauthor is an accurate construction and no certainty that we have discovered the author's meaning through this construction. Still, we can in principle gain knowledge of the author's meaning through the urauthor even if we cannot be certain that we have. This insight and the process of validation on which it is based we take from Hirsch. The urauthor in any given case is itself open to revision, and so is the urinterpretation based on it. We are seeking the most probable and most plausible interpretation we can conceive on the basis of what we know, that is, on the basis of the urauthor we have formed. Even an urinterpretation that appears highly valid is always subject to being completely wrong. We are always open to new evidence, and so the process of validation becomes, as Hirsch calls it, a "survival of the fittest."[31]

How much effort we put into constructing the urauthor is a function of how much evidence we have, how clear the text as indicator seems to be, and how concerned we are that our interpretation be faithful. We may, for example, put little to no effort into the construction of the urauthor of a newspaper article and a great deal of effort into the construction of the urauthor of a literary or philosophical text. Of course, we may do just the opposite as well; there may be a great deal of information available about the author of a newspaper article, and it may significantly inform our interpretation of the text. For example, after reading Pete Hamill's autobiography, *A Drinking Life*,[32] we can bring a highly developed urauthor to our interpretation of his newspaper articles. We may in fact form the urauthor of a text through interpreting other texts by the same author. The urauthor we form, then, is a coherent picture of what we have read and interpreted. An urauthor formed in this way, just as in any other way, is potentially inaccurate and so should always be kept open to revision.

Urinterpretation, then, involves a rigorous process of validation, assuming we are sufficiently concerned with achieving the correct interpretation. The correct interpretation is understood to be the one that reproduces the meaning of the text, that is, the author's intended communication. Can there, however, be definitive interpretations?[33] The answer is yes, at least in a limited sense. Any interpretation that exactly and completely captures the author's intended communication would be a definitive interpretation. One problem, as we have noted, is that we are never certain that this has occurred. Another problem is that an interpretation will itself be manifested in a text, a text that may have practical limitations to its understanding. The rules of the natural language the interpretation is presented in are likely to change over time, and what needs to be said to convey the author's meaning will vary with the audience. The elliptical aspects of the interpretation may be easily accessible to one audience but not to another.

We should conclude, then, that an interpretation can be definitive for a given audience. More importantly, however, the meaning indicated by the text of the interpretation can certainly be definitive; it can be an exact match for the author's meaning—though, as we have noted, we can never be certain of when this occurs.

The author's meaning is what she intended to communicate by her text. This raises a problem, however, because it is not clear that authors always, or ever, have intended texts in mind. Jorge J.E. Gracia has argued that there is in fact no such thing as an intended text.

The author may have some general intentions and some vague ideas he or she wants to convey, but those can hardly be regarded as a completely determined meaning, for those intentions and meanings could produce very different texts and, moreover, could change in the process of textual production.[34]

[O]ne may also argue that there is no such thing as the intended text for the simple reason that authors never have a clear and complete idea of the texts they intend to produce prior to the moment in which they actually produce them by writing, speaking, or thinking. . . . [T]here is never such a thing as an intended text. And this is so in turn because a text is always a result of a process of production and also does not precede such a process in any way.[35]

Though he makes an important point, Gracia has overstated his case. He is correct to say that we do not always have an intended text in the sense of one fully present to the mind before the text's actual composition. There probably is no full and complete intended text prior to the composition of any text of much length or complexity. It is difficult to imagine that Tolstoy had an intended text in any detailed sense before the actual composition of *War and Peace*, for example.

Still, it is practically possible to have an intended text for a relatively short and simple text, and theoretically possible for even a long and complex text. Take the following example: A student nervously rehearses the answer, "Albany is the capital of New York," only to say, "Atlanta is the capital of New York," when her teacher calls on her. It seems that in this case we do have an intended text that is imperfectly produced; the actual text differs in a crucial way.

Gracia would likely respond that in this case we do not truly have an intended text but an actual mental text.[36] The student developed an actual mental text, "Albany is the capital of New York," and produced a different actual spoken text, "Atlanta is the capital of New York." In some sense this analysis would be correct; both texts are actual. The mental text, however, is also the intended one. It was intended to be produced in speech, although this intention was not realized. There is no reason a text cannot be actual in one medium, for example, the mental, and intended for another medium, for example, the spoken.[37] To be clear, however, the mental text and the spoken text are two different texts, differentiated by the media in which they are composed. What is intended is that the mental text be duplicated as far as possible in the spoken word.

It is at least possible that an author could produce a written text through a series of short intended mental texts, some of these accurately reproduced in writing and some not. It is also possible that an author could have a very long and complicated mental text intended for writing. That the *Iliad*, among other works of antiquity, was carried on by oral tradition bears witness to the ability of the human mind to store long and complex texts. Neither of these possibilities does much for establishing that there need always be an intended text, however. And indeed there need not always be; it is only a possibility.

What we are concerned with in urinterpretation, however, is not intended texts but intended communications—meanings. Texts act as indicators of meanings, and so we are concerned only with what the author intended by the text. As with intended texts, intended communications may precede their texts, develop in part along with their texts, or develop somewhat contemporaneously with their texts. The author may have a meaning firmly in mind before producing the first word of the text; she may have a meaning firmly in mind before producing each part of the text; or she may develop the meaning while producing the text. As Stein Haugom Olsen says of texts, "Every particular element is conceived in intentional terms, i.e., under the perspective of serving an end."[38] And, as even W.K. Wimsatt admits, "[I]t [art work] is in a sense (and this is especially true of the verbal work of art) made of intentions or intentionalistic material,"[39] and "whatever does get into a poem is presumably put there by the poet."[40] Intentions need not be well formed in advance, but they are the very "stuff" of which the text is made; they are indeed what the author "puts" in the text—that which gives the text meaning.

Often in the process of producing the text itself the author's intended communication becomes most clear to him. Even then, however, the meaning itself is still prior to the text. It is just that the author's conscious awareness of his meaning comes to light in the text's production. Indeed, even this may not happen. It is possible, and in fact common, for an author to produce a text, have a meaning in mind, and not be consciously aware of that meaning. Some meanings, that is, intended communications, as Hirsch has shown, are unconscious. Some of these can be brought to the author's awareness by the interpreters of his text, and some meanings may resist being brought to awareness in this way. In the end, though, the author did have a meaning, the text serves to indicate that meaning, and it is the task of the urinterpreter to find and articulate that meaning.

INTENTIONALIST INTERPRETATION OF LITERARY TEXTS: MEANING AND SIGNIFICANCE

Finding significance is an essential activity in keeping literary texts fresh, alive, and read with each passing generation and era. In large measure this task falls on the shoulders of the teacher. Shakespeare's *Macbeth*, for example, is foreign, odd, and inaccessible to the average high school student, and it is the job of the teacher to bring the text to life. Part of this will include interpretation, making the meaning clear through historical background and clarification of early modern English, but the more vital task is demonstrating the relevance of the text to our own time—showing that what Shakespeare wrote was indeed timeless. This need not be at odds with the meaning the author intends, however. As Hirsch says of Shakespeare's "Sonnet 55" ("Not marble, nor the gilded monuments / Of princes, shall outlive this powerful rhyme."[41]), "The author's intention in this poem (and this is characteristic of literature, law, and religion) includes an intention to communicate effectively into the future."[42] This underscores the point that authors of literary texts may have intentions of various types. (Consider the case of Hermann Hesse, who makes clear that his *Steppenwolf* has been widely misinterpreted as a pessimistic book.[43]) An author's intention may be specific or vague, firmly grounded in the present or open to future applications, productive of logical reasoning or of aesthetic experience. The possibilities are endless. As A.J. Close says, "Intentions in literature . . . include such non-tangible 'aims' as the cerebral Jamesian interest in presenting the ambiguous complexities of a moral issue or Quevedo's delight in the dramatic dissonances of a conceit."[44] Whatever the author intended to communicate is the meaning of the text.

A literary text, as an effort to communicate, is a speech act,[45] and thus involves an illocutionary act and a perlocutionary act. An illocutionary act has a certain conventional force and to be successful must secure uptake, bringing about an understanding of the meaning and the force of the locution.[46] This is to be distinguished from producing effects, which is characteristic of the perlocutionary act. A perlocutionary act is what we bring about or achieve by saying something, such as convincing, persuading, deterring, and surprising.[47] Often, then, the author of a literary text will intend a certain perlocutionary effect, and inasmuch as this is what she intends, it is part of the meaning to be sought. Authors of literary texts are often concerned with producing aesthetic experiences in their audiences, and such experiences can be the intended perlocutionary effects of their texts. Among other criteria, one may even judge the success of a literary work by the extent to which its perlocutionary effect is achieved. As Gregory Currie says, "[S]uccess in the aesthetic sense is a matter of perlocutionary effect, not of illocutionary uptake."[48]

In teaching a literary text we should indicate when what we are presenting is significance rather than meaning. In a written hermeneutic examination, significance and meaning will often be interwoven. This, too, should be properly indicated. There is an ethical transgression involved in presenting a significance of a text as if it were the meaning of the text; the author is misrepresented and the audience deceived.[49] The author of a literary text may have broad, suggestive, and inclusive intentions, but surely these have their limits. Finding these limits is difficult, and to some extent must be addressed on a case-by-case basis.[50] Hirsch himself has come to express a similar view. As he says of future-directed intentions, their "purpose could embrace an indefinite number of future applications that no human being could foresee in precise detail."[51] We must approach such future-directed intentions on an individual basis. There will be cases in which a given interpretation no longer bears any resemblance to the author's intention, and such interpretations are not to be accepted. "The genuine difficulty of the problem presents itself when future fulfillments depart further and further from what one might originally have expected."[52]

Let us consider briefly the value of significance that departs from what the author intended to communicate. Feminist, Marxist, and Freudian readings are often of this kind. As long as such hermeneutic examinations indicate their aim and methodology, presenting significance rather than intended meaning, they need not misrepresent the author or deceive the audience, and, in fact, they may be quite valuable in stirring ideas. We are often, however, the best producers of significance ourselves. Most of us have, for example, found personal significance in a work of literature we later discovered we had misinterpreted. This should not, however, profoundly devalue the significance we had formerly found in the text. The significance I find in *King Lear* may well have a more profound effect on me than that which a noted Shakespearean scholar finds. Her interpretation is likely to be better than mine, based as it would be on a superior knowledge of Shakespeare and all that relevantly concerns him, but in what sense could the significance the scholar finds be better than mine? Other readers of Shakespeare might find it more appealing and engaging, but this is a matter of taste. Whereas meaning is rigorously objective and can be judged by objective standards, significance is less rigorously objective and can, to some extent, be judged by subjective standards.

It is possible, we should note, for a literary text to lose its appeal through time. In such a case, however, what shall we do? Shall we ferret out ever more creative significance of the work, departing further and further from its meaning? Perhaps not. Perhaps we should draw the line and recognize that at some point a given literary text may lose its appeal, that its meaning may no longer be of much interest no matter how far significance departs from that meaning. As Hirsch has properly suggested, in such cases we should "introduce truer and more valuable works into the traditional literary canon to replace those that are outdated."[53]

NOTES

1. See William Irwin, *Intentionalist Interpretation: A Philosophical Explanation and Defense* (Westport, CT: Greenwood Press, 1999), pp. 39–72.

2. E.D. Hirsch, Jr., *Validity in Interpretation* (New Haven: Yale University Press, 1967), p. 259 (hereafter *VI*; emphasis added).

3. *VI*, pp. 242–43, emphasis added.

4. For Hirsch's earliest major article on the subject see E.D. Hirsch, Jr., "Objective Interpretation," *PMLA* 75 (1960): 463–79.

5. E.D. Hirsch, Jr., "Transhistorical Intentions and the Persistence of Allegory," *New Literary History* 25 (1994): 551. Here he argues for the "persistence of intention." Even in the case of Foucault, he argues, there is an author function. For Foucault it is the reader who fulfills the author function.

6. *VI*, p. 18. P.D. Juhl would agree to a certain extent. See his *Interpretation: An Essay in the Philosophy of Literary Criticism* (Princeton, NJ: Princeton University Press, 1980), pp. 191–92.

7. *VI*, p. 220, bracketed comment added.

8. The author construct with which Hirsch must concern himself is based very much on the historical person, and in this sense is very different from Booth's implied author.

9. E.D. Hirsch, Jr., "Counterfactuals in Interpretation," in Sanford Levinson and Steven Mailoux, eds., *Interpreting Law and Literature: A Hermeneutic Reader* (Evanston, IL: Northwestern University Press, 1988), p. 58. Bracketed comment added to reflect Hirsch's note, which says he has in mind Foucault and Barthes.

10. Juhl, *Interpretation,* p. 191.

11. Ibid.

12. Ibid., pp. 185–86, emphasis added.

13. Jerrold Levinson, "Intention and Interpretation in Literature," in *The Pleasures of Aesthetics* (Ithaca: Cornell University Press, 1996), pp. 175–213, see especially pp. 207–208. See also Jerold Levinson, "Intention and Interpretation: A Last Look," in Gary Iseminger, ed., *Intention and Interpretation* (Philadelphia: Temple University Press, 1992), pp. 221–56.

14. Noël Carroll has done a convincing job of this. See his "Interpretation and Inten-

tion: The Debate between Hypothetical and Actual Intentionalism," *Metaphilosophy* 31 (2000): 75–95; and idem, "Andy Kaufman and the Philosophy of Interpretation," in Michael Krausz, ed., *Is There a Single Right Interpretation?* (University Park: Pennsylvania State University Press, forthcoming).

15. Carroll, "Interpretation and Intention," p. 85; cf. Robert Stecker, "Apparent, Implied, and Postulated Authors," *Philosophy and Literature* 11 (1987): 266 [p. 136].

16. I would argue that this is consistent with ordinary conversational interpretation and thus supplements Carroll's view. Cf. Noël Carroll, "Art, Intention, and Conversation," in Gary Iseminger, ed., *Intention and Interpretation* (Philadelphia: Temple University Press, 1992), pp. 97–131.

17. Cf. Juhl, *Interpretation*, pp. 88–89. Despite Juhl's rejection of an author construct, he is very helpful in our project of assembling the various elements that constitute the urauthor. Juhl argues throughout his book that there is a logical connection between an author's intention and a number of things on which interpretation is often based (biographical information and other external evidence, the text itself, context, use of language, and aesthetic qualities of a text). He argues that in making reference to these things, in placing our interpretive stock in them, we are actually referring to the author's intentions.

18. Cf. Juhl, *Interpretation*, pp. 54–65. Juhl's discussion of allusion and irony sheds much light on this issue.

19. Cf. ibid., pp. 106–112, 66–89.

20. Cf. ibid., pp. 90–99, 141. For our purposes we shall consider audience as part of context, though Juhl does not specifically do so himself.

21. Cf. ibid., pp. 103, 261–68.

22. Juhl would argue that in appealing to any of these we are, logically speaking, appealing to the author's intentions.

23. Of course not all authors have always literally "written" their texts. The Homeric epics, for example, were produced and carried on for a time orally. When I speak of writing, then, I mean to include all ways of composing texts. Texts can in fact be written, spoken, and even nonphysical (i.e., mental) entities. Cf. Jorge J.E. Gracia, *Texts: Ontological Status, Identity, Author, Audience* (Albany, NY: SUNY Press, 1996), pp. 18–26.

24. In this volume Jason Holt calls this "the presumption of intent" and argues it provides only a "marginal" life for the author (pp. 70–73).

25. What is conventional will vary, among other ways, according to the genre in which we place the text. For example, placing a text in the genre of poetry will usually be quite different from placing it in the genre of ordinary discourse.

26. Cf. Merold Westphal, "Kierkegaard and the Anxiety of Authorship," in this volume (pp. 23–43).

27. I have argued for the soundness of this distinction. See Irwin, *Intentionalist Interpretation*, pp. 46–50.

28. Regardless of what the text may seem to say in accord with the conventions of language. See Irwin, *Intentionalist Interpretation*, pp. 56–58, for my defense of even Humpty Dumpty's use of language. See also Keith Donnellan, "Putting Humpty Dumpty Together Again," *Philosophical Review* 77 (1968): 203–15; Michael Hancher, "Humpty Dumpty and Verbal Meaning," *Journal of Aesthetics and Art Criticism* 40 (1981): 49–58; Jonathan Bennett, "The Meaning-Nominalist Strategy," *Foundations of Language* 10 (1976): 141–68.

29. Non-urinterpretation and significance are discussed in greater detail in Chapter 5 of Irwin, *Intentionalist Interpretation*.

30. As well as its "extreme actual intentionalist" account of meaning. See Irwin, *Intentionalist Interpretation*, pp. 56–61.

31. *VI*, p. 169.

32. Pete Hamill, *A Drinking Life* (Boston: Little, Brown and Company, 1994).

33. Gracia broaches this question in *A Theory of Textuality: The Logic and Epistemology* (Albany, NY: SUNY Press, 1995), pp. 169–70.

34. Ibid., p. 113.

35. Ibid., p. 77.

36. For a discussion of mental texts see Gracia, *Texts*, pp. 23–26.

37. This argument was originally made in William Irwin, "Review of Jorge J.E. Gracia's *A Theory of Textuality: The Logic and Epistemology*," *Sorites* 3 (1995): 64–68.

38. Stein Haugom Olsen, "Interpretation and Intention," *British Journal of Aesthetics* 17 (1977): 215.

39. W.K. Wimsatt, "Genesis: A Fallacy Revisited," in David Newton-De Molina, ed., *On Literary Intention* (Edinburgh: Edinburgh University Press, 1976), p. 116.

40. Ibid., p. 120.

41. William Shakespeare, "Sonnet 55," in *The Norton Anthology of Poetry*, 3rd ed. (New York: W.W. Norton & Company, 1983), pp. 187–88.

42. E.D. Hirsch, Jr., "Meaning and Significance Reinterpreted," *Critical Inquiry* 11 (1984), p. 205.

43. Hermann Hesse, "Author's Note—1961," in *Steppenwolf* (New York: Henry Holt and Company, 1990), pp. v–vi.

44. A.J. Close, "*Don Quixote* and the 'Intentionalist Fallacy,' " *British Journal of Aesthetics* 12 (1972): 23.

45. I cannot argue at length for this assertion within the scope of this project. For a defense of this position see Juhl, "Interpretation," pp. 218–19. See also Hirsch, "Counterfactuals," p. 64.

46. J.L. Austin, *How to Do Things with Words*, 2nd ed. (Cambridge, MA: Harvard University Press, 1962), pp. 116–17.

47. Ibid., p. 109.

48. Gregory Currie, "What Is Fiction?" *Journal of Aesthetics and Art Criticism* 43 (1985): 391. Cf. Close, "*Don Quixote*": "The recognition that poets, novelists, and dramatists intend to arrest our attention, and engage our interest, in certain ways is basic to our response to literature" (p. 36).

49. For the argument concerning the ethics of misrepresenting the author, see Irwin, *Intentionalist Interpretation*, pp. 50–54.

50. Cf. Hirsch, "Counterfactuals," pp. 62–63. Hirsch argues that a counterfactual conditional does have a truth value, and so thinking in terms of counterfactuals is a valuable way of determining if an interpretation is a valid accommodation of the past to the present. Hirsch discusses counterfactual interpretations of Blake's "London."

51. Hirsch, "Meaning," p. 206.

52. Ibid., p. 207.

53. Ibid., p. 219.

CHAPTER 13

The Death of Cervantes and the Life of *Don Quixote*

Eric Bronson

Spanish existentialist Miguel de Unamuno has a problem. He loves *Don Quixote*. What he loves most is Don Quixote's burning desire to achieve immortality through others' recognition of his name. But that is not Unamuno's problem. The problem is that Don Quixote's creator, Miguel de Cervantes Saaverdra does not seem to share Unamuno's viewpoint. Cervantes introduces Don Quixote as a likeable, but pitiable, man who has lost his mind reading frivolous books of knight-errantry, hardly the stuff of epic heroism. Has Unamuno misread his favorite text?

Unamuno understands there are often discrepancies in interpretations. However, rather than amend his own reading of *Don Quixote*, Unamuno attacks Cervantes. "I consider myself more Quixotist than Cervantist," Unamuno writes, taking pains to "disagree with the manner in which Cervantes understood and dealt with his two heroes."[1] Taken at face value, this seems an outrageous statement. Is it possible for a reader to understand a text more accurately than the author? Does the author have a voice in deciding how her text should properly be read? Is there ever one definitive interpretation of a text? Such questions cut to the core of the philosophical issues surrounding authorial intent.

When Roland Barthes proclaimed the death of the author, he was attempting to break the author's monopoly over her own text. If the author could be eliminated, then the reader would have much greater autonomy in forming his own interpretations. With such new-found freedom, Unamuno's rebellion against the author of his beloved book is not as radical as it may first appear. Unamuno believes Cervantes would oppose his existential, twentieth-century interpretation, and therefore calls the value of authorial intention into question. Like

Barthes, Unamuno calls for a metaphorical killing of the author. In this chapter, though, I will argue that Unamuno's reading of *Don Quixote* does not present a difficult challenge to Cervantes or to the life of the author. Cervantes, I believe, encourages innumerable interpretations of his hero, including Unamuno's. If Unamuno read Cervantes's intentions more carefully, he would save the interpretive life of the author by understanding how his interpretation actually *coincides* with Cervantes's.

THE PHILOSOPHY OF AUTHORIAL INTENT

Unamuno is not the only one to reexamine *Don Quixote* in light of its contemporary hermeneutic issues. Notably, Jorge Luis Borges presents us with "Pierre Menard, Author of the *Quixote*" (or, more specifically, author of two chapters of *Don Quixote*). In this short story, Borges introduces Menard, a profound thinker, bent on re-creating the 400-year-old text. Menard independently reproduces pages of Cervantes's work, "word for word and line for line."[2] Although Menard might seem to be plagiarizing *Don Quixote*, Borges makes it clear that he is not. Indeed, the two texts should be understood differently. For example, Menard (and Cervantes) writes about truth, "whose mother is history, rival of time, depository of deeds, witness of the past, exemplar and adviser to the present, and future's counselor."[3] Borges notes that when Cervantes wrote the above statement in Chapter 9 of *Don Quixote* in the beginning of the seventeenth century, it read like a well-written exaltation to history. However, when Menard writes the exact same words in the twentieth century, it reads like a contemporary pragmatist view of truth, and the style is outdated and pretentious.

Borges informs us that this is not the first time Menard has challenged the way we understand texts. Among Menard's few surviving papers is "an invective against *Paul Valéry*, in the *Papers for the Suppression of Reality*."[4] As it turns out, Valéry and Menard were friends and the latter's invective is "the exact opposite of his true opinion of Valéry." Behind Menard's re-writing of the *Quixote* and his invective against Valéry is a formidable defense of the author. If we didn't know that the "historical" Menard was a friend of Valéry and we didn't know the context of his text was the "Suppression of Reality," we would likely come to the erroneous conclusion that Menard meant exactly what he wrote. Knowledge of the historical author, Borges implies, should affect the way we understand a text. Although the words are identical, we understand Cervantes in the seventeenth century differently than we understand Menard in the twentieth century.

The debate concerning *Don Quixote* mirrors the current philosophical debate concerning the role of the author in the interpretation of texts. Contemporary to Menard's literary achievement (as conceived by Borges), the New Critics (notably Wimsatt and Beardsley) claimed that readers were placing too much emphasis on authorial intention.[5] The author was becoming a repressive figure, anxiously pacing "like a nervous cook, waiting to supply some condiment that was left out of the soup."[6] The reader, Beardsley argued, need only examine the text. If she has trouble understanding the passage then she should read it again. If questions still arise, perhaps the text is poorly written and she should judge it accordingly. From Beardsley's position, it is only a step to Barthes's argument that the author's interpretive role is no longer viable. Since Beardsley's author is repressive, he should be done away with altogether, freeing the reader for her own constructed reality.

More recently, philosophers such as Jerrold Levinson,[7] Alexander Nehamas,[8] and Jorge J.E. Gracia have attempted to strike a compromise by resurrecting the author in a way that does not diminish the importance of textual evidence. Their position is sometimes called "hypothetical intentionalism."[9] Let us focus our attention on Gracia, who has argued for the author playing an important, but not all-important, role in helping the reader understand the meaning of the text. "A text," Gracia argues, "is a complex entity whose meaning and significance depend on a variety of factors. The author has a key role among these, and in some cases is the determining factor."[10] In other cases, the text and its cultural function should have the ultimate say.

Knowing something extra about the author can aid the reader in understanding the text. Gracia uses the example of the text of Shakespeare's *Hamlet*, rich with philosophical issues about life and death. Wouldn't our understanding of the text be called into question if it were discovered that *Hamlet* was in fact written by a monkey who randomly pushed keys on a computer? Would the text still carry the same meaning? Would it have any meaning? Or, as Gracia asks, should the monkey's *Hamlet* even be considered a text at all? Like Borges, Gracia values the historical context in which a text is written, but like Beardsley, Gracia understands that the author can, at times, mislead the reader about the meaning of the text.

We can surely sympathize with the reader who finds herself caught in a vicious cycle. Gracia admits the "well-known principle that effects tell us something about their causes and so we should expect for texts to tell us something about their author."[11] The reader should know the author's intentions to help her carefully read the text, but in order to understand the author's intentions she must carefully read the text. What conclusion are we to draw? Gracia argues, "[T]here is only one meaning for every text, but that meaning is to be understood broadly so as to encompass much more than particular authors or audiences have in mind when they understand the texts."[12] In other words, we need to study both the author and the text to arrive at the best possible understanding of the text. There is one correct meaning of the text, hidden among a network of interpretations and interpretive processes.

Of course, the reader can never be certain that she correctly understands the author's intentions. No one can know beyond a shadow of a doubt the intentions of another person. At times, we cannot even be sure of our own intentions. The truth is out there, but, according to Gracia, the reader cannot be certain that she knows it. Therefore, the reader must (in the words of Plato) take the second best route. The reader should find as many clues as she can from the text itself, and from outside the text, by studying all the relevant information available about the writer's life and times. Then the reader will be well prepared to make an educated conjecture concerning the author's intentions.

Following Gracia's argument, the author is not dead. Instead, there are (for our purposes) two authors: the historical author whose intentions we may never know with certainty, and the pseudo-historical author whose intentions we construct based on all the available evidence. As long as there are only two authors to consider, the project of interpretation is manageable. But what happens when there are many different authors? If the careful reader is to take into account Gracia's multifaceted guide to interpretation, she must first discover exactly who is writing the particular passage. This is difficult but hardly impossible, particularly if the writer is still alive. Now imagine a scenario in which a text has four authors, three of whom are fictional characters and none of whom are completely reliable. Throw in a seemingly irrational hero with a fabricated love interest, and it becomes increasingly clear why philosophers such as Unamuno and Borges have used *Don Quixote* to help them sort through the thorny issues of authorial intent.

Three hundred and fifty years ahead of his time, Miguel de Cervantes deliberately puts the reader of *Don Quixote* in a confusing position. Long before Gracia, Beardsley, and Borges, Cervantes experimented with the idea of the disappearing author and challenged the reader to rethink the way she interprets texts.

THE AUTHORS OF *DON QUIXOTE*

Philosophers are naturally drawn to *Don Quixote* because of its rich exploration of the hermeneutic issues surrounding authorial intent. In the novel, Cervantes claims different fictional authors wrote various sections, challenging readers to rethink their interpretations. Ahead of his time, Cervantes takes himself out of the novel, perhaps putting into literary practice the critical theory of the death of the author.[13] Or was Cervantes doing something else altogether? By focusing on this literary example, we shall be in a better position to reach more general conclusions about the author's place in textual interpretation.

Cervantes is, as Gracia would say, the historical author of *Don Quixote*. He was born in Spain in 1547. In 1605, he published the first part of his masterpiece, followed ten years later with Part Two. In 1616, Cervantes died. At the time of Cervantes's writing, books of knight-errantry were still enjoying enormous popularity, and physician Juan Huarte de San Juan had published his well-received casebook of patients, including some who had gone mad with delusions of grandeur.[14] Could these facts about Cervantes and his time period help the reader in her interpretation of *Don Quixote*? Borges and Gracia would likely say yes, since they believe that the author's biographical information can, and sometimes should, influence the reader's understanding of the text. Beardsley and Unamuno would dismiss Cervantes's personal history since they argue the author's role oftentimes hinders the reader's free interpretations.

But what does Cervantes say? He gives us very little information about himself, and the information he does give does not seem helpful. In fact, he continuously distances himself from his own creation. Already in the Prologue, the reader is given the power to form her own judgments about *Don Quixote* without asking the author for approval. Cervantes writes:

But I, though in appearance Don Quixote's father, am really his stepfather [*padrastro*], and so will not drift with the current of custom, nor implore you, almost with tears in my eyes to pardon or ignore the faults you see in this child of mine. For you are no relation or friend of his. Your soul is in your own body, and you have free will with the best of them . . . and so you can say anything you think fit about this story, without fear of being abused for a bad opinion, or rewarded for a good one.[15]

Cervantes deliberately invokes an ironical tone and we should not take him too seriously. However, we also should not lightly gloss over his attempt to kill himself as author of the text. Because he chooses to be a stepfather (metaphorically speaking, of course), he absolves himself from full responsibility for his main character. Cervantes will not be Beardsley's repressive author because he opts out of the responsibility. But neither is he Barthes's deadbeat author, wholly distant from his own creation. From early on in the novel, Cervantes pokes fun at the reader's innocent trust of the author. We might recall the discussion between the priest and the barber over the burning of Don Quixote's books. When it is revealed that among the many unworthy novels is Cervantes's *Galatea* (published in 1585), the priest observes, "That Cervantes has been a great friend of mine for many years, and I know that he is more versed in misfortunes than in verse. His book has some clever ideas; but it sets out to do something and concludes nothing."[16] Again, his self-deprecating humor belies an important philosophical point. The author, Cervantes implies, is hardly the final authority concerning his own text. Through Cervantes's healthy dose of self-deprecation, the reader is made less trustful of later authorial interventions. As John J. Allen notes, the confusion caused by Cervantes's abandonment of his own creation inevitably disorients the reader: "[T]he conviction grows that the author is just as helpless as the reader," forcing the reader to judge future dilemmas "from the characters and situations themselves, rather than from authorial commentary."[17]

In Chapter 9 of *Don Quixote*, Cervantes completes his suicidal attempt, taking himself out of the book altogether by inventing a new author, the lightly esteemed Cide Hamete Benengeli. It is no coincidence that Borges's Menard chooses Chapter 9 as the section of the text to reproduce. Through its peculiar shifting of authors, this chapter calls into question the relevance of the author's intentions. Just as Don Quixote and his newest enemy, the gallant Basque, are poised to strike violently at one another, the story is abruptly interrupted. The rest of the story is left unfinished. Cervantes, painting himself as "the second author," informs us that the first author's story (to which Cervantes is only the narrator) is missing. "At this critical point our delightful history stopped short and remained mitigated, our author failing to inform us where to find the missing part" (I, p. 9).

From Chapter 9 on, not only is the original author's text never recovered but the author mysteriously disappears as well. The narrator, or second author, serendipitously discovers the remaining text of the adventurer-knight at a silk merchant's shop in Toledo. The narrator realizes his discovery when a Spanish-speaking Moor instructs him that within the Arabic text is a line about the ravishing Dulcinea del Toboso and her unsurpassed ability in salting pork. Within six weeks, the narrator's nameless interpreter translates the entire text of *Don Quixote* written by Hamete.

Even the most assiduous reader would be more than a little confused. The first author, who the reader naturally, but erroneously, believes to be Cervantes is no longer directly involved in the text. Writing in his place is the unknown Hamete, who is made accessible only through an equally unknown translator. The first author, to be sure, was hardly the most reliable narrator; he is not even sure of Don Quixote's real name.[18] The reader, in the unlikely event that she cares at all, is already confused about the veracity of the first author. Therefore, one might suspect that a change in authors might help reduce some of her earlier difficulties in interpreting the text. Such hopes, though, are quickly dashed as the narrator observes that our new storyteller, Cide Hamete, comes from a nation of liars and all further discrepancies should be attributed to the "dog of an author."

What is the reader to make of all this? From the Prologue, we are to believe (seemingly from Cervantes) that the book *Don Quixote* is a parody and a farce, a work not to be taken too seriously. And yet, alongside the humorous stories and philosophical musings is a continuous string of irrelevant details by unreliable sources and invented authors. At first glance, it certainly seems as though Cervantes is making Beardsley's argument against the author. If the author is as unreliable as Cervantes repeatedly observes, then perhaps we should stop thinking about the author's intentions altogether and concentrate entirely on the text itself. This seems to be exactly what Cervantes endorsed in his Prologue.

Unfortunately, the case cannot be settled so easily. Before Cervantes published his second part, another illegitimate *Don Quixote* was allegedly composed by Avellaneda, pretending to be Cervantes. A disgruntled Cervantes attempts to clear the air in his Prologue to Part Two, using his usual sharp wit. But jokes aside, Cervantes's tone becomes unusually serious when defending the authenticity of his own text, imploring the reader "to notice that this second part of Don Quixote, which I place before you, is cut by the same craftsman and from the same cloth as the first." Cervantes accuses the rogue author of succumbing to the "*tentaciones del dominio*," the temptations of the devil. For an author who previously took great pains to distance himself from ownership of his text,

Cervantes's distaste for rogue authors using his name seems more than a little hypocritical. Or is it?

It must be that Cervantes *does* want the reader to pay attention to the author's intentions. Otherwise, there would be no need to mention these made-up authors at all. If Cervantes truly meant to kill the author altogether, in the later spirit of Barthes, then he would not throw in a multitude of fictional authors. The surest way to make someone laugh is to remind him constantly not to laugh. Similarly, by continuously calling attention to the questionable Cide Hamete and the suspect translator, Cervantes forces the reader to pay closer attention to the author. The author, Cervantes tells us, is not reliable, and this *should* affect the way the reader reads the text. By disguising authors, Cervantes does not disguise his intentions; on the contrary, he reveals them.

INTENTIONS OF A DEAD AUTHOR

To summarize, Cervantes willfully kills himself off early in the novel to distance himself from his text. However, by continuously forcing the reader to examine the author's accuracy, he is still carefully directing the reader's interpretation. Cervantes turns surly when confronted with another author who writes a different *Don Quixote* with presumably different intentions. His anger in the Prologue to Part Two shows the reader that Cervantes believes the author does play an important role. The reader, he warns, should remember that Cervantes is the true author. Cervantes's own intentions are important to him and should be important to readers.

But just what are Cervantes's intentions? Is *Don Quixote* an entertaining book of knight-errantry, or is it a parody and critique of such books? Is the character Don Quixote an intelligent, romantic hero, or is he a deranged madman who should be stopped? These questions have aroused much contentious debate over the years and are not peripheral; they are questions that probe the very meaning of Cervantes's novel.

Soon after its publication, *Don Quixote*'s interpreters took Cervantes at his word. In the Prologue to Part One, Cervantes insists that his novel "aims at no more than destroying the authority and influence which books of chivalry have in the world and among common people." Don Quixote himself is portrayed as a simple gentleman carried away by reading too many books of medieval chivalry. He read so much that "his brain dried up and he lost his wits" [*de manera que vino a perder el juicio*] (I, p. 1). The reader should laugh at Don Quixote as he mistakes windmills for giants, prostitutes for maidens, and common criminals for well-meaning martyrs. Each adventure is understood as a joke at the expense of the all-too-common adventure heroes of his time.

As Western civilization became more and more specialized and bureaucratized, however, readers began to see Don Quixote as the romantic hero, tossing aside his petty privileges to pursue his heart's desire. The Knight of Sad Countenance was everything the average person wished to be: passionate, eloquent, and fiercely independent. According to many readers in the romantic age, Don Quixote did not lose his wits, as Cervantes humorously observes, but rather held complete command over his sanity. The nineteenth-century "romantic" commentators[19] emphasize passages in which Don Quixote soberly discusses the reasons for his adventures. "I know who I am," Don Quixote tells the skeptics, "and I know, too, that I am capable of being not only the characters I have named but all the Twelve Peers of France" (I, p. 5). Such interpreters are also quick to point out that it is Sancho, the more practical voice of reason, who observes "that there's nothing so pleasant in the world for an honest man as to be squire to a knight errant, that seeks adventures" (I, p. 52). Many of those who fall into the romantic camp argue that if Don Quixote is mad, it is a madness greatly envied by we saner, duller dreamers.

Most recently, a third interpretation of *Don Quixote* has gained favor. Cervantes's masterpiece is read as a psychological metaphor for our own fragile identities. The adventures are not to be taken literally, but should be understood as a mirror to the reader's soul. Some of these commentators[20] focus on Cervantes's second part. Under the "psychological" interpretation, Don Quixote's brief foray into the underworld via the cave of Montesinos (II, p. 22) should be read as man's struggle to find salvation in a corrupt and violent world. And when Don Quixote inexplicably destroys Master Peter's puppet show (II, p. 26), he demonstrates to the reader how her own constructed reality is little more than an awkward dance of pasteboard cutouts.

As should be clear, the literal, romantic, and psychological interpretations are not at all similar and are thus difficult to reconcile. If Don Quixote is a hero, then it is wrong to whimsically dismiss previous stories of knight-errantry. But if Don Quixote is a joke then he should certainly not be our paradigm for "seizing the day." And furthermore, if the reader is to take the psychological approach then nothing is what it seems. So who is right?

Cervantes, as was noted, deliberately hides behind poorly translated and loosely recorded disguises. These disguises reveal his intentions. The various interpretations discussed above are not due to uncritical readings, but rather are byproducts of the author's deliberate confusion. By blurring his own identity, Cervantes consciously encourages the reader to engage himself in questions of identity. As Ruth El Saffar observes, "Through a focusing on the function of the main fictional narrator, Cide Hamete, it is clear that it is not the character of Don Quixote, but the dialectic represented by the opposition of Don Quixote and Cide Hamete that forms the basis of the novel."[21] Understanding the repeated discrediting of the author is therefore the key to understanding the text.

When the author is not reliable, all bets are off. Without an authoritative voice, the character of Don Quixote can be interpreted however the reader pleases. This must be Cervantes's wish, inasmuch as we can know it. If Cervantes really wanted to articulate a particular spin, then he needed to speak as himself (as he did against the illegitimate *Don Quixote*) or through a trustworthy narrator or character. Even Sancho Panzo, the simple peasant skeptical of his master's adventures, is prone to his own delusions of grandeur. Cervantes encourages mutually inconsistent interpretations of his hero by discrediting himself and all other seemingly reasonable voices in his novel. No character in *Don Quixote* is reliable and therein lie Cervantes's intentions. Through his unorthodox narrative technique, Cervantes allows and even encourages multiple interpretations of his novel.[22]

So is Don Quixote a hero or a fool? According to Cervantes, he can be either. The careful reader comes to this inevitable conclusion by examining the author's intentions. Cervantes attempts to take himself out of the novel early on, but as we have seen, disappearing authors are never really dead. The disappearing author reveals his intentions as surely as the clear and present author. Cervantes is the author of *Don Quixote*, and his intentions help the reader to understand his text. Though Cervantes could never have anticipated all the past and future interpretations of his text, he did knowingly create and intend the conditions for so many analyses to prosper.

Therefore, with its confusing multilayering of fictional authors and confusing characters, *Don Quixote* can be read as an affirmation of the author's life. The author's role need not be as repressive as Beardsley claims. As Gracia argues, taking into account other considerations, such as the context of particular lines, the reader can come to understand the author's intentions. Since Cervantes's intention seems to be to allow many different interpretations, Unamuno can have back his valiant Don Quixote without disagreeing with the hero's author.

In *Don Quixote*, the author is far from dead, a point Unamuno himself should have realized. In 1914, Unamuno published a novella entitled *Mist* (*Niebla*). In typical Unamuno fashion, the characters engage in existential questioning of the meaning of existence. However, on a few occasions, Unamuno disrupts the traditional role of the narrator in the spirit of Cervantes. One of his own fictional characters is the alleged writer of the Foreword, and, in the end, the reader is treated to a funeral oration occurring in the mind of a dog. *Mist*, like *Don Quixote*, challenges the reader to account for the peculiar disappearances of the original author.[23] In one particularly unusual scene, Unamuno himself is paid a visit by his protagonist, Augusto Pérez. The conversation is civil until Augusto threatens to kill Unamuno. The mere notion of a fictional character killing an author certainly stretches the imagination, and Unamuno (character or author?) is rightfully perplexed. "Y luego has insinuado la ida de matarme," he writes. "And now you have conceived the idea of killing me. Of killing me—*me*? And you? Am I to die at the hands of one of my creatures?"[24] In the end, Unamuno asserts his power as author by killing Augusto and dismissing the threat.

As Unamuno himself seems to make clear, characters cannot take on a life wholly independent from their author.[25] If Unamuno wants to interpret *Don Quixote* correctly, he must do so under the guidance of Cervantes's intentions. Unamuno's own interpretation of Don Quixote as a beautiful person bent on achieving immortality falls within the many plausible interpretations because

Cervantes, even in his absence, still has a claim on how his text should properly be read.

Interpreting *Don Quixote* is certainly confusing, but only as confusing as its author intended.[26]

NOTES

1. Miguel de Unamuno, "The Life of Don Quixote and Sancho," in *The Selected Works of Miguel de Unamuno* (Princeton: Princeton University Press, 1967), Foreword to the second edition.

2. Jorge Luis Borges, "Pierre Menard, Author of the *Quixote*," in *Labyrinths* (New York: New Directions Publishing, 1962), p. 39.

3. Ibid., p. 43.

4. Ibid, p. 38.

5. W.K. Wimsatt and Monroe C. Beardsley, "The Intentional Fallacy," in *The Verbal Icon: Studies in the Meaning of Poetry* (Lexington: University of Kentucky Press, 1954), pp. 3–18.

6. Monroe C. Beardsley, "The Authority of the Text," in *The Possibility of Criticism* (Detroit: Wayne State University Press, 1970), p. 37.

7. Jerrold Levinson, "Intention and Interpretation in Literature," in *The Pleasures of Aesthetics* (Ithaca, NY: Cornell University Press, 1996), pp. 175–213.

8. Alexander Nehamas, "The Postulated Author: Critical Monism as a Regulative Ideal," *Critical Inquiry* 8 (1981): 133–49. See also idem, "Writer, Text, Work, Author," in this volume, pp. 95–115.

9. Cf. Noël Carroll, "Interpretation and Intention: The Debate between Hypothetical and Actual Intentionalism," *Metaphilosophy* 31 (2000): 75–95; and Gary Iseminger, "Actual Intentionalism vs. Hypothetical Intentionalism," *Journal of Aesthetics and Art Criticism* 54 (1996): 319–26.

10. Jorge J.E. Gracia, *A Theory of Textuality: The Logic and Epistemology* (Albany: SUNY Press, 1995), p. 141.

11. Jorge J.E. Gracia, *Texts: Ontological Status, Identity, Author, Audience* (Albany: SUNY Press, 1996), p. 100.

12. Gracia, *Theory of Textuality*, p. 110.

13. Nickolas Pappas makes a similar point about reading Plato, Nietzsche, and Proust. See his "Authorship and Authority," in this volume, pp. 117–28.

14. For a brief discussion of Huarte's influence on Cervantes, see Brian McCrea, "Madness and Community," *Indiana Journal of Hispanic Literature* 5 (1994): 213–24.

15. All English quotations of *Don Quixote* are taken from the J.M. Cohen translation (New York: Penguin Books, 1950). The original Spanish is quoted from *Don Quijote de la Mancha* (Barcelona: Collección Austral, 1998).

16. Cervantes, *Don Quixote*, p. 62.

17. John J. Allen, *Don Quixote, Hero or Fool?: A Study in Narrative Technique* (Gainesville: University Press of Florida, 1979), p. 13.

18. On the very first page we are told that while other more dubious historians believe the knight's name to be "Quixada or Quesada . . . by very reasonable conjecture we may take it that he was called Quexana." But not more than two pages later we are informed by the author that the deranged gentleman will call himself Quixote, all but proving "that

his name must have been Quixada and not Quesada as other authorities would have it."
Is Don Quixote's "true" name Quixana or Quixada? There is a similar confusion as to
"the place in La Mancha" where Don Quixote lived. See Allen, *Don Quixote*, pp. 18–
19.

19. For a good summary of the romantic interpretation, see Anthony Close, *The Romantic Approach to Don Quixote* (Cambridge: Cambridge University Press, 1978).

20. For example, see Henry W. Sullivan's *Grotesque Purgatory* (University Park: Pennsylvania State University Press, 1996).

21. Ruth El Saffar, *Distance and Control in Don Quixote* (Chapel Hill: University of North Carolina Press, 1975), p. 25.

22. For the argument that it is possible to intend such multifaceted meanings, see William Irwin, *Intentionalist Interpretation: A Philosophical Explanation and Defense* (Westport, CT: Greenwood Press, 1999), p. 117.

23. About *Mist*, Alexander Parker writes, "This deliberate breaking of the law of artistic consistency accounts for the unease that some critics, and doubtless many readers, have felt about the writer." "On the Interpretation of *Niebla*," in *Unamuno: Creator and Creation* (Berkeley: University of California Press, 1967), p. 134. As we have seen, *Don Quixote* elicits a similar discomfort.

24. Miguel de Unamuno, *Niebla* (Quito, Ecuador: Libresa, 1996), p. 218; Miguel de Unamuno, *Mist*, trans Warner Fite (Champagne: University of Illinois Press, 2000), p. 302.

25. Unamuno does, ultimately, side with Barthes's death of the author theory. But throughout his life, he is particularly troubled about the high status attributed to the Other, in this case, the reader. Cf. Frances Wyers, "Unamuno and 'The Death of the Author,' " *Hispanic Review* 58 (1990): 325–46. Unamuno "reacts to the thought of the author's death with an apprehension and denial that color and determine all his conceptions of subjectivity, language, and the writing subject" (p. 329).

26. I wish to thank Mark Mascia and Michael J. McGrath for helpful comments on an earlier version of this chapter.

Selected Bibliography

Allen, Graham. *Intertextuality*. London: Routledge, 2000.

Arthur, Christopher E. "Gadamer and Hirsch: The Canonical Work and the Interpreter's Intention." *Cultural Hermeneutics* 4 (1977): 183–97.

Austin, J.L. *How to Do Things with Words*. 2nd ed. Cambridge: Harvard University Press, 1962.

Barnes, Annette. *On Interpretation*. Oxford: Basil Blackwell, 1988.

Barthes, Roland. "From Work to Text." In *Textual Strategies: Perspectives in Post-Structuralist Criticism*, trans. and ed. Josué V. Harari, pp. 73–81. Ithaca, NY: Cornell University Press, 1979.

———. "The Death of the Author." In *Image, Music, Text*, trans. Stephen Heath, pp. 142–48. New York: Hill and Wang, 1977.

———. *The Pleasure of the Text*, trans. Richard Miller. New York: Hill and Wang, 1975.

———. *S/Z*, trans. Richard Miller. New York: Hill and Wang, 1974.

———. "La Mort de l'Auteur." *Manteia* 5 (1968): 12–17.

Beardsley, Monroe C. *Aesthetics: Problems in the Philosophy of Criticism*. Rev. ed. New York: Macmillan, 1980.

———. "The Authority of the Text." In *The Possibility of Criticism*, pp. 16–37. Detroit: Wayne State University Press, 1970.

Benjamin, Walter. "The Author as Producer." In *Reflections: Essays, Aphorisms, Autobiographical Writings*, trans. Edmund Jephcott, pp. 220–38. New York: Schocken, 1978.

Bennett, Jonathan. "The Meaning-Nominalist Strategy." *Foundations of Language* 10 (1976): 141–68.

Berger, Karol. *A Theory of Art*. New York: Oxford University Press, 2000.

Bernauer, James William, and David Rasmussen, eds. *The Final Foucault*. Cambridge: MIT Press, 1988.

Biriotti, Maurice, and Nicola Miller. *What Is an Author?* Manchester: Manchester University Press, 1993.

Biro, John. "Intentionalism in the Theory of Meaning." *The Monist* 62 (1979): 238–58.

Blondel, Eric. "Interpreting Texts with or without Nietzsche." In G.L. Ormiston and A.D. Schrift, eds., *Transforming the Hermeneutic Context: From Nietzsche to Nancy*, pp. 69–88. Albany: SUNY Press, 1990.

Bloom, Harold. *The Anxiety of Influence: A Theory of Poetry*. New York: Oxford University Press, 1973.

Booth, Wayne C. *The Rhetoric of Fiction*. Chicago: University of Chicago Press, 1961.

Brand, Myles. *Intending and Acting*. Cambridge: MIT Press, 1984.

Brand, Peg Zeglin, and Myles Brand. "Surface Interpretation: A Reply to Leddy." *Journal of Aesthetics and Art Criticism* 57 (1999): 463–65.

———. "Surface and Deep Interpretations." In Mark Rollins, ed., *Danto and His Critics*, pp. 55–69. Cambridge: Blackwell, 1993.

Brest, Paul. "The Misconceived Quest for the Original Understanding." In Sanford Levinson and Steven Mailoux, eds., *Interpreting Law and Literature: A Hermeneutic Reader*, pp. 69–96. Evanston, IL: Northwestern University Press, 1988.

Brophy, Kevin. "What Is a Foucault? A Note on Foucault's Essay, 'What Is an Author?' " *Southern Review: Literary and Interdisciplinary Essays* 28 (1995): 4–9.

Brown, Andrew. *Roland Barthes: The Figures of Writing*. New York: Oxford University Press, 1992.

Burke, Seán. *The Death and Return of the Author: Criticism and Subjectivity in Barthes, Foucault and Derrida*. 2nd ed. Edinburgh: Edinburgh University Press, 1998.

Cain, William E. "Authors and Authority in Interpretation." *Georgia Review* 34 (1980): 617–34.

———. "Authority, 'Cognitive Atheism,' and the Aims of Interpretation: The Literary Theory of E.D. Hirsch." *College English* 39 (1977): 333–45.

Carroll, Noël. "Andy Kaufman and the Philosophy of Interpretation." In Michael Krausz, ed., *Is There a Single Right Interpretation?* University Park: Pennsylvania State University Press, forthcoming.

———. "Interpretation and Intention: The Debate between Hypothetical and Actual Intentionalism." *Metaphilosophy* 31 (2000): 75–95.

———. "The Intentional Fallacy: Defending Myself." *Journal of Aesthetics and Art Criticism* 53 (1997): 305–309.

———. "Anglo-American Aesthetics and Contemporary Criticism: Intention and the Hermeneutics of Suspicion." *Journal of Aesthetics and Art Criticism* 51 (1993): 245–52.

———. "Art, Intention, and Conversation." In Gary Iseminger, ed., *Intention and Interpretation*, pp. 97–131. Philadelphia: Temple University Press, 1992.

Caughie, John. *Theories of Authorship: A Reader*. London: Routledge & Kegan Paul, 1981.

Champagne, Ronald A. "Resurrecting RB: Roland Barthes, Literature, and the Stakes of Literary Semiotics." *Semiotica* 107 (1995): 339–48.

Cioffi, F. "Intention and Interpretation in Criticism," *Proceedings of the Aristotelian Society* 64 (1964): 85–106.

Clayton, Jay, and Eric Rothstein, eds. *Influence and Intertextuality in Literary History*. Madison: University of Wisconsin Press, 1991.

Close, A.J. *"Don Quixote* and the 'Intentionalist Fallacy.' " *British Journal of Aesthetics* 12 (1972): 19–39.

Connolly, John M. "Gadamer and the Author's Authority: A Language Game Approach." *Journal of Aesthetics and Art Criticism* 44 (1986): 271–78.

Culler, Jonathan. *Structuralist Poetics: Structuralism, Linguistics, and the Study of Literature*. London: Routledge and Kegan Paul, 1975.

Gregory Currie. "Work and Text." *Mind* 100 (1991): 325–39.

———. "What Is Fiction?" *Journal of Aesthetics and Art Criticism* 43 (1985): 385–92.

Danto, Arthur C. "Deep Interpretation." In *The Philosophical Disenfranchisement of Art*, pp. 47–67. New York: Columbia University Press, 1986.

Davies, Stephen. "The Aesthetic Relevance of Authors' and Painters' Intentions."*Journal of Aesthetics and Art Criticism* 41 (1982): 65–76.

Derrida, Jacques. *Positions*, trans. Alan Bass. Chicago: University of Chicago Press, 1981.

———. "Signature Event Context." *Glyph* 1 (1977): 172–97.

———. *Of Grammatology*, trans. Gayatri Chakravorty Spivak. Baltimore: Johns Hopkins University Press, 1976.

Dickie, George, and Kent Wilson. "The Intentional Fallacy: Defending Beardsley." *Journal of Aesthetics and Art Criticism* 53 (1995): 233–50.

Diengott, Nilli. "Implied Author, Motivation and Theme and Their Problematic Status." *Orbis Litterarum: International Review of Literary Studies* 48 (1993): 181–93.

Dilthey, W. *Selected Writings*, ed. and trans. H.P. Rickman. Cambridge: Cambridge University Press, 1976.

Donnellan, Keith. "Putting Humpty Dumpty Together Again." *Philosophical Review* 77 (1968): 203–15.

Dreyfus, Hubert L., and Paul Rainbow. *Michel Foucault: Beyond Structuralism and Hermeneutics*. 2nd ed. Chicago: University of Chicago Press, 1983.

Dutton, Dennis. "Why Intentionalism Won't Go Away." In Anthony J. Cascardi, ed., *Literature and the Question of Philosophy*, pp. 194–201. Baltimore: Johns Hopkins University Press, 1987.

———. "Criticism and Method." *British Journal of Aesthetics* 13 (1973): 232–42.

Eaton, Marcia Muelder. "Intention, Supervenience, and Aesthetic Realism." *British Journal of Aesthetics* 38 (1998): 279–93.

Ellis, A.J. "Intention and Interpretation in Literature." *British Journal of Aesthetics* 14 (1974): 315–25.

Ellis, J.M. *Against Deconstruction*. Princeton: Princeton University Press, 1989.

Epstein, William, ed. *Contesting the Subject*. West Lafayette, IN: Purdue University Press, 1991.

Eribon, Didier. *Michel Foucault*, trans. Betsy Wing. Cambridge: Harvard University Press, 1991.

Fish, Stanley. "Biography and Intention." In William Epstein, ed., *Contesting the Subject*, pp. 9–16. West Lafayette, IN: Purdue University Press, 1991.

———. *Is There a Text in This Class? The Authority of Interpretive Communities*. Cambridge, MA: Harvard University Press, 1980.

Foucault, Michel. "Nietzsche, Freud, Marx." In G.L. Ormiston and A.D. Schrift, eds.,

Transforming the Hermeneutic Context: From Nietzsche to Nancy, pp. 59–68. Albany: SUNY Press, 1990.

———. "What Is an Author?" trans. Josué V. Harari. In Paul Rainbow, ed., *The Foucault Reader*, pp. 101–20. New York: Pantheon Books, 1984.

———. "What Is an Author?" trans. Josué V. Harari. Originally published in *Textual Strategies: Perspectives in Post-Structuralist Criticism*, trans. and ed. Josué V. Harari, pp. 141–60. Ithaca, NY: Cornell University Press, 1979.

———. "What Is an Author?" trans. Donald F. Bouchard and Sherry Simon. In Donald F. Bouchard, ed., *Language, Counter-Memory, Practice: Selected Essays and Interviews*, pp. 113–38. Ithaca, NY: Cornell University Press, 1977.

———. *The Archaeology of Knowledge*, trans. A.M. Sheridan Smith. New York: Pantheon, 1972.

———. *The Order of Things: An Archaeology of the Human Sciences*, trans. Alan Sheridan. London: Tavistock, 1970.

———. "Qu'est-ce Qu'un Auteur?" *Bulletin de la Société Francaise de Philosophie* 63 (1969): 75–95.

Frank, Manfred. "The Interpretation of a Text." In G.L. Ormiston and A.D. Schrift, eds., *Transforming the Hermeneutic Context: From Nietzsche to Nancy*, pp. 145–176. Albany: SUNY Press, 1990.

Frege, Gottlob. "On Sense and Reference." In *Translations from the Philosophical Writings of Gottlob Frege*, trans. and ed. P. Geach and M. Black, pp. 56–78. Oxford: Basil Blackwell, 1952.

French, Patrick, and Roland Francois Lack, eds. *The Tel Quel Reader*. New York: Routledge, 1998.

Friedman, Susan Stanford. "Weavings: Intertextuality and the (Re)Birth of the Author." In Jay Clayton and Eric Rothstein, eds. *Influence and Intertextuality in Literary History*, pp. 146–80. Madison: University of Wisconsin Press, 1991.

Gadamer, Hans-Georg. *Truth and Method*, trans. Joel Weinsheimer and Donald G. Marshall. 2nd ed. New York: Continuum, 1989.

———. "Text and Interpretation," trans. Dennis J. Schmidt. In Brice R. Wachterhauser, ed., *Hermeneutics and Modern Philosophy*, pp. 377–96. Albany: SUNY Press, 1986.

———. *Philosophical Hermeneutics*, ed. and trans. David Linge. Berkeley: University of California Press, 1976.

Gasché, Randolphe. *The Tain of the Mirror*. Cambridge: Harvard University Press, 1986.

Gaut, Berys. "Interpreting the Arts: The Patchwork Theory." *Journal of Aesthetics and Art Criticism* 51 (1993): 597–609.

Geller, Jeffery. "Painting, Parapraxes, and Unconscious Intentions." *Journal of Aesthetics and Art Criticism* 51 (1993): 377–87.

Gough, Martin. "The Death of the Author and the Life of the Subject." In Karl Simms, ed., *Language and the Subject*, pp. 227–36. Amsterdam: Rodopi, 1997.

Gracia, Jorge J.E. *How Can We Know What God Means? The Interpretation of Revelation*. New York: Palgrave, 2001.

———. "Relativism and the Interpretation of Texts." *Metaphilosophy* 31 (2000): 43–62.

———. "The Interpretation of Revealed Texts: Do We Know What God Means?" *American Catholic Philosophical Quarterly* 72 (1998): 1–19.

———. *Texts: Ontological Status, Identity, Author, Audience*. Albany: SUNY Press, 1996.

————. *A Theory of Textuality: The Logic and Epistemology*. Albany: SUNY Press, 1995.

————. "Author and Repression." *Contemporary Philosophy* 16 (1994): 23–29.

————. "Can There Be Definitive Interpretations? An Interpretation of Foucault in Response to Engel." In Barry Smith, ed., *European Philosophy and the American Academy*, pp. 41–51. La Salle, IL: The Hegeler Institute, 1994.

————. "Can There Be Texts Without Historical Authors?" *American Philosophical Quarterly* 31 (1994): 248–53.

————. "Can There Be Texts Without Audiences?" *Review of Metaphysics* 47 (1994): 711–34.

————. "Texts and Their Interpretation." *Review of Metaphysics* 43 (1990): 495–542.

Gracia, Jorge J.E., Carolyn Korsmeyer, and Randolphe Gasché, eds. *Literary Philosophers?: Borges, Calvino, Eco*. New York: Routledge, 2002.

Grondin, Jean. *Introduction to Philosophical Hermeneutics*, trans. Joel Weinsheimer. New Haven: Yale University Press, 1994.

————. "Hermeneutics and Relativism." In Kathleen Wright, ed., *Festivals of Interpretation: Essays on Hans-Georg Gadamer's Work*, pp. 42–62. Albany: SUNY Press, 1990.

Hamlyn, D.W. "Unconscious Intentions." *Philosophy* 46 (1971): 12–22.

Hancher, Michael. "Humpty Dumpty and Verbal Meaning." *Journal of Aesthetics and Art Criticism* 40 (1981): 49–58.

————. "Three Kinds of Intentions." *Modern Language Notes* 87 (1972): 827–51.

Heidegger, Martin. *Being and Time*, trans. John Macquarrie and Edward Robinson. San Francisco: HarperCollins, 1962.

Hermerén, Göran. "Allusions and Intentions." In Gary Iseminger, ed., *Intention and Interpretation*, pp. 203–20. Philadelphia: Temple University Press, 1992.

————. "Intention and Interpretation in Literary Criticism." *New Literary History* 7 (1975): 57–82.

Hicks, Jim. "Partial Interpretations and Company: Beckett, Foucault, et al. and the Author Question." *Studies in Twentieth Century Literature* 17 (1993): 309–23.

Hilpinen, Risto. "Authors and Artifacts." *Proceedings of the Aristotelian Society* 93 (1993): 155–78.

Hirsch, E.D., Jr. "Transhistorical Intentions and the Persistence of Allegory." *New Literary History* 25 (1994): 549–67.

————. "Counterfactuals in Interpretation." In Sanford Levinson and Steven Mailoux, eds., *Interpreting Law and Literature: A Hermeneutic Reader*, pp. 55–68. Evanston, IL: Northwestern University Press, 1988.

————. "Meaning and Significance Reinterpreted." *Critical Inquiry* 11 (1984): 202–25.

————. "On Justifying Interpretive Norms." *Journal of Aesthetics and Art Criticism* 43 (1984): 89–92.

————. *The Aims of Interpretation*. Chicago: University of Chicago Press, 1976.

————. "Three Dimensions of Hermeneutics." *New Literary History* 3 (1972): 245–61.

————. *Validity in Interpretation*. New Haven: Yale University Press, 1967.

————. "Truth and Method in Interpretation." *Review of Metaphysics* 18 (1965): 488–507.

————. "Objective Interpretation." *PMLA* 75 (1960): 463–79.

Hix, H.L. *Morte d'Author: An Autopsy*. Philadelphia: Temple University Press, 1990.

Hollier, Denis. "Foucault: The Death of the Author." *Raritan* 5 (1985): 22–30.

Holt, Jason. "A Comprehensivist Theory of Art." *British Journal of Aesthetics* 36 (1996):
    424–31.
Hoy, David C. *Foucault: A Critical Reader*. Oxford: Blackwell, 1986.
———. "Must We Say What We Mean?" *University of Ottawa Review* 50 (1980): 411–
    26.
———. *The Critical Circle: Literature, History, and Philosophical Hermeneutics*. Berke-
    ley: University of California Press, 1978.
Hunt, Lynn. "The Revenge of the Subject/the Return of Experience." *Salmagundi* 97
    (1993): 45–53.
Irwin, William. "A Critique of Hermeneutic Truth as Disclosure." *International Studies
    in Philosophy* 33 (2001): 63–75.
———. "Philosophy and the Philosophical, Literature and the Literary, Borges and the
    Labyrinthine." In Jorge J.E. Gracia, Carolyn Korsmeyer, and Randolphe Gasché,
    eds., *Literary Philosophers? Borges, Calvino, Eco*, pp. 27–45. New York: Rout-
    ledge, 2002.
———. "What Is an Allusion?" *Journal of Aesthetics and Art Criticism* 59 (2001): 287–
    97.
———. "An Author Construct There Must Be." *Diálogos* 74 (1999): 169–77.
———. *Intentionalist Interpretation: A Philosophical Explanation and Defense*. West-
    port, CT: Greenwood Press, 1999.
Iseminger, Gary. "Interpretive Relevance, Contradiction, and Compatibility with the Text:
    A Rejoinder to Knight." *Journal of Aesthetics and Art Criticism* 56 (1998): 58–
    61.
———. "Actual Intentionalism vs. Hypothetical Intentionalism." *Journal of Aesthetics
    and Art Criticism* 54 (1996): 319–26.
———. "An Intentional Demonstration?" In Gary Iseminger, ed., *Intention and Inter-
    pretation*, pp. 76–96. Philadelphia: Temple University Press, 1992.
Iser, Wolfgang. "The Reading Process: A Phenomenological Approach." In Jane P.
    Tompkins, ed., *Reader, Response, Criticism*, pp. 50–69. Baltimore: Johns Hop-
    kins University Press, 1980.
Juhl, P.D. *Interpretation: An Essay in the Philosophy of Literary Criticism*. Princeton:
    Princeton University Press, 1980.
———. "The Appeal to the Text: What Are We Appealing To?" *Journal of Aesthetics
    and Art Criticism* 36 (1978): 277–287.
Keefer, Donald. "Reports of the Death of the Author." *Philosophy and Literature* 19
    (1995): 78–84.
Kivy, Peter. "The Authority of Intention." In *Authenticities: Philosophical Reflections on
    Musical Performance*, pp. 145–87. Ithaca, NY: Cornell University Press, 1995.
Knapp, Steven. *Literary Interest: The Limits of Anti-Formalism*. Cambridge: Harvard
    University Press, 1993.
Knapp, Steven, and Walter Benn Michaels. "Against Theory 2: Hermeneutics and De-
    construction." *Critical Inquiry* 14 (1987): 49–68.
———. "Against Theory." *Critical Inquiry* 8 (1982): 723–42.
Knight, Deborah. "Not an Actual Demonstration: A Reply to Iseminger." *Journal of
    Aesthetics and Art Criticism* 56 (1998): 53–58.
———. "Selves, Interpreters, Narrators." *Philosophy and Literature* 18 (1994): 274–86.
Krausz, Michael. "Interpretation and Its 'Metaphysical' Entanglements." *Metaphilosophy*
    31 (2000): 125–47.

————— *The Limits of Rightness*. Lanham, MD: Rowman & Littlefield, 2000.

—————. "Intention and Interpretation: Hirsch and Margolis." In Gary Iseminger, ed., *Intention and Interpretation*, pp. 152–66. Philadelphia: Temple University Press, 1992.

Krukowski, Lucian. "Artist—Work—Audience: Musings on Barthes and Tolstoy." *British Journal of Aesthetics* 30 (1990): 143–48.

Lamarque, Peter. "Objects of Interpretation." *Metaphilosophy* 31 (2000): 96–124.

—————. *Fictional Points of View*. Ithaca, NY: Cornell University Press, 1996.

—————. "The Death of the Author: An Analytical Autopsy." *British Journal of Aesthetics* 30 (1990): 319–31.

Lamarque, Peter, and Stein Haugom Olsen. *Truth, Fiction, and Literature: A Philosophical Perspective*. Oxford: Clarendon Press, 1994.

Lang, Berel. "The Intentional Fallacy Revisited." *British Journal of Aesthetics* 14 (1974): 306–14.

Leddy, Thomas W. "Against Surface Interpretation." *Journal of Aesthetics and Art Criticism* 57 (1999): 459–63.

—————. "Iseminger's Literary Intentionalism and an Alternative." *British Journal of Aesthetics* 39 (1999): 219–29.

Levinson, Jerold. "Intention and Interpretation in Literature." In *The Pleasures of Aesthetics*, pp. 175–213. Ithaca, NY: Cornell University Press, 1996.

—————. "Intention and Interpretation: A Last Look." In Gary Iseminger, ed., *Intention and Interpretation*, pp. 221–56. Philadelphia: Temple University Press, 1992.

Livingston, Paisley. "From Work to Work." *Philosophy and Literature* 20 (1996): 436–454.

Loptson, Peter. "Hume, Multiperspectival Pluralism, and Authorial Voice." *Hume Studies* 24 (1998): 313–34.

Lyas, Colin. "Wittgensteinian Intentions." In Gary Iseminger, ed., *Intention and Interpretation*, pp. 132–51. Philadelphia: Temple University Press, 1992.

—————. "Anything Goes: The Intentional Fallacy Revisited." *British Journal of Aesthetics* 23 (1983): 291–305.

Lyon, Arabella. *Intentions: Negotiated, Contested, and Ignored*. University Park: Pennsylvania State University Press, 1998.

MacCabe, Colin. "The Revenge of the Author." *Critical Quarterly* 31 (1989): 3–13.

Macey, David. *The Lives of Michel Foucault*. London: Hutchinson, 1993.

Magnus, Bernd. "Author, Writer, Text: The Will to Power." *International Studies in Philosophy* 22 (1990): 49–57.

Manns, James. "Intentionalism in John Dewey's Aesthetics." *Transactions of the Charles S. Peirce Society* 23 (1987): 411–23.

Margolis, Joseph. "Relativism and Interpretive Objectivity." *Metaphilosophy* 31 (2000): 200–26.

—————. "Robust Relativism." In Gary Iseminger, ed., *Intention and Interpretation*, pp. 41–50. Philadelphia: Temple University Press, 1992.

McCoy, Heather. "Foucault and the Use of Biography." *Symploke* 3 (1995): 165–78.

Meiland, Jack W. "The Meanings of a Text." *British Journal of Aesthetics* 21 (1981): 195–203.

—————. "Interpretation as a Cognitive Discipline." *Philosophy and Literature* 2 (1978): 23–45.

Michelfelder, Diane P., and Richard E. Palmer, eds. *Dialogue and Deconstruction: The Gadamer-Derrida Encounter*. Albany: SUNY Press, 1989.

Miller, James. "Foucault's Politics in Biographical Perspective." *Salmagundi* 97 (1993): 30–44.

———. *The Passion of Michel Foucault*. New York: Simon & Schuster, 1993.

Mitscherling, Jeff. "Philosophical Hermeneutics and 'The Tradition.' " *Man and World* 22 (1989): 247–50.

Morgan, Michael. "Authorship and the History of Philosophy." *Review of Metaphysics* 42 (1988): 327–55.

Morris, David Copland. "The Life of the Author: Emerson, Foucault, and the Reading of Edward Abbey's Journals." In Peter Quigley, ed., *Coyote in the Maze: Tracking Edward Abbey in a World of Words*, pp. 242–62. Salt Lake City: University of Utah Press, 1998.

Nathan, Daniel O. "Irony, Metaphor, and the Problem of Intention." In Gary Iseminger, ed., *Intention and Interpretation*, pp. 183–202. Philadelphia: Temple University Press, 1992.

———. "Categories and Intentions." *Journal of Aesthetics and Art Criticism* 31 (1973): 539–41.

Nehamas, Alexander. *The Art of Living: Socratic Reflections from Plato to Foucault*. Berkeley: University of California Press, 1998.

———. "Writer, Text, Work, Author." In Anthony J. Cascardi, ed., *Literature and the Question of Philosophy*, pp. 265–91. Baltimore: Johns Hopkins University Press, 1987.

———. "What an Author Is." *The Journal of Philosophy* 83 (1986): 685–91.

———. "The Postulated Author: Critical Monism as a Regulative Ideal." *Critical Inquiry* 8 (1981): 133–49.

Nelles, William. "Historical and Implied Authors and Readers." *Comparative Literature* 45 (1993): 22–46.

Newton-De Molina, David. *On Literary Intention*. Edinburgh: University of Edinburgh Press, 1976.

Norris, Christopher. *Derrida*. London: Fontana, 1987.

Novitz, David. "Interpretation and Justification." *Metaphilosophy* 31 (2000): 4–24.

Olsen, Stein Haugom. "Conventions and Rules in Literature." *Metaphilosophy* 31 (2000): 25–42.

———. "Interpretation and Intention." *British Journal of Aesthetics* 17 (1977): 210–18.

Palmer, Richard E. "Phenomenology as Foundation for a Post-modern Philosophy of Literary Interpretation." *Cultural Hermeneutics* 2 (1973): 207–22.

———. *Hermeneutics: Interpretation Theory in Schleiermacher, Dilthey, Heidegger, and Gadamer*. Evanston, IL: Northwestern University Press, 1969.

Pappas, Nickolas. "Authorship and Authority." *Journal of Aesthetics and Art Criticism* 47 (1989): 325–31.

———. "Plato's 'Ion': The Problem of the Author." *Philosophy* 64 (1989): 381–89.

Park, Clara Claiborne. "Author! Author! Reconstructing Roland Barthes." *The Hudson Review* 43 (1990): 377–98.

Pletsch, Carl. "The Self-Sufficient Text in Nietzsche and Kierkegaard." *Yale French Studies* 66 (1984): 160–88.

Plett, Heinrich F., ed. *Intertextuality*. Berlin: Walter de Gruyter, 1991.

Rajan, Tilottama. "Intertextuality and the Subject of Reading/Writing." In Jay Clayton and Eric Rothstein, eds., *Influence and Intertextuality in Literary History*, pp. 61–74. Madison: University of Wisconsin Press, 1991.

Reid, Ian. "The Death of the Implied Author? Voice, Sequence, and Control in Flaubert's *Trois Contes*." *Australian Journal of French Studies* 23 (1986): 195–211.

Rockmore, Tom. "Interpretation as Historical, Constructivism, and History." *Metaphilosophy* 31 (2000): 184–99.

Rose, Mark. *Authors and Owners: The Invention of Copyright*. Cambridge: Harvard University Press, 1993.

Rosebury, Brian. "Irrecoverable Intentions and Literary Interpretation." *British Journal of Aesthetics* 37 (1997): 15–30.

Rosen, Stanley. "The Limits of Interpretation." In Anthony J. Cascardi, ed., *Literature and the Question of Philosophy*, pp. 213–41. Baltimore: Johns Hopkins University Press, 1987.

Ross, Valeric. "Too Close to Home: Repressing Biography, Instituting Authority." In William Epstein, ed., *Contesting the Subject*, pp. 135–65. West Lafayette, IN: Purdue University Press, 1991.

Schleiermacher, F.D.E. *Hermeneutics and Criticism: And Other Writings*, ed. and trans. Andrew Bowie. Cambridge: Cambridge University Press, 1998.

———. *Hermeneutics: The Handwritten Manuscripts*, ed. Heinz Kimmerle, trans. James Duke and Jack Frostman. Missoula, MT: Scholars Press, 1977.

———. *Hermeneutik*, ed. Heinz Kimmerle. Heidelberg: Carl Winter, 1959.

Schmidt, Lawrence K. *The Specter of Relativism: Truth, Dialogue, and Phronesis in Philosophical Hermeneutics*. Evanston, IL: Northwestern University Press, 1995.

———. *The Epistemology of Hans-Georg Gadamer: An Analysis of the Legitimization of Vorurteile*. Frankfurt: Peter D. Lang, 1985.

Schrift, Alan D. "Reading, Writing, Text: Nietzsche's Deconstruction of Author-ity." *International Studies in Philosophy* 17 (1985): 55–64.

Shusterman, Richard. "Interpretation, Intention, and Truth." In Gary Iseminger, ed., *Intention and Interpretation*, pp. 65–75. Philadelphia: Temple University Press, 1992.

———. "Interpreting with Pragmatist Intentions." In Gary Iseminger, ed., *Intention and Interpretation*, pp. 167–82. Philadelphia: Temple University Press, 1992.

Siegle, Robert. "The Concept of the Author in Barthes, Foucault, and Fowles." *College Literature* 10 (1983): 126–38.

Sirridge, Mary. "Artistic Intention and Critical Prerogative." *British Journal of Aesthetics* 18 (1978): 137–54.

Sluga, Hans. "Foucault, the Author, and the Discourse." *Inquiry* 28 (1985): 403–15.

Sparshott, Francis. "The Case of the Unreliable Author." *Philosophy and Literature* 10 (1986): 145–67.

Stecker, Robert. "The Constructivist's Dilemma." *Journal of Aesthetics and Art Criticism* 55 (1997): 43–52.

———. *Artworks: Definition, Meaning, Value*. University Park: Pennsylvania State University Press, 1996.

———. "Art Interpretation." *Journal of Aesthetics and Art Criticism* 52 (1994): 193–206.

———. "The Role of Intention and Convention in Interpreting Artworks." *Southern Journal of Philosophy* 31 (1993): 471–89.

————. "Incompatible Interpretations." *Journal of Aesthetics and Art Criticism* 50 (1992): 291–98.

————. "Fish's Argument for the Relativity of Interpretive Truth." *Journal of Aesthetics and Art Criticism* 48 (1990): 223–30.

————. "Apparent, Implied, and Postulated Authors." *Philosophy and Literature* 11 (1987): 258–71.

Stopford, John. "The Death of the Author (as Producer)." *Philosophy and Rhetoric* 23 (1990): 184–91.

Stout, Jeffrey. "The Relativity of Interpretation." *The Monist* 69 (1986): 103–18.

————. "What Is the Meaning of a Text?" *New Literary History* 14 (1982): 1–14.

Sutrop, Margit. "The Death of the Literary Work." *Philosophy and Literature* 18 (1994): 38–49.

Tatar, Burhanettin. *Interpretation and the Problem of the Intention of the Author: H.-G. Gadamer vs. E.D. Hirsch*. Washington, DC: Council in Values and Philosophy, 1998.

Taylor, Carole Anne. "Authorship without Authority: Walden, Kierkegaard, and the Experiment in Points of View." In Ronald Schleifer and Robert Markley, eds., *Kierkegaard and Literature: Irony, Repetition, and Criticism*, pp. 164–82. Norman: University of Oklahoma Press, 1984.

Thom, Paul. *Making Sense: A Theory of Interpretation*. Lanham, MD: Rowman & Littlefield, 2001.

————. "On Changing the Subject." *Metaphilosophy* 31 (2000): 63–74.

Tillyard, E.M.W., and C.S. Lewis. *The Personal Heresy: A Controversy*. London: Oxford University Press, 1939.

Tolhurst, William E. "On Textual Individuation." *Philosophical Studies* 35 (1979): 187–97.

————. "On What a Text Is and How It Means." *British Journal of Aesthetics* 19 (1979): 3–14.

Trivedi, Saam. "An Epistemic Dilemma for Actual Intentionalism." *British Journal Aesthetics* 41 (2001): 192–206.

Wachterhauser, Brice R. "Interpreting Texts: Objectivity or Participation?" *Man and World* 19 (1986): 439–57.

Wachterhauser, Brice R., ed. *Hermeneutics and Truth*. Evanston, IL: Northwestern University Press, 1994.

————. *Hermeneutics and Modern Philosophy*. Albany: SUNY Press, 1986.

Walker, Cheryl. "Feminist Literary Criticism and the Author." *Critical Inquiry* 16 (1990): 551–71.

Walton, Kendall L. "Style and the Products and Processes of Art." In Berel Lang, ed., *The Concept of Style*, pp. 72–103. Ithaca, NY: Cornell University Press, 1987.

Weberman, David. "A New Defense of Gadamer's Hermeneutics." *Philosophy and Phenomenological Research* 60 (2000): 45–65.

————. "Cambridge Changes Revisited: Why Certain Relational Changes Are Indispensable." *Dialectica* 53 (1999): 139–49.

————. "Reconciling Gadamer's Non-Intentionalism with Standard Conversational Goals." *The Philosophical Forum* 30 (1999): 317–28.

————. "The Nonfixity of the Historical Past." *Review of Metaphysics* 50 (1997): 749–68.

————. *Historische Objektivität*. Frankfurt am Main: Peter D. Lang, 1991.

Weinsheimer, Joel C. *Gadamer's Hermeneutics: A Reading of Truth and Method*. New Haven: Yale University Press, 1985.

Weiss, Gail. "Reading/Writing between the Lines." *Continental Philosophy Review* 31 (1998): 387–409.

Westphal, Merold. *Becoming a Self: A Reading of Kierkegaard's Concluding Unscientific Postscript*. West Lafayette, IN: Purdue University Press, 1996.

———. "Kierkegaard and the Anxiety of Authorship." *International Philosophical Quarterly* 34 (1994): 6–22.

———. *Kierkegaard's Critique of Reason and Society*. Macon, GA: Mercer University Press, 1987.

———. "Hegel, Pannenberg and Hermeneutics." *Man and World* 4 (1971): 276–93.

Wimsatt, W.K. "Genesis: A Fallacy Revisited." In David Newton-De Molina, ed., *On Literary Intention*, pp. 116–38. Edinburgh: University of Edinburgh Press, 1976.

Wimsatt, W.K., and Monroe C. Beardsley, "The Intentional Fallacy." In *The Verbal Icon: Studies in the Meaning of Poetry*, pp. 3–18. Lexington: University of Kentucky Press, 1954.

Wiseman, Mary Bittner. *The Ecstasies of Roland Barthes*. London: Routledge, 1989.

Wyers, Frances. "Unamuno and the 'Death of the Author.' " *Hispanic Review* 58 (1990): 325–46.

Index

About the Contributors

ROLAND BARTHES, social and literary critic and Professor of Semiology, was born in Cherbourg, France, in 1915. At the Sorbonne he received degrees in classical letters and grammar and philology. Among other places, Barthes taught in Rumania and Egypt, and at the École des Hautes Études en Sciences Sociales and Johns Hopkins University. Barthes was appointed to the Collège de France in 1977. He died in 1980. Barthes's most important books include: of *Le degré zéro de l'écriture* (1953, trans. *Writing Degree Zero*); *Mythologies* (1957, trans. *Mythologies*); *Essais critiques* (1964, trans. *Critical Essays*); *Sur Racine* (1965, trans. *On Racine*); *S/Z* (1970, trans. *S/Z*); *L' Empire des signes* (1970, trans. *Empire of Signs*); *Sade, Fourier, Loyola* (1971, trans. *Sade, Fourier, Loyola*); and *Le Plaisir du texte* (1973, trans. *The Pleasure of the Text*).

ERIC BRONSON teaches Philosophy and World Civilizations at Berkeley College in New York City. He is also a Visiting Professor at Altai University in Barnaul, Russia.

MICHEL FOUCAULT, philosopher, social critic, and historian of thought, was born in Poitiers, France, in 1926. He studied philosophy and psychology at the École Normale Supérieure in Paris. During the 1960s, he taught and served as head of the philosophy departments at the University of Clermont-Ferrand and the University of Vincennes. In 1970 he was elected to the highest academic post in France, the Collège de France, where he took the title of Professor of the History of Systems of Thought. He died in June 1984. Foucault's most important books include *Folie et déraison* (1961, trans. *Madness and Civiliza-*

tion); *Naissance de la clinique* (1963, trans. *The Birth of the Clinic*); *Les Mots et les choses* (1966, trans. *The Order of Things*); *L' Archéologie du savoir* (1969, trans. *The Archaeology of Knowledge*); *Surveiller et punir* (1975, trans. *Discipline and Punish*); and the unfinished *Histoire de la sexualité* (1976–84, trans. *The History of Sexuality*).

JORGE J.E. GRACIA holds the Samuel P. Capen Chair and is SUNY Distinguished Professor of Philosophy at the State University of New York at Buffalo. He is the author of numerous scholarly articles, the editor of more than a dozen books, and the author of the following books: *How Can We Know What God Means? The Interpretation of Revelation* (2001); *Hispanic/Latino Identity: A Philosophical Perspective* (2000); *Metaphysics and Its Task: The Search for the Categorial Foundations of Knowledge* (1999); *Texts: Ontological Status, Identity, Author, Audience* (1996); *A Theory of Textuality: The Logic and Epistemology* (1995); *Philosophy and Its History: Issues in Philosophical Historiography* (1992); *The Metaphysics of Good and Evil According to Suarez* (1989); *Individuality: An Essay on the Foundation of Metaphysics* (1988); *Introduction to the Problem of Individuation in the Early Middle Ages* (1984, 1986); and *Suarez on Individuation* (1982). He is currently working on two books: one on race, ethnicity, and nationality and one on tradition.

JASON HOLT teaches philosophy at the University of Manitoba. He has published scholarly papers in aesthetics, metaphysics, and the philosophy of mind, and is the author of the first book-length study of the interconnections between blindsight and the nature of consciousness (forthcoming). He has also published a novel, *Fragment of a Blues* (2001) and two books of poetry, *Feeling Fine in Kafka's Burrow* (1994) and *Memos to No One* (1999).

WILLIAM IRWIN is Associate Professor of Philosophy at King's College, Pennsylvania. He has published scholarly articles on the theory of interpretation and aesthetics, and is the author of *Intentionalist Interpretation: A Philosophical Explanation and Defense* (1999), and the co-author of *Critical Thinking: A Student's Introduction* (2001). He is the editor of *Seinfeld and Philosophy* (2000) and the co-editor of *The Simpsons and Philosophy* (2001).

PETER LAMARQUE is Professor of Philosophy at the University of York in England. He is editor of the *British Journal of Aesthetics*, author of *Fictional Points of View* (1996), and co-author, with Stein Haugom Olsen, of *Truth, Fiction, and Literature: A Philosophical Perspective* (1994). He also edited the *Concise Encyclopedia of Philosophy of Language* (1997) and *Aesthetics in Britain* (2000), a special issue of the *British Journal of Aesthetics*. He was Philosophy Subject Editor of the ten-volume *Encyclopedia of Language and Linguistics* (1994).

ALEXANDER NEHAMAS, Edmund N. Carpenter II Professor in the Humanities and Professor of Philosophy and Comparative Literature at Princeton University, is the author of *Nietzsche: Life as Literature, The Art of Living: Socratic Reflections from Plato to Foucault*, and *Virtues of Authenticity: Essays on Plato and Socrates*, as well as numerous scholarly articles. He is also interested in problems in the philosophy of art and culture, and is currently writing about beauty, aesthetics, and ethics.

NICKOLAS PAPPAS is Associate Professor of Philosophy at the City College and the Graduate Center, the City University of New York. He has written the *Routledge Philosophy Guidebook to Plato and the Republic*, articles on Plato, Aristotle, Kierkegaard, and topics in aesthetics, film, and literary theory. Forthcoming works include a book-length study of causation and birth in Nietzsche, and an interpretive study of Plato's *Menexenus*.

ROBERT STECKER is Professor of Philosophy at Central Michigan University. He is the author of *Artworks: Definition, Meaning, Value* and numerous papers on the philosophy of art, philosophy of mind, and the history of modern philosophy. He is currently completing *Interpretation and Construction*, a book about the interpretation of art, literature, and the law.

CHERYL WALKER is Richard Armour Professor of Modern Languages at Scripps College. She is the author of *The Nightingale's Burden: Women Poets and American Culture before 1900* and *Masks Outrageous and Austere: Culture, Psyche, and Persona in Modern Women Poets*, both published by Indiana University Press. Her most recent book is *Indian Nation: Native American Literature and Nineteenth-Century Nationalisms* (1997). Her current project is a book on Elizabeth Bishop and religion.

DAVID WEBERMAN is Assistant Professor of Philosophy at Georgia State University. He is the author of *Historische Objektivtät* (1991) and papers on figures such as Heidegger, Sartre, Foucault, and Gadamer and on topics in metaphysics, the philosophy of history, political philosophy, and race theory. He is currently working on a book-length defense of interpretive pluralism.

MEROLD WESTPHAL is Distinguished Professor of Philosophy at Fordham University. He is the author of numerous scholarly articles and the following books: *History and Truth in Hegel's Phenomenology*; *Hegel, Freedom and Modernity*; *Kierkegaard's Critique of Reason and Society*; *Becoming a Self: A Reading of Kierkegaard's Concluding Unscientific Postscript*; *God, Guilt, and Death: An Existential Phenomenology of Religion*; *Suspicion and Faith: The Religious Uses of Modern Atheism*; and *Overcoming Onto-theology: Toward a Postmodern Christian Faith*.